AUTUMN PASSAGES

A DUCKS UNLIMITED TREASURY OF WATERFOWLING CLASSICS

Illustrations by Francis Lee Jaques

Ducks Unlimited, Inc.
Memphis, Tennessee
1995
and
Willow Creek Press
Minocqua, Wisconsin
1995

Autumn Passages : a Ducks unlimited treasury of waterfowling classics
  / illustrations by Francis Lee Jaques.
      p. cm.
    1. Waterfowl shooting—United States. 2. Waterfowl shooting—Canada.
3. Hunting stories—United States. 4. Hunting stories—Canada.
I. Ducks unlimited
SK331.A87 1995
799.2′44—dc20   95-23523
                                                          CIP

Published August 1995
Printed in the United States of America

Table of Contents

Foreword

WATERFOWLING IS A CHOOSING THAT OCCUPIES A UNIQUE NICHE among the many hunting venues with which we are blessed. I first experienced it half a century ago, and the die was cast even before my first duck, a splendid canvasback drake, made his splashdown.

In the fleeting decades since then I've passed a good time, savoring a wide array of hunting opportunities near and far. Driven birds in Europe, goose-bump-raising points by ramrod-stiff pointers locked on Georgia bobwhites, doves aplenty on several continents, a lion at seventeen feet, a magnificent desert ram way out there, and...well, life is good. And over those great years one question crops up repeatedly: If you had to give up all kinds of hunting except one, what would you keep?

Waterfowl! You know why. Pursuing ducks and geese involves such a tremendous variety of pleasurable accoutrements...blinds and boats, calls and calling, decoys and dogs, shotguns and shotshells. And it takes place in diverse, beautiful locales that never grow old. Finally, of course, there are the birds...magnificent in their variety and their personalities.

Just browsing through the titles and authors in this book triggers an overload of sensory memories. Mist rising from the duckweed-laced swamp, flooding me with aromas unknown to common, non-hunting folk; moon sinking rapidly behind the treetops, chased by the brightening east while the whisper of wings in the dark overhead sings of good things to come.

"Bull Cans of the Delta", "How Come?", "Memories of Mallards." Nash Buckingham, Robert Ruark, Gene Hill, Jimmy Robinson, W. B. Leffingwell, Zack Taylor. All these and more. It doesn't get any better than this.

Enjoy.

Grits Gresham
Natchitoches, LA
June, 1995

Introduction:
Wildfowling's Best

In the pages of every waterfowler's memory are tales worth sharing. Like a vintage decoy, the stories grow in value with time until they are savored for the treasures they are. Perhaps no other American sporting pastime has inspired a greater fraternity of master storytellers. The marshes, tidewaters, and flooded bottoms have long been the venues of sometimes musing, often hilarious, but always entertaining yarns that chronicle the life of the wildfowler.

This book is a collection of such anecdotes, a celebration of the rich literary heritage that is unique to waterfowling. Imagine sharing a duck blind with Gene Hill, Jimmy Robinson, Gordon MacQuarrie, Nash Buckingham, Robert Ruark, Aldo Leopold, and others whose prose has survived the rough seas of literary criticism to become timeless entries into our sporting heritage. With every turn of the page, you'll join these sporting notables as they share their thoughts and passion for wildfowling. They'll tug at your shirt sleeve, pulling you into their stories until you're seated beside them, contemplating the world through their eyes.

You'll witness the evolution of waterfowling, for each work captures a slice of history. Who could forget Nash Buckingham and "Bo-Whoop," his famous Burt Becker twelve-bore magnum. For Buckingham disciples, the gun came to develop an aura and personality of its own. Even today, what waterfowler wouldn't hope for a Bo-Whoop of his own? In "How Come," the duo joins a congenial group of Cajuns whose boathouse retreat becomes the setting for an essay that captures the spice of fabled Louisiana duck hunting as only Buckingham could.

Jimmy Robinson's adventures on Manitoba's Delta Marsh became legendary over the years, for he shared his tales with countless *Sports Afield* readers who came to know him through his energetic prose. "Bull Cans of the Delta" remains a classic, for it combines Jimmy's often-frequented hunting haunt and his favorite quarry. "Lucky is the hunter whose time and convenience can put him on the Delta," he writes, "at the precise instant of the bull can arrivals." In case you've never been there, Jimmy will take you as he has many before you.

What would a duck hunt be without an old friend? For a generation of readers, that favorite blindmate has been Gene Hill. His "Calling Ducks" essay shares the dreams of every waterfowler to one day master this beguiling sport. Like many of us, however, Hill's hunting prowess falls short of his wishes—or he leads us to believe it does anyway—but that's what makes him one of us.

We should remember, too, that in their day many of these writers, in addition to their distinguished reputations for storytelling, were important voices for wildlife preservation—they were conservation visionaries and activists as well as writers and hunters. Sigurd Olson, Aldo Leopold, Nash Buckingham, Gordon MacQuarrie, Jimmy Robinson, and others whose works are contained here helped shape public opinion and influence legislation beneficial to conserving wildlife and wildlife habitat.

There are works of many other writers here who love wild places and there inhabitants as well. Lean back and let them show you their special places, hideaways where wet dogs, weathered guns, and good sports are always welcomed.

Matthew B. Connolly, Jr.
Executive Vice President,
Ducks Unlimited, Inc.

Acknowledgments

Ducks Unlimited, Inc., gratefully acknowledges the courtesies extended by our copublisher, Willow Creek Press of Minocqua, Wisconsin, and the following copyright holders who permitted reprinting the material contained in this anthology.

Text Acknowledgements: Page 203, "You Got To Be Crazy to Be A Duck Hunter" from THE OLD MAN AND THE BOY by Robert C. Ruark. Copyright 1953, 1954 (c), 1955, 1956, 1957 by Robert C. Ruark. Reprinted by permission of Henry Holt and Co., Inc. Page 127, "The Wheatfields of Alberta" from A BOOK ON DUCK SHOOTING by Van Campen Heilner; copyright 1939 by Penn Publishing Co. and renewed 1967 by Van Campen Heilner. Reprinted by permission of Alfred A. Knopf, Inc. Page 191,"Red Legs Kicking" from A SAND COUNTY ALMANAC, AND SKETCHES HERE AND THERE by Aldo Leopold; copyright 1949 by Oxford University Press. Reprinted by permission of Oxford University Press. Page 257, "Russian Agents on Chesapeake Bay" from PARADISE: STORIES OF A CHANGING CHESAPEAKE by J.H. Hall; copyright 1994 by J.H. Hall. Reprinted by permission of Rappahannock Press, Inc. Page 157, "In the Presence of Mine Enemies" from MORE STORIES OF THE OLD DUCK HUNTERS; Page 89, "The Belated Neighbor" from LAST STORIES OF THE OLD DUCK HUNTERS; and Page 185, "Armistice Day Storm" from MACQUARRIE MISCELLANY by Gordon MacQuarrie. Copyright Ellen Gibson Wilson; copyrights in compilations by Willow Creek Press. Reprinted by permission of Willow Creek Press, et. al. Page 267, "Marsh Tales" from MARSH TALES: MARKET HUNTING, DUCK TRAPPING, AND GUNNING by William N. Smith; copyright 1985 by Tidewater Publishers. Reprinted by permission of Cornell Maritime Press. Page 223, "Missouri River Sandbar Geese" from GOOSE SHOOTING by Charles L. Cadieux. Copyright 1979. Reprinted by permission of the author. Page 167, "How Come?" from OLE' MISS, copyright 1937, 1946 and reprinted by permission of Dr. Dyrk Halstead and Robert Urich. Page 283, "The Life of a Decoy" by Zack Taylor reprinted from

Shooting on the Gulf Coast

BY W.B. LEFFINGWELL

1899

M Y BOYHOOD DAYS WERE SPENT WHERE GAME WAS PLENTIFUL, AND nothing but the exigencies of urgent business has been powerful enough to deprive me of outing afield in each of the passing years. Last year I was a bond slave to business in Chicago, while the fever of old-time sport ran with more than its wonted vigor; yet the summer days glided by, and less and less seemed the probabilities that the yoke of labor would be lightened. But the fates were working my emancipation in the person of the Hon. Frank Holland, of Dallas, Texas, who sang the siren song of "A hunter's and angler's paradise, where you can hunt geese, ducks, snipe, curlew or quail, catch tarpon, trout, red fish or Spanish mackerel, and dine on oysters, shrimp and terrapin within a few yards from where your boat is anchored."

Was Anthony ever tempted thus?

I fell from the grace of business, and as such turpitude, like poverty, loves company, I drew into my net, as my chosen companion, the hard-worked secretary of Montgomery, Ward & Co., Mr. George A. Thorne. Together we left Chicago on a wintry morning bound for Rockport, Texas. Our journey was a most delightful one; on the following day we were speeding through the scenic Ozark Mountains, that afternoon through the Indian Territory and at night through Texas.

Our host had gathered his party at Kennedy, where our land journey ended and our outdoor life was to commence, and, mindful that variety is no less the soul of sport than of life, had yoked on a worthy triumvirate of other sportsmen in the persons of three as good Nimrods as ever pulled trigger, Mr. Kirk Hall, of Dallas, and Col. I.L. Elwood and C.W. Marsh, of De Kalb, Ill.

The first morning of our hunt broke as beautiful and fresh as June;

the sun arose across the bay as bright and clear as in summer days; at the wharves the little schooners rocked with gentle undulations, for the wind was just astir and the waters were tremulous. All had been prepared for our trip; and soon the *Alice* and *White Rose* spread their canvas wings.

Captain William Armstrong, of our boat, *Alice*, assumed command, and we profited by his lore of land and sea. The first day we sailed perhaps twenty-five miles up Matagorda Bay, a beautiful sheet of water dotted here and there with islands of green, some small, some quite large, and all beached with myriad oyster shells. We stopped only once, and then to get oysters sufficient for our supper. That night the wind went down, the bay was as calm as a sleeping child and the heavens filled with stars of unusual brilliancy. Not a breath of air stirred, and it was so warm that we sat out of doors in our shirt sleeves. How the stars twinkled that night and were reflected in the sleeping waters! Our voices seemed unusually loud, but were hushed when the whistling wings of belated ducks were heard overhead, or the cry of a loon pierced the atmosphere and was answered by another apparently miles away. The next morning we did our first shooting.

The party was divided, Messrs. Holland, Elwood, Marsh and Thorne preferring to go after ducks and geese, and Mr. Hall and myself for quail. We landed on Matagorda Island—an island perhaps twenty-five miles long and from one to four miles wide—where we found a team awaiting us. It was a mule team, reins of rope, tugs of chain, but a wagon of excellent proportion. The parties placed at ponds for geese, Mr. Hall and I remained with the wagon and went in pursuit of quail.

As we drove over the island I could not but notice the scenery and soil. Here and there little bunches of chaparral shot above the weeds and grass and gave a deeper tinge to the waving fields of brown and green, and the sandy soil was made more apparent at the foot of the cactus bushes. These bushes are the places where quail enjoy their midday siestas, for they seek them from ten o'clock till four, and there bask in the warm sunshine and dust themselves. And such quantities of quail! Never had I seen them quite so plentiful before; almost every cactus bush had its covey of quail. We shot many, and as we drove we were told there were many deer on the island, and that possibly we might get a shot.

Our course took us along the margin of a dry slough, and suddenly there sprung ahead of us from the grass a splendid doe. Instantly the Captain cried to me: "Put in a shell with big shot; there's a buck in the grass."

I did not see the deer, but my comrades did, and almost simultaneously two reports rang out, the buck gave one wild plunge, his head fell heavily against his shoulders, and he crushed to earth. We put the deer into the wagon, and then moved slowly along looking for quail under the cactus. I watched the bush, but I did not change my heavy shells, and 'twas lucky for me that I did not, for as we approached the bush a magnificent yearling buck plunged from it not more than twenty-five yards away. He made a few jumps before I caught him, and, at the discharge of my gun, he made one wild leap and fell dead, his neck filled with No. 3 shot—my wild goose load. Congratulations were showered upon me, and we thought we had achieved quite glory enough for one day, but I was destined to still more and continued sport at the fresh-water pond, where we found Mr. Thorne already busy. I liked the looks of that pond and, as I knew it was the only one for miles, ducks and geese would surely come there for water. Unfortunately I had but a few shells, but I decided to spend the balance of the day there, whilst the genial Captain and friend Hall went to the boat for shells.

The day was quite warm and summer-like, and I divested myself of my coat, awaiting the flight of game. At times a few scattered flocks of ducks came in, and almost invariably paid toll. The noon hour was a drowsy one. The flight of ducks and geese began about two, and I looked longingly in the distance for my companions. I was willing to go thirsty, I was willing to go hungry, but how I did wish for more ammunition! As it was, however, I killed a big bag of ducks and Canada geese before my companions returned.

It was late when we reached the boat. I had gone hungry for most of the day, and, even had I not, I could have done ample justice to the venison, the quail, the oysters, and the hot biscuits that awaited me.

The next morning we sailed further up the bay, passing islands of the same character as seen before, and saw hundreds of swans and pelicans on the island bars. We were now in pursuit of "redheads," for, while they were abundant in portions of the bay, we were prevented by first one thing, then another, from getting at them. Sailing all the forenoon brought us to a little island which the Captain said was the first redhead grounds. With numerous decoys we sought the coves and inlets, but missed the flight. We killed a few ducks, but others of the party were more successful.

The following morning we started again. Much time was wasted in an endeavor to locate the flight, yet the afternoon enabled us to make the score for the day good. The afternoon was one of observation for me, and, as I had noticed the flight of geese about two miles west of us, I knew that flight led to a fresh-water pond, and I determined to find that pond on the morrow and to get in line of a flight that had been undisturbed for days, possibly weeks. "I am with you," volunteered my colleague, Thorne, true sportsman that he is. Our "Captain," of course, was included.

We had an early breakfast, and a tramp of about two miles brought us to a dried-up swale or low land, through which a belt of dried mud showed where fresh water had recently been. To an inexperienced hunter there was not so much to indicate that one would obtain good shooting here, but, having marked the location the day before, and knowing the scarcity of fresh water, it was a certainty to me that the geese would come here some time during the day for water. We dug pits for blinds, each on the opposite side of the pond; we stuck weeds into the soft soil which margined our blinds and were soon ready for the coming of the geese. At first they did not come, and Mr. Thorne, becoming impatient, wandered away to another pond where ducks were pitching in.

From my post I had ample opportunity to take in my surroundings. On every side the prairie grass met the horizon; to the south the sand dunes protected the island from the roaring gulf, whose proximity was constantly heard, and once a schooner's topmast glided along as if on the distant land; to the west the hill arose with gentle slope, and cactus bushes and weeds and grass parted here and there disclosing the blue sky; at the north the dried bed island ponds were traced, and far away an old windmill stood like a sentinel. Less than a hundred yards was an old barbed-wire fence, which to our memories will be ever dear, for over it the geese came in trios, sextets and flocks, and oftentimes were compelled to raise their flight to prevent striking it. Those who have hunted geese, or who have studied their habits, know with what regularity they come and go, and I knew that if we were in their line of flight we would enjoy the finest sport of our lives.

The day was beautiful and clear; the wind blew from the east just sufficiently strong to at times catch the strong pinions of the birds and veer them slightly. I had been in my blind perhaps half an hour, had killed eight ducks which I set up as decoys, when afar in the west I saw the first flight of Canada geese trailing along the dried pond beds. I watched them closely, for they were the forerunners of a great army, and I knew that their trail would be followed for the balance of the day by those who straggled behind. Along they came, nearer and nearer; they reached the old wire fence and, responding to my *"Ah-unk!" "Ah-unk!"* they ceased vibrating their wings, sails were set, and, with vociferous cries, they hovered over my decoys.

I doubled up one with each barrel and the balance hurried away in wild affright. The killing of the two geese afforded me pleasure, but the greater pleasure came from the fact that I had circumvented the birds, had found their line of flight, and was promised a day of rare sport. The geese came every few minutes. Those I killed I set up for decoys, and, although I signaled after the first geese were killed, I had bagged eight before I could get my companion back.

The main flight was now on and, as we waited for the birds to come between us, few flocks escaped paying toll. I will not describe the many doubles we made, how we at one time killed all of six which hovered over our decoys, and how we often killed birds at seemingly impossible distances and heights, nor will I confess to easy misses which we made by misjudging height, distance and speed.

During a lull in the flight the Captain stopped at my blind, and when I complimented the beautiful day and the mild wind, which had now increased in force, he replied, "The day has been beautiful, but what will the night or the morrow be?" "The same as today," I responded. "Don't depend on that," he replied; "the wind is increasing, the cranes are uneasy, the flight of ducks is erratic, and the sky had taken on a darker tinge at the north, and to-night or to-morrow I look for a 'norther.'" "A norther?" I replied. "I should be more than pleased to see one, for, coming from the

North, I would like to see what our winds are like after they have reached you and passed over the entire South." "Don't you jest about a 'norther.'" he replied, "for they are mighty serious affairs, and I reckon when you have encountered one you will not care to see another."

About four o'clock the wind increased in force; it veered to the north and at five o'clock it was blowing a gale. The Captain was extremely anxious to reach his boat, and we reluctantly left our blinds. The ride to the boat was a cold one, and our skiffs were tossed like corks, for a "norther" was upon us and the water was crested with white caps.

Messrs. Hall and Marsh had put in a portion of the day after quail, and we found that unitedly we had bagged seventy-three geese, forty-one ducks, thirty-seven quail, two cranes and one wildcat. Mr. Hall shot the wildcat as it bounded from beneath a cactus bush.

It had been our intention to have gone farther north and to Heinz Bay after red-heads and canvas-backs the next morning, but a head wind prevented, and, acting upon the advice of the Captain, we lifted anchor and started on our return to Rockport, for we were assured the "norther" would last several days and we could not fish or hunt.

We were much disappointed for this, for the Captain of the *White Rose* had promised to draw his immense seine, when he would catch anywhere from a barrel to a half a dozen barrels of the famous "diamond-back terrapin." Our trip to Rockford was a stormy one; the wind blew a gale, the bay was very rough, and we all escaped seasickness by the narrowest of margins. Our sloop tossed and rolled in the trough of the sea, our mainsail was torn into shreds, our boats were enveloped at times in spray, so, taking it altogether, we experienced a "norther" which justified the Captain's prediction. We have no desire to encounter another.

When the gale had blown itself out, Thorne and I decided to return with Captain Armstrong to the land of the "red-heads," and so we sailed north again, this time destined for Heinz Bay, other red-head resorts and Port Lavaca. But we were destined not to reach either that night. After sailing an hour after dark we reached the harbor where we had previously landed and killed so many geese. We could not go farther, so decided to visit the geese again in the morning, and once more see that good old wire fence; then in the afternoon to sail for Port Lavaca.

At break of day we were in the blinds. The day broke dark and dismal, and rain had filled all the ponds. I at once saw that we were apt to lose the line of flight, for there was so much water that the geese could find hundreds of fresh-water ponds now. So it proved. We got shots at only four geese and bagged two of them. But the lowering day and north wind, the late "norther" and another approaching, stirred up the ducks so they came in flocks large and small to our decoys. At first, a mist moistened our hands and faces; then it rained, and it kept on raining until we, in spite of corduroys, were soaked. Rain and sand played havoc with our guns. I felt several times like surrendering to the weather, and finally, at about four o'clock, Mr. Thorne's extractor refused to work any longer and we gave up.

One more day we put in on duck, and it was our last. We found a better flight about half a mile east of our former blinds. Then, as the time set for our outing was up, we put about and had a pleasant sail to Rockport. We had found all that Mr. Holland had promised.

The Death of the Red-Winged Mallard

BY H.S. CANFIELD

1900

I T TOOK ROBERT LEE BRIGGS FIVE YEARS, WORKING OFF AND ON, TO SLAY the red-winged mallard. The pursuit got to be so much of a passion with him that it hurt his business, for he was a market-hunter on the southwestern coast of Texas. In summer he caught red-snappers, pompanos, sheeps-heads, and turtles. All winter he shot ducks, snipe, and wild geese, which he sold to produce dealers in Corpus Christi. He put in so much time trying to kill the drake with the crimson feathers that the dealers were wroth. They said he was ruining one of the brightest careers that ever opened before a young man in the Southwest. If he had been a "lit'ry person" he would have thought of "John Burley," who was a constant fisher for a certain one-eyed perch, which as constantly gave him the perch-laugh. The perch-laugh consists of making three bubbles rise in rapid succession, then two slow bubbles, and then two fast ones.

Briggs was not a "lit'ry person." He held that to look straight over the gun-barrels in all sorts of weather, to judge correctly, distance, speed of the flying quarry, and wind velocity; to be wise in the habits of beasts and birds, to be able, by a glance at the sun, to tell the time of day within five minutes; to be expert in the building of blinds and the use of decoys, were enough for any man. Nature was his book, and he studied it. He had three maxims handed down to him by his father, who died just after the last Indian raid, and these governed his life:

"When you've got money, he'p a feller that hain't got money.

"Shootin' on Sunday makes bad luck on Monday.

"Pers'verunce and feesh-ile on the gun-locks 'll do a heap."

It was the last maxim which sustained him during his five years' chase—off and on—of the bird that he came to know as "Red Wing," and he was proud of the ending of this contest of wits.

Back of Corpus Christi the land rises and rolls away to the northward in a prairie covered by rich grasses. Between the rolls are hollows or swales, in many of which there are ponds of fresh water, averaging a mile in length by a half-mile across. They are not generally more than waist-deep in the center, and are grown up thickly with senna weeds. Senna weeds are tall and slender and bear long, slim, bean-like pods, which rattle in ghostly fashion in the winds of winter nights. Each of the pods contains several round, jet-black, shiny seeds, and of these seeds wild fowl are fond.

The ducks roost upon the gulf, but they feed in the senna ponds all day, flying from one to another in clouds. So thick are they that if a camera were focussed on a pond and the ducks flushed, the negative would show a solid black wall of them. When they are scared by the down-swooping of a hawk, the thunder of their wings may sometimes be heard two miles away, and a man, crouched at one end of a pond, though the day be clear, will be shaded by the mass of birds streaming two hundred yards above him as completely as if he held an umbrella. With the sun flashing upon heads and wings, the tens of thousands of them show every hue of the jewels of the mines, yellow and pink and bronze and carmine, white and brown and gray and purple—"blue, glossy green and velvet black," like the snakes of the Ancient Mariner. It is gorgeous.

Here and there are groves of live-oaks, sometimes covering acres, and often circular in form. They are called "mottes," and, viewed from a distance, are not unlike islands of darker green, rising from the sea of grass around them. Mustang motte stands fifteen miles northeast of Corpus Christi, and near it is one of the larger senna ponds.

On an early day in November, Briggs was making his way on horse-back to this pond. When he reached it he staked out the horse with a rope fifty feet long, and walked to the edge of the pond, where he hid himself in the weeds which grew up to the shore. A gadwall buzzed past, which he shot. Wading out, he picked up the duck and went back to his hiding-place. There he sharpened a dark stick, three feet long. One end he stuck into the mud twenty yards from the bank. He pressed it down until only two inches of it protruded. On this end he hung the gadwall by inserting the point in its throat, just under the head. The duck floated, with its bill slightly raised, as if it were alive and swallowing a tasty morsel. This was his decoy. In an hour a half-dozen ducks of various kinds were set out and they made a flock.

The afternoon had grown old and there was a cessation in the flight. Briggs decided to permit himself a pipe. Suddenly he heard a splash, and, peering cautiously, saw something which kept him thinking for a long time. A hundred yards away, in a lake-like expanse of the water, sat a mallard drake of great size. The nearly level rays of the declining sun beamed on him ruddily, and every feather of him shone like the facet of a gem. Briggs marked the lustrous emerald of his massive head, the reddish bronze of his neck, the pearly gray of his breast. He was instinct with life and vigor, a beautiful, powerful wild thing, as noble a masterpiece as ever came from Nature's incessant workshop. Glorying in his strength and loveliness, he swam in small, rapid circles, or floated idly, gazing down at his own reflection and pleased with himself to the last degree. He preened his feathers until each lay as smoothly as if ironed, dived boldly and reappeared twenty yards away, merely to show that he could do it, spurted for fifty feet at lightning speed, checked suddenly, whirled as if upon a pivot, then threw his bill high and uttered a hoarse, strident challenge, that boomed upon the mild air like the bellow of some huge horn.

The man, his pipe forgotten, crouched until the ooze came up to his waistband. Then, as he looked and longed, the bird threw half of his body out of water, spread his wings upwards to their full reach and revolved slowly. The sunlight rested upon the pinions, and Briggs, to his wonder, saw that in each wing were brilliant crimson feathers. They were not more than four or five in number, but were of the largest, and deeply hued. He knew that the fowl was a freak, of course, just as there are birds that are albinos, but he believed that it was the only one of its kind in the world. He wished to possess it, as a collector of coins will wish to possess an ugly circular bit of copper, not half so attractive as a new nickel.

He raised his chin slightly and emitted a soft noise, much similar to the sound made by man when clucking to a lazy horse. This is a note of mallards when swallowing acorns. It was his deadliest call. In response the great drake became motionless and listened intently. The fowler waited a full minute, then repeated the cluck. The mallard, his crimson pinions flashing like the wings of the cardinal, sprang twenty feet in the air and was away like a shot, dropping a squawk of derision as he went. Briggs rose, stretching his cramped limbs. Then he said:

"Sure, he ain't no this year's bird. He's smart. That swaller call oughter got him. I never done it better. Howsomever, pers'verunce and feesh-ile on th' gun-locks 'll do a heap."

He stayed at Mustang motte three days, but he did not see the red-winged mallard again. When he returned to Corpus Christi he sold his ducks, and before the wood-fire in Nic Constantin's smoking room told the story of the red-wing.

'Lige Hawkins, skipper of the schooner *Oriole*, felt his pulse and asked him to put out his tongue; Andy Faulkner, a surveyor who never surveyed, said that he was "daffy," and "Doc" Payne, who had had two patients in three years, prescribed boneset tea and castor oil.

Standing at Chiltapin dam in the first part of the following October, engaged in killing teal, he noted a solitary flyer moving quietly but fast out of the north, the long neck stretched forwards and the wings sharply elbowed. Something in its size and poise sent a reminiscent thrill, and he stood with rapt gaze. Soon, with a steady rush, each pulsation of the smitten air distinctly audible, the bird passed over him and the crimson feathers shone like a tongue of flame in each broad wing.

The man set himself to guard the pond at Mustang motte. He waited and watched with admirable patience and skill through the cold months. Thrice he was rewarded by a sight of the quarry, and always alone. Once the drake passed above him, not more than fifty yards up. Making allowance for speed and trusting to a stray pellet to do the work, he pitched up his 10-gauge and pulled the hindward trigger. A red feather floated downwards. Briggs took it to Corpus Christi and showed it to the hotel doubters.

The next two years were depressing to him. In 1898, however, he met a Mexican who had been shooting over the salt marshes which lie to the north of Brownsville, and he had seen a large mallard with crimson pinions. He said, too, that the bird was with a hen of lighter gray than is common to the females. He supposed that she was of the summer's breeding.

Briggs wrote to several acquaintances living near to the mouth of the Rio Grande. He heard from only one of them. This man wanted to know where he got his opium.

Being determined to shake off what he called his "hoodoo," he got together a supply of provisions, mounted his "grulla" pony and went into the field early in September, 1899. Only blue-winged teal had reached the Gulf country at that season.

He worked on, without putting much heart into it, until one day in December, when, walking along the edge of Rincon marsh and hoping to pick up a jacksnipe or two, he saw a brace of ducks pitch near the center of an arm of the sea, miscalled "Swan Lake." They were three hundred yards from him, but he could discern that they were mallards, that they were male and female, and as they descended he caught a gleam of fiery red in the wings of one which set his temples hammering.

Here was his old opponent in the game of venery, this time bringing his wife with him. The gloss upon his plumage said that he was in the best of health. The hen was shades lighter than she should have been—a duck that had barely missed being an albino. Indeed, as she swam on the greenish wavelets of the inlet in certain lights she seemed white. Intent only on discovering what portion of the country the birds affected after their daily bath of salt water, Briggs discharged both barrels in the air. They rose instantly, spiraled high and shot away northwest by west, headed straight for Mustang motte, twelve miles distant. That night the market-hunter broke camp and when morning dawned he was in his old place.

Then began a campaign of two weeks. It was prosecuted with all of the skill, patience, watchfulness and woodcraft which his twenty years in the field had taught him. It seemed to him that "Red Wing" had more than human intelligence. He practised every lure within his large knowledge. He gave the assembly note. He gave the feeding note. He gave the fighting challenge. He gave the love call. He gave the low, deep recitation which means: "I have found a wonderful new kind of food in great plenty. Come and have a lot of it." He used decoys of painted wood, silhouette decoys made of tin, dead mallard decoys. He even rode to Corpus Christi and returned with a couple of tame Muscovies. These set out with strings hitched to their legs, and they quacked merrily. Other mallards came to them in plenty, but "Red Wing" and his mate kept aloof. They were at the Mustang pond for hours each day, but the drake did not swim within a hundred yards of the man, though he devised a fresh blind in a new part of the water each night and occupied it at daybreak.

He noticed a temerity on the part of the hen. She was less intelligent or less cautious than her companion. Several times he could have killed her with a long shot, but he cared nothing about her. When she showed a disposition to approach him closely she was brought back by a muttered warning from her spouse, who had eyes, as the hunter said, "in his head, in his tail, in both wings, and in his flippers." Finally, determined, it seemed, to make his days as miserable as possible, the pair forsook the pond at large and confined their visits to a part of it which, for two hundred yards in every direction, was bare of weeds or cover of any kind.

Here, safe from harm, they floated and made love. So surely as Briggs drew near to the edge of the clear water, the male's deep voice sounded and they were away to the gulf for another plunge into salt waves. They did not roost on the pond, and Briggs spent some time in endeavoring to find where they did roost, thinking that he might get near to them with a "fire-boat" in the black dark, but he failed. As distance is nothing at all to a mallard, he concluded that they went fifty miles down the coast-line before pitching upon some still, inland bay. They returned each morning at sunrise, getting their feed by diving to the bottom, which was thick with senna seeds.

Then he absented himself from the pond for several days, and did his shooting miles away. When he returned he bore, besides his game, a large bundle of senna weeds. He amassed a pile of them. The fourth day he spent in considering the making of his armor of deception. On the fifth day he went to Corpus Christi, bought a cheap shotgun and had the barrels cut to a foot in length, so that it could be used easily with one hand. On the sixth day he went back to camp, feeling composed and hopeful. The seventh day was Sunday, and, in obedience to the maxim of his father, he loafed heartily. The remainder of the time he put in binding the senna weeds about an iron barrel-hoop, just big enough to go over his head and rest firmly on his shoulders. When he had finished he had a most natural clump of stalks, massy enough to deceive any bird, no matter how super-duck its intellect might be. He tried on the thing, and, turning it round and round, found that there was one crevice through which he could see with his right eye. Then he went to sleep.

At daybreak he was at the edge of the pond's clear space, with all his body submerged. The shortened gun was held up among the weeds about his head. His teeth chattered, but he clenched them and waited. When the sun was two degrees above the horizon "Red Wing" and his wife pitched in the center of the open water. They swam about each other and clucked mutual congratulations on the day and the certainty of a good breakfast. The clump of senna, inch by inch, drifted out from the tangle of growth. So slowly it moved that it might have been driven by the gentlest and most fitful of breezes.

One thing troubled the man in the moving weeds: The hen was nearest him. She dashed gaily about, but always came back to her position between him and the drake, which was forty yards further away, the crimson pinions lying like smears of blood against his sides.

Not more than a hundred feet separated Briggs and the female, when "Red Wing," moved by a sudden impulse, no man can say what—a slight disarrangement of the disguise of weeds, something too swift in its advance, some recognition that it had no place in the clear space—threw back his emerald head, gave the danger note and launched himself afar. The hen followed instantly, upspringing with the activity of the dragonfly, but she was too late. Jets of smoke leaped from the weed clump and she checked, a shapeless mass in air, then struck the water, dead, making a shower of spray.

Muttering volubly in anger, the hunter threw off his covering, waded to the body, grasped a limp wing and made his way to shore. The warm rays of the sun fell on him and took away something of the chill. He was stooping over the wife, noting the beauty of her pale plumage, when a rush of wings startled him. He glanced up. Not seventy-five yards distant the male was darting by. He went a half-mile down the wind, came back, circled out of gunshot and headed for the gulf. As he went he uttered a despairing call. Briggs whistled softly, put on dry clothing, boiled a pot of coffee, smoked a pipe and sprawled upon his blanket.

Next morning, just as the last few stars were paling in the west, he placed the dead bird as a decoy only twenty yards from the weeds which ringed the open space. At sunrise "Red Wing" came flying swiftly, not turning to the right or to the left, speeding as an arrow, seeking his lost love. Made desperate by loneliness, and all caution gone, he darted downwards and hovered for a moment above his consort. That instant the gun spoke and he dropped beside her, shot through head, throat, and heart.

Briggs told this tale before the wood fire in Nic Constantin's smoking-room, holding the body of the red-winged mallard in his hands. He felt hurt because the men did not praise him.

A Close Call

BY ALEXANDER HUNTER

1905

T HE SHOOTING OF ALL OTHER KIND OF WATERFOWL IS A MERE PASTIME as compared to hunting the brant. One can build a blind in the reeds at the end of a peninsula, promontory, or an island, for wild ducks and geese, where, well protected from the icy winds, warm and comfortable, royal pleasure may be had in shooting canvas-back, red-head, black duck, pin-tails and shovelers, over the decoys; or he can build a cozy shelter on the banks of some creek that runs through the marshes and sea-meadows, and try his marksmanship on the black ducks. But he may sit in those land blinds during the whole winter and never see a brant hovering over the decoys, for that wary gamebird gives a wide berth to marsh, cape, island or mainland and feeds only in the open a half mile or more away from shore.

You may call the suspicious wild goose to the decoys, and even induct the cautious swan to some within shot, but there is no call, no lure ever devised that will induce that king of the waterfowl, the brant, to come within range of the heaviest caliber shot-gun. Unlike the black duck, they love a crowd, and like the canvas-back they gather in great flocks of their own species. In the early morning and evening they ride the waters in vast numbers and are quick to leave the water at the sight of any craft. They do not investigate, and have no sense of curiosity, and take wing at the slightest alarm. At low water the sand shoals are black with unnumbered thousands, and it is simply exasperating for the sportsman to gaze at them and know that if he tries to creep up within shot, their sentinels, well post-ed a hundred yards or so on the front, rear and flank, will give the alarm and in a second, with a noise like thunder, the huge mass will rise high in air and alight only when they reach a wide expanse of water where there is no boat in sight. Yet brant hunting is the most fascinating sport of all water shooting. To knock over one of these birds, going like the wind, fully repays the sportsman for many a long wait, and the risk only gives the sport a keener flavor.

Just before one Christmas I wrote to Roy Masters and Bruce Singleton that I was going after brant, and arranged to meet them at Bayview, a hamlet close to the coast. Going down a day earlier to get things in shape I found Jake Martin the master of the little sloop, and Jerry, his assistant, with everything in readiness. The next evening when my companions arrived, we all went immediately aboard the vessel, and were soon humming down the broadwater before a stiff breeze, running into an estuary at dark, not over a mile from Smith Island.

The first three or four days were windy but clear, and we had some good sport shooting black duck in the creeks, marshes, and sea-meadows, with spasmodic luck among the shovelers; but not a crack at the brant which we saw by the thousands only half a mile away. However, a sportsman must take the fat with the lean, so we enjoyed the days fully, knowing a change of weather must soon occur to give us the chance we longed for.

One morning the skipper awoke us, saying "there is going to be a change of weather, and I think you all will have a good chance at the brant to-day."

My companions hurriedly got out of their bunks and began to dress in the dim light of the swinging lantern, but as it was not my day out I turned over and was soon in a profound slumber. It seemed to me I had hardly closed my eyes when I was aroused by Jerry shaking me violently, who said a storm seemed likely, and he had signaled the two men in the blind to come back; but they did not appear to understand, and were banging away at ducks right and left. Dressing quickly I went on deck where the two boatmen were working with a will to lower a boat and go after my companions.

The weather outlook was certainly portentous. It was after dawn but the sky was black as ink, with the wind rising. For a while I clung to the mast, watching the war of the elements; but as a tornado swept across the wide waste of waters, with snow in a great, gray cloud, I hurriedly retreated below and closed the hatches. The sloop heaved, dipped and heeled until I thought she would be blown over on her side, while every mast, spar and rope creaked, rasped and hummed, each in its own language. I felt no anxiety about the absent ones for their guides, born and bred on the coast, could outface any storm that blew, and I fancied my companions, by now, must be safe on land.

The whole day passed with the storm showing no sign of dying, and when the next morning dawned and nobody came, I grew seriously alarmed; but I was as much a prisoner as if I were an inhabitant of a convict ship off Boulogne. There was no boat—not even a skiff about the vessel, so it was with a glad heart I welcomed a boat of the life-saving service, which shortly brought me news of the safety of the crew and guests. When I reached camp, Bruce told me the following story of their experience. He said:

It was pitch dark when we reached the deck, and we had to be very careful in getting into our boat, for the wind had risen during the night and the water was choppy and rough. By the light of the lantern we stowed away our traps. Jake, who had already loaded the other boat with decoys, started off first and we soon followed, guided by the gleam of the ship's lamp which Jerry had placed in the bow of the boat. It was bitterly cold, and the salt spray on our clothing froze as it fell. We could not see a yard ahead but the air was vibrant with sounds that were sweetest melody to the sportsman's ear: the swish of the wildfowl's wings, the splash as they sprang from the water, was all around us. In a half-hour we reached the blind, and the two guides anchored the last of the decoys: some two hundred and fifty in number. After our boat was shoved into its place of concealment, the skipper said he and Jerry were going back to the sloop, but would hover around the blind when day broke and gather in any game we might kill. The two then disappeared and we were left alone.

When day broke we looked around and took in the scene. A half-mile off was the lofty lighthouse tower at Smith Island silhouetted against the murky sky; close to it was the life-saving station. In front, about two hundred yards away, was the sand beach that separated the ocean from the broadwater; in the rear, in plain sight, was our sloop tugging at her anchors, and pitching violently. The surf was booming sullenly on the bar, and as the morning advanced the clouds grew denser and blacker.

Roy called my attention to the sloop, and turning, I saw the skipper and his companions waving their hats frantically. Now, whether they were signaling us to return or wishing us good luck we did not stop to speculate, for just at that moment a big bunch of mallard came heading straight for the decoys, that were riding the waves like things of life, and it was a pretty sight to see the ducks set their wings as they approached. We used our number twelves as they hovered over the decoys, and then dropped. We had hardly replaced ourselves when we both hurriedly exchanged our guns for heavy-caliber ones, and instead of using the standard No. 4 shot, we took shells loaded with double B, for a lot of wild geese and a couple of swans, borne on the pinions of the wind that was now rising into a gale, were coming with a grand sweep toward our blind. We sat silent and allowed them to come directly over us. How large the swans looked; their necks seemed as long as fishing-poles! I chose the one on the right and I could catch the gleam of his questioning eyes as he turned his head first on one side and then the other.

"Now give it to them," I shouted, and raised my gun. In an instant the powerful wings of the great bird beat the air with tremendous strokes; he was soaring upward when I pulled trigger, and slantwise he hurtled downward. Roy killed his bird and it fell dead among the decoys with outspread wings.

It then began to snow and trouble was brewing, for protected as we were by the cedar trees that formed the blind, yet we could feel the swell of the billows as they came in rapid succession; but we had no time to think of our situation for the brant flocked around the decoys in a way I had never seen in all my experience. The tempest had scattered the flock into fragments, and in flying about they had caught sight of our immense raft of decoys and came up circling around us fearlessly. Such sport as we had for a quarter of an hour surpassed our wildest hopes.

Had it been raining, one could say it came in torrents, but being snow, it seemed to blot out the world; so fierce was the wind that the flakes came horizontally and we had to turn our backs to the blast. We could not see the wildfowl until within a few feet of us, and then we found it was like aiming at shadows. We did not realize our position; the roar of the tempest, the shrieks of the seafowls, the blinding gale, the darting birds, the firing and loading gave us a sporting fever that made us temporarily mad. How long it lasted we did not know, but we were recalled to our senses by the sight of our decoys dragging off. The water was about three feet deep and each decoy had six feet of line held by a four-pound mushroom anchor, yet such was the fury of the wind that they were blown away as literally as if unhampered. We laid our guns down and looked into each other's eyes; then Roy shouted to me to hang onto the cedar bushes which were nearly submerged, for if the boat should get loose we would be gone.

"Where are the guides?" yelled Roy.

I screamed back that they couldn't find us in such a blinding snow storm.

After a little while I told my companion to shoot off his gun at regular intervals of ten or twenty seconds. The tide had swept in from the sea and our boat had risen to the top of the blinds, but the cedars still held, and I clung to them for all I was worth. Our boat was narrow, shallow and flat-bottomed and could not have lived a minute in such a sea. It was only the cedar blind that broke the impact of the waves and kept our craft from turning upside down, and I knew it to be only a question of minutes before the waters would submerge the blinds entirely. Our small quarter-of-a-minute gun called for help, faintly perhaps, but as earnestly as the minute guns of a doomed ship in mid-ocean. I got my flask from the depths of my pocket, unscrewed the top, took a heavy drink and handed it to my partner; it looked like it was to the be the last one we would take in this world. I forced my comrade to hold on to the cedars, while I slipped off my big, hip, india-rubber boots, and when I resumed my hold he did the same. Just at that moment the storm held up, the skies lightened, and the air became clear, and then our guides sighted us and their boat darted to the blind.

"Jump! jump!" they cried, and as Roy started to gather his traps together the skipper with his face ashy white, screamed, "My God, man, don't stop, it is a matter of life and death!" and we were fairly hauled head-foremost into the boat. Then the guides, with furious haste, made for the sand beach of Cape Charles.

The boat was big, roomy and well keeled, capable of carrying a dozen people, and had they put her before the wind we would have fetched up somewhere on the Virginia mainland; but the attempt to reach the sand dunes, a couple of hundred yards away, with the heavy surf breaking over the bar, was a bad error of judgment, for when we reached the sandy bar the oncoming breakers were beating with terrific force. The guides of course were ignorant of this. They could not see a boat's length ahead and naturally struck for the nearest land. The wind and tide were against us, and the rowers had to fight their way inch by inch. At last we reached the bar and found ourselves in a vortex of swirling waters; the boat was swung around and a great wave striking it broadside, turned it completely over and emptied its living freight and the guns and ammunition into the white-foamed surf. We got upon our feet and grasped hands and clung to each other; the water was waist high but the league-long rollers were way over our heads and we would duck to let them sweep by, then rise and wait for another. We dared not move for we were on the highest point of the bar. There was nothing to do but wait. In a few minutes the icy waters numbed our limbs; the struggle for life waxed feebler with every onrush of the waves, and it seemed to us we must soon be where tempest and storms could harm us no further. And then George and his boat crew loomed beside us to our great relief.

Just as the dawn broke that morning, John Goffigan, the keeper of the Cape Charles' lighthouse extinguished the great lantern, and stretching his arms, after his long and lonely night's vigil, prepared to descend the spiral stairway, when he happened to notice the barometer, and the rapidly dropping mercury which foretells a great storm. Lifting a spy glass from the rack he stepped out on the gallery and swept the scene with his glass. What he saw caused him to rush back into the room, open the trap-door and go down the winding steps faster than he ever did in his life before. Once outside, he ran at full speed to the Coast-guard Station, a few steps distant, where the guardsmen were sitting around the stove waiting for breakfast, and breathlessly shouted, "George there are two d__ fools sitting in a blind off Little Clam Bar, and a big storm is right on us; they be doomed as sure as fate."

It brought all of them to their feet and before long a boat was launched under direction of Captain George Hitchings and on its way to the duck hunters. The guardsmen kept outside the breakers and made their way parallel to the shore until they were opposite the stranded men, and then went on with a magnificent rush through the raging surf.

The Cape Charles' surfmen are the pick of the watermen of the coast, and make a crew which for efficiency and daring, is unequaled. They did their very best that morning, and strained their muscles to the uttermost tension as Captain Hitchings, who held the steering oar, yelled to them to put every pound of steam on. The rowers were half blinded by the spray, but the white-crested billows that mocked and sported with the strongest ship, found their master at last as, safely and steadily, the lifeboat pushed through the caldron and reached the half-drowned men, with not a minute to spare. Over the gunwale the half-dazed sportsmen and guides were hauled; the boat then put about and watching its chance, rode out in the open sea, and in a brief time the sufferers were safe in the Coast Station house, where they were stripped of their clothing, rubbed dry, stimulated and put to bed. The next day Captain Hitchings sent a boat to bring back the lone sportsman on the sloop.

We found the guns three days after, but the ammunition was ruined. Both boats were stove in and were literally things of shreds and patches. The two pairs of boots were thrown back into the water after a hasty examination. Of the two hundred and odd decoys, not a dozen were ever recovered; they were undoubtedly carried out to sea, and some of them may still be riding the billows thousands of miles from where they were anchored.

Duck Shooting in the Old Days

By Fred Kimble
1911

MEMORY NOW TAKES ME BACK MORE THAN FIFTY YEARS TO THE Illinois River and the happiest days of my life, and I seem to see the old camp grounds, bluff, points of timber, bends in the river, sloughs, shooting grounds and everything, just as I saw them in the long, long ago. In 1868 I lived in Chillicothe, 18 miles north of Peoria, on the Illinois River. The river bottoms were low and marshy on the opposite side, and the best duck shooting was to be found there.

Duck Island marsh and lake, 32 miles below Peoria, was my favorite shooting ground, back as far as 1869. In that year Joe Long, Henry Doty, Alden Wilky and myself started down from Chillicothe on a trip to the Sunny South, intending to hunt on our way down the river in a small houseboat belonging to Wilky. Our fist stop was Duck Island and camps of duck hunters were in evidence all along the west bank. We arrived in the night and carried our boats over the ridge that lies between the river and the rice pond. The wild rice was as thick as you ever saw wheat in a field. Other boats had been taken as far as the edge of the pond, but no boats thus far had penetrated more than a boat length into the thick rice. The water was but a few inches in depth, but the soft mud went down to Jericho, I guess, and then some.

Before leaving Chillicothe we had shot in the Crow Creek rice pond and had come prepared for just such an emergency, and each had a push pole, the kind shown in Long's book. The cuts of boats, decoys, batteries and sink box shown in his book were taken from my outfit. With the push poles, or mud sticks, we were enabled to navigate all over the rice pond, while about all our neighbors could do was to climb the willow trees that grew around the edge of the pond and watch the ducks fall as we would kill them above the rice.

We would shoot till noon, then put in the balance of the day picking up, and it was a man-sized job. On coming ashore we would hide our new-fangled push poles under the rice a few feet out from the shore and wade and wallow through the mud, pulling or pushing our boats the rest of the way, to be met by the other hunters. We shot and worked in this way for about two weeks, when the pond froze over and the ducks left for the South, and we followed them as far as New Madrid, Missouri, making the trip down the Illinois and Mississippi rivers. When we left our duck-shooting friends were still wondering how we could stand it to wade and wallow in the mud, all over the rice pond, day after day, as we had done!

Discovery of Choke Boring Guns

We had our camp outfit hauled over to Little River, seven miles from the Mississippi, a famous resort of ducks and geese, where we camped for the Winter. We were in a part of the Sunken Lands district of Missouri, Arkansas, Tennessee and Kentucky, caused by an earthquake in 1811. I had a double-barrel muzzle-loader, built by O.P. Secor of Peoria, and a single-barrel muzzle-loader, built by Joseph Tanks of Boston. Joe had a breech-loader built by Tonks, and Doty had two muzzle-loaders. My two guns were the first guns ever choke-bored; Joe's was the second. Doty's two guns were open shooting guns. The barrels of my Secor gun were too thick to stand much of a choke, but the single gun had a good thick barrel, and Mr. Tonks made a great shooting gun out of it. I bought it because it outshot my double gun.

The single gun would shoot in a 26-inch circle at 40 yards, Joe's breech-loader in a 30-inch circle, and Doty's two guns would scatter four and a half feet. The single gun was good for single ducks up to 70 yards, Joe's breech-loader up to 60-yards, my double gun up to 50 yards, Doty's guns about 40 yards. My reason for describing our guns in detail is because the knowledge of choke-boring spread from these guns to all parts of the civilized world.

Wildfowl Shooting in the Sunken Lands

After we had got settled in our Little River camp we killed a lot of game, both ducks and geese, and shipped to Cincinnati by boat. On certain days the ducks would come out in the big timber, where most of our shots would be over the tops of the cypress trees, fully 200 feet high. I stepped a fallen tree and found it to be 200 feet long. The single gun was the only gun in camp and, in fact, the only gun known that would reach ducks flying over the tops of these cypress trees. I think Alden Wilky was the best shot of any of us, and learned to shoot the single barrel before I did before we had left the Illinois River country. Ducks would cross the Duck Island rice pond over to Clear Lake on the opposite side of the river, but would fly so high as to be out of reach of ordinary guns. Wilky stood on the river ridge on the Clear Lake side one day and started practicing with the old single barrel. After making a few high shots, something like 70 yards, he succeeded in killing one and found it had been struck with quite a number of No. 4 shot and in a little while, after getting the proper lead, he began to kill them quite regularly. Finally he got so he had no use for any other gun in camp on the Illinois.

While at New Madrid it froze up and the ducks left us the second time, but the geese remained and we gave them the best we had. One day I killed 40 of the big fellows and a number of days I killed upwards of 30 each day. Some of them weighed 12 to 16 pounds and it was all I could do to get them to camp in my paddle boat. The more I used the old single gun the better I liked it. When we came north in the Spring we stopped off at the mouth of the Sangamon River, just above Browning. Here I had a good chance to practice shooting over the tops of the timber with this gun and was able to shoot it fairly well, killing some days as many as 30 and 40 mallards without a miss. These ducks were all the way from 40 to 70 yards, and it took careful holding and fine calculation to do it. I had sold my double gun and depended on this single-barrel muzzle-loader for all my shooting, until I got the 6-bore muzzle-loader, which became quite famous.

What My Noted Single-Barrel Gun Would Do

I am the man who discovered choke boring as now used by all gun manufacturers. I started experimenting in the gun shop of Charley Stock, in Peoria, Illinois. At first I used musket barrels left over from the Civil War

as they were heavy and would stand lots of boring. Then I procured regulation gun barrels to bore after I had obtained results by repeated boring
and calipering.

After I had finished boring the 6-bore I found I had a gun good up to
80 yards. I used 6 drams of coarse grain powder and No. 3 shot, 1-1/2
ounces. This gun would shoot through an inch board at 40 yards, 1/2-
inch board at 60 yards, 1/4-inch board at 80 yards. The velocity up to 40
yards was very great; at 60 yards it slowed down one-half and at 80 yards
it had slowed down another half. Therefore it took twice as long for the
shot to travel from 40 to 60 yards as from the gun to 40 yards.

Remarkable Trap-Shooting Scores

After the Spring duck shooting was over in 1872 I took in the
Illinois State Shoot, held in Chicago at wild pigeons. It was almost my
first experience at the traps. There were 151 entries in the main event
and the best pigeon shots in the country were on the grounds, Captain
Bogardus among them. I had the old single-barrel, and it was the only
muzzle-loader on the grounds. The event was at ten birds, 21 yards rise,
gun below the elbow until the bird was on the wing, ties to be shot off
at three birds at 26 yards, and if that didn't settle it, miss and out at 31
yards. Only ten men out of 151 were able to kill ten straight of the swift
flying pigeons. After three birds at 26 yards only Bogardus and I were left
of the entire field. After we had gone straight for 20 birds at 31 yards, he
asked me for a division, notwithstanding he had bet me $50 he would
shoot me out. The same year I shot two days at Decatur, three days at
Jacksonville, two days at Peoria and two days at Winona without a
miss—-a run of 735 straight, mostly at glass balls. Shortly after I defeat-
ed J. Frank Kleintz of Philadelphia, then the crack pigeon shot of the
East, in a match at 100 live pigeons, score 88 to 84. Daniel W. Vorhees
of Peoria backed me in this march, which was for one thousand dollars.
We both used 10-gauge guns, traps and handle, and Kleintz gave me the
hardest birds.

Novel Duck Shooting Before Large Audience

After shooting on the Sangamon until the ducks had mostly gone north, we broke camp and came home up the river. Doty lived at Henry, a town about 40 miles north of Peoria, while Wilky went home to Chillicothe.

On arriving in Peoria, I found Peoria Lake, which is a widening of the Illinois River for 18 miles, covered with bluebills, which were feeding on spill slops which were dumped in the lake from a glucose factory located on the shore only a few blocks above the foot of Main Street at the river front. The ducks would come within a hundred yards of the bank, fill up on this waste or slop, then leave and make room for others. The river was high and the lake had a strong current running south. It looked to me like one more chance for a big day's shoot. I hired a wide, flat-bottomed boat, towed it across the lake among the willows and cut a big boatload. Then I towed it back to the Peoria side and fixed up a brush battery covering the boat and building a blind to shoot from. In the morning at daylight I had the battery anchored at 100 yards from shore, with about 50 decoys set out to the east. I had sold my double gun and had only the old, despised, single-barrel muzzle-loader.

The bluebills commenced coming at daylight and I started shooting. A boy was stationed a few hundred yards below with a boat to pick up the ducks as they would float down. The day was bright and still, the water as smooth as glass, and the shooting the easiest I ever had in my life. The ducks would come to the decoys and when within about 40 yards I would rise up in my blind and they would start to climb, either to the left or right. I could take all the time needed and fill a duck full of No. 4 shot. I made one run of 57 straight without missing, being one of my longest straight runs on ducks.

Peoria was then a city of about 25,000 people, and soon spectators began to collect on the shore until the bank was lined with people watching me shoot, many of whom probably had never seen birds of any kind shot in the air before. My father was among the crowd. We lived only a short distance from the shore, and at noon he brought a dinner pail with a hot oyster stew and had it sent out to me. To eat a hot oyster stew out of a duck blind in the presence of a large, refined and appreciative audience was something new in the duck shooting line. I was the whole show and was surely "it." Later I shot in great crowds at tournaments; have shot individual matches before large numbers of people; have given skating exhibitions, played banjo solos, violin and French accordion solos before large audiences; played checkers against state champions and won, but never was the whole show either before or since.

My boatman picked up 156 bluebills that day, and others in boats picked up quite a lot while the picking was good. It was estimated that 200 ducks were killed that day by the old one-barrel gun. Most of the people who saw my shooting that day have passed on, but I am still alive at 86 years of age and able to shoot pretty well yet. I shot a couple of days a few years ago at one of the large ducking clubs in Southern California and the members were surprised. They said my shooting was a revelation to them. I did a little trap shooting also and several times got nearly 100 straight.

Many branches of sport such as golf, baseball, lawn tennis and others allow of large galleries of spectators but this is the only time I have ever known of a large concourse of people watch a man shoot ducks.

Among the Geese and Sand Hill Cranes in North Dakota

My Parker No. 10 double gun handled large shot well, putting its charge of No. 1 or No. 2 shot into a 30-inch circle at 40 yards.

I had heard much about the goose shooting in North Dakota, so I took a trip up there. I stopped with a farmer 12 miles north of Dawson, North Dakota. A colony of New York farmers had taken up a tract of land just south of the Manitoba line, and had planted it all in wheat. It was called New York settlement and my stopping place was the nearest house to the railroad. All the other farmers had to pass the house in going to or from town.

This large tract of wheat was the first in the line of flight of the geese and cranes on their way south and it was a great feeding ground. I stopped with a farmer named Stinchcomb and W.B. Mershon knew him.

Here was a good opportunity to try out my Parker on long-range shooting and I took advantage of it. I used No. 1 shot. One afternoon, shooting from a pit in a stubble field, between 3 o'clock and sundown, I killed 46 Canada geese and 37 sand hill cranes. Five of the largest geese weighed 16-1/2 pounds each. The total weight of the game shot inside of three hours was over 700 pounds. It filled our wagon box.

I could kill both geese and cranes up to 65 yards and had no trouble in killing pairs up to 60 yards when straight overhead.

Both the old Parker gun and myself decided it was time to go home after putting in a solid month with the geese and cranes. When we arrived at Dawson on the railroad I found the reports had been brought in from day to day by the farmers and to hear them tell it, a goose couldn't fly high enough to get out of reach of that old gun. What it had done to the geese and cranes was the talk of the town. The farmers were supplied first and the game not used by them was shipped to Minneapolis and Chicago. The trip had been successful in every way. In fact, as fine a trip as I ever had in all my career and one never to be forgotten.

The Passing of the Battery

BY PERCY M. CUSHING

1912

THIRTY YEARS AGO THE MEN WHO WENT WILD FOWLING ALONG THE coasts of this country measured their sport by the number of ducks that they killed in a day. Game was plenty, and a man's rating as a gunner was determined by the size of the bag. It was only natural, therefore, that all gunners employed the methods of hunting that were most conducive to large kills, and it was the desire for heavy bags that fathered the shooting battery, sinkbox, tub, or open water blind, as it is variously called, an agent of a past generation which, without doubt, has done more to exterminate coast wild fowl than anything else.

The battery is nowadays fast becoming obsolete, forbidden by the law in many places where it once thinned the ranks of ducks, forsaken by sportsmen in others because of a realization that the number of slain birds no longer indicates the measure of sport, and because the supply of wild fowl in many localities is now too small to warrant the expense and trouble of the somewhat elaborate outfit for battery gunning.

But in the passing, this once popular mode of duck gunning has taken with it a charm which no other type of wild fowling ever possessed. True, the decline of the battery is proving to be a salutary piece of insurance against the slaughter of coast-following ducks, and of course should be commended by all sportsmen; yet it will leave a void in the hearts of those who have enjoyed it which cannot be filled by any shore shooting.

It might be inferred that this article is in favor of battery shooting, but that is not necessarily the case. If it were possible for every man who shoots to be so deeply imbued with the feeling of real sportsmanship that he could kill his fifteen or twenty ducks and then watch a hundred more wheel temptingly before his decoys without firing at them, then I would cry "Long live the battery." But it takes all kinds of people to make up a world, including those who must be placed where it is not easy for them to kill more than the legal limit of game.

The battery is doomed, and it will not be long before it is barred by law from the few places where it still flourishes, principally the Chesapeake and the Great South Bay of Long Island. But from the years of its prime, the memories crowd close, bright-faced and indelible.

Perhaps it is the very term, battery gunning, suggesting as it does somehow the time when broad coast bays held mighty rafts of ducks—rafts that numbered thousands and blackened the water sometimes for a solid mile—that lends the primary thrill to this type of shooting. It savors of the old days of the first breech-loader when the wild fowl were so plentiful that the most imaginative could not foresee the time of their depletion. It smacks of broad-backed shoals with the tide rips curling round their edges and all day, from dawn till dark, images of swift wings cutting cleanly against the autumn sky. In it, too, is the lure of abundance, the dream of the gunner of shot-out marshes, the fascination of the days that used to be.

The writer can remember when his father shot from a battery, can recall the overhauling of scores of decoys, as the fall drew on, of the repainting of the battery in the early coolness of September, and of the struggle to get the exact shade of slate-green blue which would match the winter water most closely. Out in the old carpenter shop, as a small boy, he watched with interest as the "Old Man" painted up the stool and inquired eagerly just what kind of duck each one represented. And when the Old Man's hair was whiter and his eyes dimmer, so that once in a very long time a rocketing drake got off scot free, and it became time for the boy himself to help paint the decoys against the coming of October, he could tell each without question.

But that first season when the boy went, and for the next season and the next, he had still much to learn. There were the best shoals where the mussels and sea grass lay, where the running tide did not grip the decoy lines and snarl them; there was the weather and its effects on the flight of the ducks—how a sou'wester made them "use" one shoal, and a nor'easter another. And there was the art of swinging the stool around and to leeward of the battery and of attracting the attention of game by kicking the foot. And there were many other things that the boy, starting by knowing one decoy from another, learned more or less easily. The years went by, and the Old Man sat aboard the little sloop and watched while his eyes grew dimmer and age gave the old ten-gauge weight until it no longer came to his cheek as it used to when it was young. And when at last the Old Man became tired of it and left it behind him forever, he left with it some of the wisdom they had gained together.

So the boy, brought up with the old gun and the Old Man and the old battery, cherished a memory that endured, and he has watched the old-style battery gun and the battery itself follow the Old Man into oblivion with a certain regret.

It was a drab afternoon in November a long, long time ago. The new gun was to have been a Christmas present, but the Old Man couldn't wait. There were ducks in the bay, the boy was big enough, and the mother's objections were only on the general ground that it spoiled Christmas surprises to give the presents ahead of time. The Old Man listened and stared out of the kitchen window that fronted on the bay.

"I'm with you, Caroline, under ordinary circumstances," he said, "but just look out there."

Caroline, who was my mother, went to his side and followed the indication of his big, bony finger. Streaming across the gray distances as far as the eye could reach were string on string of winging ducks.

"It's making up for a sou'wester," he said, "and they're working under the flats for a lee. What a day! What a day!"

The woman smiled a little. "Well, be careful," she said. "You know where it is—up in the storeroom behind the old cedar chest."

But the Old Man, chuckling to himself, was going up the back stairs two steps at a time.

A moment later he laid it in my hands—an oily, rough flannel case, and within, the bright, twist-barrels of a cheap little Belgian double-barrel. He had had the barrels cut to order—the Old Man—and the stock shortened, and to you who remember first-gun boyhood it would be futile to say that no high-priced piece that ever came to me in later years brought with it the thrill that leaped to my heart when the Old Man snapped on the fore-end of that little Belgian and pressed it to my shoulder for the first time.

As my hands closed on it, they sealed the beginning of a personal friendship such as only men and guns can know.

"And now," said the Old Man, "your mother has been getting your woolen clothes together. Run and get them and we'll go down aboard the *Edith*. Dan'l has her all ready, with the battery boat astern, and I've a hundred shells I loaded for your gun a month ago."

I can remember the alacrity with which I skedaddled after those clothes, the heavy flannel shirts, blue-knit jacket, woolen gloves, a set of oilers, and hip-boots with thick German socks.

The *Edith* was my father's sloop, a blunt-bowed, beamy, snug old craft with a great roomy gunning cabin, a coal range, and the story of many an eventful season. Dan'l was my father's man. He'd been before the mast of a square-rigger, had ridden a cattle range somewhere out West in between times, and was a sort of all-around sailor and landsman combined, with the strongest accent on the sailor. Once a year regularly he got drunk, and the rest of the time was sober and reliable. And moreover, he was a good cook, a good shot, and understood all about ducks and shooting.

It was late in the afternoon when we filled away from the dock, with the gray reaches of the broad coast bay sweeping lonesome and gray for miles and miles to the south.

The Old Man was at the wheel, Dan'l was at the main sheet. I stood in the cabin companionway, my head above the hatch, looking off into the tatters of the bleak, wintry day, hemmed in by the steel-blue and opal of the west, and the dusk crowding close from the east. With a full sheet and a faint northerly breeze behind us, and outshore, the dim threat of the outer breaches faint and shadowy, the *Edith* swung away into what to me was a broad sweep of the golden anticipation of youth, to the Old Man, the stamping ground of years of rough toil for the sport he loved best.

Behind us the painter of the battery boat straightened with a jerk, the cumbersome flat-bottomed craft herself, swung round in line, picked up a bone in her teeth, and I heard Dan'l's voice close in my ear. He had belayed the sheet and stepped into the companionway beside me.

"See! see!" he was saying, his bony finger pointing out into the gathering dimness. "Watch 'em, boy, watch 'em—teeterin' along as far as you can see, flock on flock of 'em, clean coverin' ev'ry point of the compass east to west. We'll teeter 'em to-morrow."

The Old Man glanced into the southeast where the gloom of evening was darkening. "If it don't blow," he corrected, "we'll have a wind by day-light, and it'll be either a snorting sou'easter or a light air from the same quarter. If it snorts, we can't lie in the battery. Those birds are working east, for smooth water under Sea Dog shoals. They read weather better than any man can read it. See 'em, see 'em, boy—redhead and broadbill, nothing but redhead and broadbill. My, my, a thousand birds in sight all the time!"

Dan'l had dived below for the marine glasses. He swept eastward with them. "There's a big bunch of birds in the water off the head of the chan-nel," he remarked. "Coots, most likely. There, they're gettin' up now. Yes, coots, all right, with a few broadbill mixed in. All working east, every one of 'em. Cracky, there'll be a powerful slue of feathers up under the lee of Sea Dog to-night."

The Old Man chuckled. "And to-morrow," he chuckled, "they'll be coming back over the mussel beds to feed. And we'll be there first."

The crow's feet about Dan'l's temples deepened and there was a twin-kle in his eyes. "If it don't blow too hard," he said innocently. "It's mean lying in a machine where there's a sou'easter snortin'."

The Old Man bit readily. "A sou'easter ain't so bad," he argued, "and when it comes to real business, it has to be blowing considerable to set that old double battery of mine awash. I guess we can lie in pretty near anything—if there's any birds flyin'. Just look at 'em out there now, Dan'l."

"Swads an' swads of 'em," agreed Dan'l solemnly. "I certain hope it don't blow."

"Darn blows!" growled the Old Man.

It was dark—black, gusty dark when the Old Man rolled the wheel down hard, the mainsail cracked like a rapid-fire gun as it spilled the wind, and the boom jerked splashingly over our heads. The Old Man held the spokes, peering ahead. Dan'l was for'ard. I heard the anchor take the water and felt it set as he choked the cable. Then he came aft.

"You hit it dead," he chuckled. "About four feet on the last of the ebb.

Mud bottom and mussels. You've got cat's eyes."

The Old Man said nothing, but I knew he was pleased. Dan'l seldom showed admiration at anything, but he once told me that he could sink a boathook anywhere in the mud in the bay, and that the Old Man could lay his course dead to it with his eyes shut on the darkest night the Heavens ever sent.

Supper aboard. You who have never had it know not its meaning—supper aboard. The cozy cabin, low-ceilinged and broad, the dim light of the swinging ship's lamp, the bunks all spread, the glowing threads of light showing up through the cracks in the cook-stove where it stands in the shadows beyond the lamp, the smell of coffee, the gurgle of water alongside, the tattoo of wind-blown halyards on the mast, and without and beyond league on league of darkened water, loneliness and mystery.

We finished. The Old Man lighted his pipe. The warm glow of the open stove played upon the face of Dan'l as he bent over the dish pan.

"Ev'ry time I lay on this bar where we're layin' now," he said, "it reminds me of the time four years ago me and Jim Ryburn laid here in a double machine. It was getting on into the afternoon, and there was nothing stirring—nothing stirring at all." Dan'l set the coffee pot down and picked up the frying pan.

"When all of a sudden," he continued, "I looked over to the beach and see what 'peared like the smoke from a steamer out to sea."

He dried the frying pan carefully.

"Only it wasn't smoke, for it was going up and down, up and down, nervous and teeterin'-like. And I poked Jim in the ribs, and says I—"

The frying pan went on its hook, and Dan'l groped around in the soap water for the forks.

"'It's birds,' says I to Jim, 'a million of 'em, and they're coming right at us.'"

Behind me I heard a gentle, mellow sound. I looked at the Old Man. He was in the bunk, his eyes closed, his mouth open. Dan'l's voice sank lower. "Jim, he saw 'em too, and next minute a million plowed right into the stool, and I sat up to lam it to 'em. Just then another million we hadn't seen, came in from behind us, and the whole mess bumped right together."

Dan'l gravely poured the dishwater down the centerboard trunk.

"And it was an awful thing," he went on, "two million ducks smashin' into each other like fightin' armies.

"And Jim jumps up, and I jumps up, and there's nothin' but ducks in sight. The whole world's made of ducks, and the shadder of movin' wings. There was so many I didn't know which to shoot first, and Jim didn't know, and by the time we got through pointin' first this way, then that, the whole swad was out of gunshot, and we hadn't fired a shell. No, sir, not a —"

But Dan'l faded slowly into the deeper shadows across the cabin; the glow of the stove died out; the melodious tattoo of halyards merged indistinctly with the gurgle of water under garboards and ceased, and—what was that? It was the Old Man's hand.

"Come, come, boy," he was saying; "it's making daylight in the east, and we've got a day before us, a whole, long day."

Slowly the surroundings came back to me, and I looked across the cabin. There was Dan'l, just as I had seen him before I dropped off to sleep, it seemed but a moment before, bending over the stove, with the red streaks from the crevices lighting up the deep lines of his weather-worn face.

The cabin was warm and comfortable. The sounds without came back to me, the tattoo of halyards, the gurgle of water, the song of wind through rigging. It would have been good to lie there a long time and listen to them, but suddenly the anticipation of what that period between sunrise and noon would bring gripped me and I sneaked into my clothes.

All was bustle aboard.

"That blow is here, but it isn't hard enough to hurt us," said the Old Man, and there was a queer thrill in his voice that I had never caught in it before.

Dan'l flopped a pancake hastily and, throwing back the cabin hatch, sniffed the air.

"You're right, and I'm glad of it," he answered.

But the Old Man was sliding the plates and coffee cups upon the hinge table that hung beside the centerboard trunk, and I turned to and helped him.

Flapjacks, sausage, coffee, toast! Oh, Lord! oh Lord! Only you who have known such a breakfast at the break of a winter's morning, with a morning of whistling wings and speaking guns before you, can understand.

But the Old Man just couldn't wait. "I know we hadn't ought to, Dan'l, but can we leave these dishes till noon. It's such a day, and we've got to be fixed before sunrise," he argued, half to himself.

On deck the chill of early morning pinched sharp. A sleepy star or two flickered uncertainly westward. To the east a ragged rent of gray cracked diagonally across the sky. The wind, wet and black from leagues of water, rushed against us.

"About a hundred yards sou'east," said the Old Man. "Four feet of water, and dark bottom with the mussels."

"About a hundred yards," agreed Dan'l, poling away in the battery boat. I stayed on the sloop and watched.

The rent in the east had spread to a vast, drab field when the double battery was rigged, and the two hundred decoys trailed off conically to leeward of it. The drab field was tinged with red when Dan'l put us in the battery with the rowboat, and the rim of the sun was looking up when he hoisted sail on the sloop and stood out into the bay to put up the huge raft of birds that he knew were lying close under the shoals of Sea Dog.

The Old Man slipped a pair of shells into the old ten-bore.

"Lie close, boy," he cautioned, "for Dan'l'll have 'em moving soon, and then they'll tower above that white bar a mile to leeward there and pitch down right for these mussel beds."

Lying flat on my back in the double battery, my eyes just level with the wings, I could see the decoys bobbing it seemed for a hundred yards to leeward of us, though in reality the outpost of them was but forty yards distant. We were completely surrounded by decoys. They pressed in close on either side, ran up to a short point a few yards at our backs to windward, and swept out in a great cone in front of us. Nothing but decoys, decoys, decoys—brant, broadbill, redheads. I tried to count them, but their bobbing heads confused me, and the next instant I felt the Old Man's hand on my arm.

"They're lifting, boy," he said quietly. "In a minute they'll be pitching down on us in little bunches. Keep your head down, and don't shoot till they hook their wings and stick out their feet. Then pick your bird. Nobody ever killed anything by shooting wild into a flock of stooling ducks."

Straining my eyes into the glare of the sun, I saw a great black cloud wheel and lift like a vast swarm of mosquitoes, circle broadly, split into smaller clouds, and the next moment I grasped hastily for my gun, for close and low to our right four spike-like birds with long, beating wings were bowling in at our stool.

"Don't shoot," whispered the Old Man at my side. "They're shell-drake trash; we want better."

It was my first close acquaintance with live wild ducks, but the Old Man knew best, so I lay low, holding back the desire to shoot, and watched the four red-billed birds swing gracefully, with set wings, over our stool, circle out, swing in again, and then beat off into the gloom that still hung westward.

Hardly had they gone when the Old Man spoke again, this time with a note of suppressed excitement in his voice.

"Now, son, down!" he whispered. "Here comes the first bunch—broadbill, I think, and at least a dozen. Not the best in the world, but swift, game, and hard to hit. Wait till I say shoot."

Looking eastward I saw a quick wedge of birds lifting sharply in the air, flaring first one white side, then the other to the sunlight, and pitch down close to the water. Then I ducked my head below the coaming of the battery and watched the Old Man's face—saw his eyes roll around to the left, saw the fire leap into them, and heard the sharp sound of his voice: "Now!"

Then I sat up, and every other thought vanished—every thought but the one I concentrated on the towering white breast, with the stiff black neck above it, that flared tremendously near at hand.

It was my first shot, and I have never forgotten it. I pulled the right barrel, saw the bird swerve like lightning to the right, knew that I had just missed, and then reached desperately for him with the second barrel.

The quick disappointment of the first hasty shot steadied me, as it so often does to gunners, and I threw everything into that last chance. The bird folded up fifty yards away, hit the water, bounced twice, and spun slowly around in circles, with its head down.

It was a thrill such as nothing before had ever furnished, and which I think no other shot, no matter how difficult, that I have since made, has ever carried. I looked at the Old Man. His eyes were shining. He laid his great hand on my shoulder.

"That was a good shot, son," he said.

Over on his side of the battery three dead birds lay in the water. I asked him how we were to pick them up.

"Dan'l will gather them as they drift down to leeward," he replied.

The next instant we were flattening low in the battery again, for more birds were coming, and more, and more. Dan'l was routing them out of Sea Dog wholesale. The first bunch passed a quarter of a mile to our left, and I was surprised to see the Old Man begin suddenly kicking his foot in the air, quickly lowering it, only to kick it up again. In a whisper I asked him why.

"To attract their attention," he answered. "To make them see our stool. From a distance it looks as though a duck in this flock was sitting up and flapping his wings."

Suddenly I saw the passing flock rise fifty feet above the water, and every bird turn toward us as though governed by a single impulse.

"Coming," breathed the Old Man. "I got their eye that time. Don't kick now," he explained. "Once you've turned your birds, lie as flat as you can and keep still."

The flock, eight of them, redheads and mostly drakes, bored straight for the battery on the Old Man's side. Fifty yards away they dropped closer to the water and set their wings. It looked as though they were going to fly straight into the box, but at the last moment, they scaled on gracefully hooked pinions right across in front of us. My, how big they looked, their long necks reaching stiffly out in front. You who have shot redheads know how easy it is to tell them from their long necks and colors. Just as they reached the center of our stool, the Old Man nudged me. "Up, boy," he spoke tensely, as we rose together, I to miss as I did usually, the Old Man to crumple up a bird with each barrel.

The flight was well under way now. Always more birds coming and still more birds. An hour flashed away, and a continuous string of white breasts reached floating away to leeward. Our guns were hot, and the shell boxes between our feet in the battery were emptying. And still the birds came, scaling up from the foot of the stool, rocketing in from either side, corkscrewing down from a hundred feet first one side, then the other, flashing in the climbing sun, or whistling down over the head fender from behind us so swiftly that we could but grab our guns and send a single shot hastening after them. And it was seldom on even these difficult chances that the Old Man's ten-gauge failed to take toll. I have since seen many men shoot, but I have seen few who could hold up with the Old Man. He was a wizard.

A long, long way to leeward we could see Dan'l working up toward us in the sloop, driving raft after raft of birds down across us, billowing them over us in an endless blanket. And when at length the last raft had broken up and he faced the half-mile of dead birds we had been sending down to meet him for three hours, we sat up in our battery, I with my shoulder aching, and the Old Man with just a trace of weariness in his face, though the fire of enthusiasm still smoldered in his eyes. One hundred shells with five drams of black powder in the old ten-bore in a morning would have been a strain on hair less gray.

Dan'l picked up seventy-four birds. I had killed two of them. The rest were the toll the Old Man had taken.

I would have gotten out of the battery in the afternoon, but the Old Man smiled and shook his head.

"No, boy," he said. "This is your first day. You have many ahead of you. I have many to look back on, and the few more I have left will be enough for me. Dan'l will shoot with you this afternoon."

We had lunch, oysters that Dan'l had raked on the beds while we had been shooting—oysters fried as I think no one else has ever fried them, coffee, chops, pie.

"Nothin' but redhead for us this afternoon," grinned Dan'l, as we got into the box. "No shell paggers, coots, or broadbill. We're partikler and we're goin' to take our pick."

And we did—took it so well that when the lonesomeness of the late afternoon streamed drably across the bay, and the lights from the setting sun glimmered uncertainly on our decoys, the Old Man luffed the sloop up alongside the battery with forty-seven redheads and one black duck on board.

Then Dan'l and the Old Man picked up. It was a long and cold task, and when the last decoy was stowed in the stool boat, and the battery unweighted and hauled aboard, the darkness was settling. And into it we filled away for home with the last of the southeast wind at our backs.

"One hundred and twenty-two," muttered the Old Man as he gave up the wheel to Dan'l and came below into the yellow light of the cabin lamp. "One hundred and twenty-two and all good birds. It's not so bad. I've killed two hundred and ten, but that was a long time ago, before you were born, son. Birds are getting scarcer now. By the time you're as old as I am, you'll be doing well to kill ten. Yes, boy, ten birds will be a bag then, and the battery will be the cause of it. Then they'll stop batteries—when it's too late. But, Lord, sonny, what sport they've been, what sport!"

The Passing of the Marshland

BY ROSS KINER

1915

P HILLIP CAME IN THE OTHER DAY BRINGING WITH HIM FOUR BEAUTIFUL ears of corn. Spreading them out on the window ledge he said: "There: Just look at that corn, raised right in the middle of what was St. Peter's marsh. I brought you those to show the boys what kind of crops could be raised right where you used to shoot ducks."

"Huh!" as if I cared how much or how good corn was raised so long as they had ruined the best duck marsh in Illinois. Corn! all corn! Corn across the flat of Nower's pasture; corn where the muskrat houses were; corn crowding in on the Meredosia's bed; corn on the Mud Creek bottoms. Kismet! It is fate!

Yesterday, only yesterday, I picked up the little 22 and leaving Rickel's store, I wandered north by west across the pasture land, along the deep "dredge ditch," until I came to that wooded island that used to lie, all marsh surrounded, in the center of the "big slough," the slough that used to run from the Green River to the Rock, with at the center a divide, the water of the southern slope sullen or rapid as the grade permitted, finally swelling the narrow and tortuous Green River, the other spinning to the north, plunging with a swirl into the Rock, at the mouth of the round bayou.

Corn, all corn! I stood beneath the black oaks and looked toward the east, there where the cattails and rushes grew: there where Harry's "pump" failed him, there where the mallards, at sunset, swinging into roost left their toll as the little Parker called *"Spang! spang! spat! spat!"* you could hear those chilled 7's strike as the Dupont drove them home. Two greenheads: and now, corn, all corn. North and westward, ah! that wild meadow on that April day, jack snipe after jack snipe, "scaiping" from the cover of fresh sprouting flag and smartweed. Again and again the 16-bore flashes to the shoulder, again and again the Dupont snaps out its challenge. "Gee!" what a dead center on that bird that hung for just a breath upwind.

Corn, all corn! Southward to that bog emerald-studded pasture where on that April evening I lay prostrate alongside that little pool, my only blind a few dead weeds stuck here and there around me. *"Querreck! querreck!"* chuckled my live decoys. *"Querreck! querreck!"* come and lunch with me. "Now! well! of all the bling, blasted misses!"

Corn, all corn! Corn where that pair of pintail met their fate. Corn, all corn, the length and breadth of the Green River marshes. Corn, all corn in the mucky beds of the Twin Lakes. "Kismet!" why rail at fate? Of times when my lusty brothers of the plow bewail the yearly and ever-increasing drouths, those continued, long-drawn out, sun-scorched summers, I say: "You have dredged and ditched and tiled too much. You cannot get the moisture from clouds over land that has no moisture." Then, those lusty square-shouldered fellows, who speak so learnedly of potash and of phosphate, of hill drop and powdered lime, laugh me to scorn and say, "Huh! if you had *your way*, all you would have would be a duck slough." Perhaps that, too, is true.

Duck Shooting on Club-Foot Lake— Reelfoot

BY ROBERT LINDSAY MASON

1916

Ah, whence dost thou come, O bird of widespread wing?
From what remotest short does thou wondrous tidings bring?
Now, wither dost thou tend? Perchance to Southern clime,
Where calm lagoons are girdled in with orange and lime.

-Isaac McLellan

UP TO THE PRESENT TIME, DUCK SHOOTING ON REELFOOT HAS BEEN attendant with risk—not for the ducks so much as for the shooters. Certain lawless elements have commanded this region so long that unless a "port" possesses the open sesame to the exclusive order of the P.C.—Pusher's Conference—of Hotel Samberg, it is an even draw as to whether he ought to venture upon these shores.

Jim Commons, Fatty Brooks, Slim Griffith, and sundry other pushers less famous, may punctuate the morning air with revolver shots which mean: "Get up, you lazy sports if you expect to get ducks today" or the signal may shout: "Look out, boys! New sport on the lake. May be a revenuer!" Or a particularly rapid staccato may scream: "Game warden!"

Claude, Jim and I did not fear the familiar perils of this watery wilderness for we were already initiated. And, too, we recognized the fact that if it were not for the pusher's patient oar which enables him to pull facing the bow, we might now be resting at the bottom of the lake, strangled in the submarine forest of trapanatans or the twisted roots of the cypress.

In the year 1812 Nature coughed, gulped mightily and a slew-footed lake two hundred square miles in extent was born in the twinkling of an eye where nothing had been but peaceful landscape in the northwestern corner of Tennessee. The basin thus created was not filled with the waters of the muddy Mississippi, for its waters are crystal.

The P.C. decided that the forming of the lake caused the earthquake! We shooters could not dispute it. We could not swear that the lake, entire, had not existed before—sub-terra—and that by mixing its own waters with the subterranean fire had not belched itself bodily from the bowels of the earth. Nature has an effective way of getting rid of her unpleasant in'ards very quickly, just as Claude does when he eats too much of Mrs. Smith's delightful cooking—which is nearly every time we go there.

At any rate, this weird stretch of water is a vast cemetery of trees. Everywhere their stumps and ragged skeletons stand stark monuments of a primeval forest. Some protrude from the depths like the sunken masts of a lost armada; others like the peaceful spiles of Venice; still other veterans like the banished admirals of the inland navy. The owls and heavy-winger "water-buzzards" have never left it, for here they find riotous subsistence upon the teeming fish. So do the furtive fishermen, not yet quite sure of their rights, though in times past they have fought—even murdered—for them in face of crooked legislation.

Our progressive pushers—Fatty and Jim—use live, trained decoys— "Dicks and Susies." These little feathered, intelligent friends trod familiarly over our legs with their pink, web feet, chattering with much joyous anticipation of the hunt as they clambered into our boats. Our guides had turned them out of their pens before daylight to "limber up." They are rarely ever fed; only when hunting is dull. We hunters had already eaten generously of Mrs. Smith's baked croppy (sic) fish, roast duck, fried coot, hot rolls, etc. Duck and man seemed ready for the fray.

Sam Applewhite's motor, after doing stunts over submerged log and snag, chugged us out beyond the pale of film ice and within reach of the sport. We soon ensconced ourselves in the curious blinds of Rat Island; the waist-high hollow stumps concealed among the curiously distorted boles and roots of the clumps of water cypress.

Our excited Dicks and Susies were soon turned loose to feed. There were only a few coots in sight. Fatty possessed one of those inimitable duck calls for which Reelfoot is famous and when his industrious decoys did not tune up with the proper duck chatter Fatty soliloquized in wild celery talk and umbrella nut conversation.

Very soon, with the help or our "pitching" Dicks and Susies, he pulled them down right out of the sky. Here they come! Our chilled veins and limbs were suddenly warmed with action. As the birds breasted against the wind to settle, we raised from our tree-clumps and let them have it.

Our decoys kept a comical eye heavenward and dodged our kill as it splashed into the half frozen waters of the lake. Down we went again. More nutty talk by Fatty, and here they came. Up we went like Jacks in boxes. Down came our feathered shower, the lifeless bodies often skidding for many feet across the firmer ice from the momentum of the fliers. We shot until our guns were too hot to hold comfortably, then we had lunch.

Unfortunately, that afternoon a great raft of coots a mile long settled off to our right; as a result the new ducks swerved off to their feeding grounds, though decoyed by us. This continued until we were compelled to bring in our faithful decoys and depart for Cane Island. Although we shot among the coots frequently we could not disperse them. After our second round at Cane Island we reached our limit. There was a furtive exchange of glances in which temptation was written.

"Well," said Fatty, "we'll be going!" That settled it. It is an inviolable rule of the P.C. never to exceed the limit nor to shoot on the grounds before sunrise or after sunset. We obeyed the mandate by paddling our way homeward.

The next morning we were upon the water early. The ice was so thick it had to be broken in the "blow-holes" to allow the staking of the decoys. Presently Dicks and Susies were working bravely. Up came great clouds of redheads, mallards, teals, and a few canvasbacks. We let them have it at close range. After desultory shooting we were compelled to decamp to Goose Basin on account of the changing wind. We did not go for geese, however, for these fair creatures did not deign to descend from the Flying Wedge—the Aerial Goose Limited, "no stop-overs." They skimmed by a mile high like a whizzing arrow winging southward.

Fatty chattered some more cunning duck talk while we battered them from the reeds. Our boatload of game at close of day spoke eloquently of our success. Jim picked up a lost "Dick" as we turned to go. He was quacking desolately in a lonesome pool. His stay with us was very brief, however. The welcome he received from the feathered brethren was not to his taste, so he put over the gunwale and dived into the depths of Reelfoot. He never came up.

He may be now feeding on rich umbrella nut and wild celery in duck heaven or perhaps he went to a hotter place reserved for feathered Judases who betray their kind. He had evidently been guilty of some infraction of the laws of Dicks and Susies. We did not stay to inquire but threaded our way back to a good, hot supper and a more hospitable welcome than he received from his kind.

Lo! The Poor Coot

BY RICHARD WARREN HATCH

1924

OWING, PERHAPS, TO THE FACT THAT I HAVE NEVER ACCUSTOMED MY palate to the rigors of a diet which should include birds' nests, raw fish, sea-gulls, and other such very questionable delicacies, I have never been a coot-hunting enthusiast. I believe that even a hunter has the right to refuse to eat some things. Furthermore, henceforth I intend to govern my actions by the strict adherence to that belief, which has come to be firmly fixed within me.

Though I now admit freely my lack of enthusiasm in the matter of coot hunting, I must also admit that last fall I was roped in on a coot-kill expedition before I knew what it was. And now I consider it a sort of solemn duty to speak on certain details relative to that expedition for the benefit of all other hunters who are uninitiated. I do it in the same spirit that would impel me to warn a dear friend from the big city not to hold the bag on a before-breakfast snipe hunt.

Well, it was late September; the ducks had been flying south in sufficient numbers to land a few brace in a nicely browned condition on my platter. From where I enjoyed the repose and sunshine of my little farm I could occasionally hear the mellow call of wild geese float down from the deep heavens. My vacation was nearly over, and I had moved back from the shore to a spot some five miles inland, about thirty miles from Boston, and about sixteen miles from Plymouth, and pleasantly secluded in the pine woods of Massachusetts.

It was about ten o'clock of a brisk night, and the dog and I were basking in the cheery glow of an open fireplace. I was bathed in the flood of warmth from the fire, and steeped in the fragrance of my oldest pipe. I had no desire to go anywhere.

Then the telephone rang impatiently, and the following harrowing conversation ensued:

"Hallo."

"Hallo. 'S that you, Dick? Say, this is Franny and Park. Come on hunting with us tomorrow."

"Where?"

"Aw, down here at the beach. Duck shooting. Mother won't let us go out in the boat without somebody that's used to boats. She's scared we'll get drowned or something."

"What d'yuh think I am, a pilot?"

"Aw listen...come on...will yuh?"

"What time?"

"Five o'clock."

"No thanks! 'S goin' to rain."

"Six o'clock. What d'yuh say, Dick? Will yuh, please?"

"Guess not, boys. Thanks just the same."

"Make it seven o'clock, then. We only got this one weekend for hunting, and we can't go out without yuh, Dick."

"Oh, well, all right. I'll be there. Goodby."

Well, you see how good all my resolutions were. I swore that I wouldn't get up early and go hunting again. I knew the boys counted on me, and I knew they counted on doing most of the shooting that was to be done. Besides, I had shipped all my artillery home, and I had nothing at the farm but one very ancient Belgian hammer gun, a twelve. It must have been a very nice gun when the man bought it who gave it to the man who sold it to the man who gave it to me. It was battered and bent, and it boasted only one hammer which took all my strength to cock.

But the gun had a virtue—the one barrel which could be shot had a wicked range. A few days previously, I had startled three country louts by knocking over a woodchuck at about forty yards.

I arrived at the beach at seven o'clock the next morning. The beach is about twenty-two miles south of Boston as the coot flies, and not far north of Duxbury Bay and the Gurnet.

The boys, of course, were sound asleep. There wasn't a sign of life around the cottage where they were staying, but a very lean, hungry-looking bird dog. He belonged to Franny, and really I pitied that dog on sight, he looked so hungry. I would have pitied him more, but he eyed me with considerable distrust, and although I have always supposed bird dogs were good-natured, this one looked positively omnivorous, and I am very bony.

By eight o'clock we were ready to start, a nice time to be setting out on a duck hunting party. My two enthusiastic companions were high-school boys, both sixteen years old. Parker, when pressed by other hunters to speak, admitted that he not only had had an exceptionally broad experience in hunting for one of his years, but also that he was an excellent shot. In fact, from the naïve remarks made at breakfast, I judged that it would be a day of very heavy casualties among the ducks and other flying game.

Francis, known always as Franny, had been with me before. I can say for him that he is the quickest shooter I have ever seen; I have watched him blow a rail to pieces enough times to know that. He usually shoots twice before he can even call "mark" while in the field. Furthermore, he has always been famous for an unbounded appetite, and a most democratic taste; in fact, for a half dollar cash he had swallowed a live frog for the benefit of the contributors to the pool. I mention his appetite because it has a bearing on this story.

We had hardly climbed into the dory in which we were going to navigate, when the sun went in and a chill wind from the ocean began to make itself felt. There were signs of a cold, drizzling rain. We rowed about a half mile before I thought to ask about decoys.

"They're under there," said Parker pointing to some tarpaulin in the bow.

The rain came—a gentle but firm rain, cold, chill, a regular damper on any party. And then we rowed past the last possible duck stand on the river, and headed for the mouth. I felt that all was not right.

"Where are you going?" I protested. "I thought you were after ducks; we passed the last stand."

"Sure," said Parker gently. "You know the black boys that fly down the coast all day? We're after them!" He even took pride in that statement.

"Oh, boy!" said Franny, "there's a million of 'em. Betcha we fill the dory!" He expanded proudly. "How those ducks do fly out there!"

Ducks—the word sent a chill through me. They meant coot—not the true coot or mud hen of fresh water, but those heavy bullet-proof sea ducks known to the ornithologist as scoters. It seemed to me that suddenly the rain felt colder and wetter. I made a feeble motion for adjournment; I suggested that it might be a bad day on the open sea in a dory...it was getting foggy. The realization that I was on a coot hunt appalled me!

"Can't you handle a dory on a day like this?" asked Parker cruelly.

"Aw, Dick could take a boat anywhere." This from Francis whom I had trusted.

Modesty and a natural dread of untruth forced me to admit my natural ability, and so we went on.

Now coot shooting is done in this fashion on the New England coast. Block decoys are floated on the sea at a distance of from a half mile to a mile off shore. Then a dozen dories line up on either side of the decoys. The coot fly from six to twenty feet over the water, in an endless string from morn till night. Some of them run the gauntlet, and once they start no amount of shooting will deter them. Coots are brave birds; and they fly at a good speed, too.

I have sat on shore and counted, yes, actually counted thirty-eight shots in one barrage at a flock of coot in less than forty seconds. I have counted a dozen shots from one dory in eight seconds. At Brant Rock, during the coot shooting, one can always hear what sounds more like a rapid fire naval engagement than a hunt. At such times I am sure that coot were designed for the special benefit of the manufacturers of gun powder and shells.

On the way out the river mouth our hunting began when a little black helldiver appeared off the port bow. Francis shot rapidly, as fast as he could load and re-load and get a bead on the diver. I think he only shot eight times before Parker let go a broadside. For a minute or two there was considerable gunnery practice, and then the boys decided to let the bird go.

"Darn things aren't any good to eat," said Franny philosophically. I wondered at the time about his experiences with coot, but I didn't say anything.

The sea was choppy, a little too choppy, I figured, for comfort in an open dory. It was hazy and cold and wet. How I wished that I had stayed at home! Finally we shipped our oars about a half mile out, and Parker picked the tarpaulin off the decoys. I said "decoys"—well, that's because I'm naturally polite. They were just three coal-black blocks of wood on a rope—three of them. One of them had no head; and the head on another was so loose that it rotated round and round with the rise and fall of the waves. Those decoys would have made me laugh if they had not looked so tragic that miserable day. I can see them yet: the headless one leading the string, the next one lying on its side half the time, and the last one with its head pointing at its tail. Gosh!

Then the coot hunting began in earnest. We sat and watched the decoys and the sky and the other hunters who were out. I soon discovered that there were four more boatloads of fools that morning. That's one of the pleasures of coot hunting; you're never alone.

I wrapped up in the tarpaulin and made believe that I was comfortable. As time passed I realized that I had made a dreadful mistake. The heaving up and down of that dory soon produced an unpleasantly similar motion deep down in my vital parts where the two shredded wheat and the scrambled egg were resting. I began to feel that some strong force was at work within me, a force that would demand recognition. I looked at the beautiful land only a half mile away. I have never seen anything to compare to the beauty of the coast line from that boat; it was a sight never to be forgotten.

I should like to have had a coot's-eye view of the peaceful scene. Rain...wind...and three lunatics huddled in a pitching dory. But there were no coots there to see us; they all must have slept late that morning. I had never been wild about coot shooting, as I have said, but now I grew wilder and wilder and seasicker and seasicker. From appearances I was not the only member of the party suffering from seasickness.

Then..."Look!"...and two coot came down the wind, looking casually at our decoys from a distance, and went and got themselves shot by the men in the outside dory. Only seven shots were fired before they fell. Pretty good for coot hunting.

Then a dim shape came suddenly out of the fog, and Franny let go twice. *Pow!! Pow!!* It was lovely shooting and the bird fell, a big gray gull, almost black, that it cost only fifty dollars to shoot. Two hours out; game, one sea gull.

Five minutes later a lone coot came hurrying along and we watched him run the gauntlet of the outside boats. There were just nine shots fired, and then the last man in the third boat turned loose with an automatic and dropped the bird on his fourth shot. Not bad for coot.

We began to perk up a bit about then. It looked as though the coot were beginning to fly, but it looked as though they were all scared by our decoys. The neck on the third one would turn around at the wrong time, or the second one would lie down on its side.

"Here he comes!" sang out Franny suddenly.

I looked for a sea gull, but I saw a lone coot headed to pass our stern at long range. He was headed down wind and going ninety miles an hour; probably he was flying so fast that his eyes watered and he couldn't see our decoys, because he kept right on coming. "Take your time," I said.

At about fifty yards' range Franny threw up his cannon and simply tore the atmosphere all to pieces. *Bang! Bang!* The coot came on, undismayed.

At thirty yards, as near as he would come, Parker took a calm aim and fired. *Bang! Bang!* The noble bird sped on.

In desperation I raised the old cripple and fired my one barrel. Someone had to save the reputation of the hunt.

We rowed over and picked up the coot; he was no blacker than real dark coal.

"Gosh!" said Franny. "Dead as a door nail. We must 'a filled him with lead."

"We just naturally socked him," said Parker magnanimously. I looked down at my battered old fowling-piece and said nothing at all. After that we waited another hour, during which I longed more and more for land; then we rowed home.

I believe that experience, which some author has said is the name we give our mistakes, is a mighty good teacher for young hunters. And I knew when Franny and Parker were preparing that coot for cooking that that experience was going to be one of their mistakes, but I didn't say a word.

But I do know two good ways of preparing coot that are guaranteed to make it delicious for the most epicurean hunter, and I pass this information along right now. The easiest way is to place the coot in a pot to boil with a good flat-iron or an anvil. Let it boil long and merrily, and when you can stick a fork in the flat-iron or the anvil, as the case may be, then that coot will be ready to eat. If that takes too much patience, take the goodly coot and nail it firmly to a hardwood board. Put the board in the sun for about a week. At the end of that time, carefully remove the coot from the board, throw away the coot, and cook the board.

But there are some Yankees who eat coot. I guess some of those New Englanders are just as tough as they used to be.

Now the boys neglected to try one of these tested recipes for cooking their black wildfowl. Gradually the smell of the bird permeated the cottage. I smelled it, and I want to say that although I have walked the beaches for years, I have never seen or heard of sea food strong enough for coot to feed on, judging by that smell.

Finally I moved to a room remote from the kitchen. The smell persisted. It was at this point in the game that I made a rough draft of an amendment to the Federal Migratory Game Law forbidding the killing of coot. I felt pity...for hunters like me.

The coot finally got cooked. Franny, who had eaten live frogs, sniffed it keenly. Parker took a good big bite and remarked that he wasn't very hungry, and he guessed he'd wait a while. Franny ate two mouthfuls and then went and got a drink. He was gone quite a long time, I thought.

By nightfall the moaning of the bird dog aroused them. "Gosh, he's always hungry and he hasn't had anything to eat today," said Franny.

"Give him the coot," said Parker sadly.

The dog was on the back porch and we threw the coot out by the garage. An hour later, when I was departing, the coot lay where it had fallen. The dog retreated to the other side of the garage.

Now I want to ask just one question: "What becomes of all the coot that the coot-shooters shoot?"

Canada Geese

By Martin Bovey

1926

I KILLED MY FIRST GOOSE THE DAY AFTER CHRISTMAS, 1921, AT Currituck. I was the only guest at the lodge, and Henry, the Negro cook, and I celebrated Christmas with a banquet of roast Canada goose and corn whisky. Inside the lodge we became more and more cheerful, while outside the weather became progressively gloomier as the rising wind flung short, sudden bursts of rain against the windowpanes.

The goose was but a heap of well-picked bones, and the supply of "corn" was fast dwindling, when Carl Hubbard, goose guide extraordinary, came in through the kitchen door.

"Why aren't you home playing Santa Claus to your kids?" I asked him as he dumped his sou'wester and dripping oilskin slicker on the wood box.

"Got that over with this morning," he said. "I'm aimin' to play Santa Claus to you now. Like to kill some geese?"

My answer was most emphatic.

"Wind's veerin' into the north," Carl declared, motioning with the tumbler of corn Henry had already poured for him. "May freeze some before mawnin'. Anyway the rain'll stop, and it'll sure 'nough blow. Fetch your truck along and sleep at my place tonight. It'll save an hour's run in the boat, and my missus'll be right glad to see you. We're havin' our Christmas dinner this evenin'," he finished, his eyes sweeping the ruins of our goose.

I explained that more food—or drink—was superfluous.

Carl waved the notion aside. "After you been pitchin' around in Cyclone for ten miles, you'll eat aplenty. Red clay and Cyclone sure give a fellow exercise."

Carl and Henry polished off the corn, while I changed into shooting clothes. Then with Henry's blessing we shoved across the channel in a skiff and loaded my gun and stuff into Carl's battered Model T. Carl spun the crank long and fast. Apparently there was more water than gas in the tank, but finally the motor ceased its passive resistance, and we shot away over the combination of ruts, gullies, sinkholes, and craters that the maps of the region maliciously proclaim a road.

Carl drove with the fury of a man who scorns natural obstacles and with the abandon of one well fortified by strong drink. Through a crack in the mud that coated the windshield I saw another car rushing toward us. Carl advanced his hand throttle, and we bounded forward. Just as sudden death seemed inevitable, we slid to a stop, front bumper a yard short of the other fellow's.

Carl leaned out and shouted through the downpour, "Snow, you old so-and-so! Merry Christmas!"

"Merry Christmas yourself!" Snow bellowed back. A moment later he appeared alongside, pulled the cork from a large bottle, and thrust it toward me. "Merry Christmas, an' here's how."

We had a drink. Then from a bottle that Carl produced from the pocket of his slicker we had another.

"Merry Christmas!"

Snow climbed back into his Ford; both cars went into reverse, then leapt forward and lurched past each other.

We careened down the road for perhaps half a mile before I saw another car approaching. Again we halted with a splendid flourish—inches apart.

"Merry Christmas!"

This time it was Lem Saunders. We climbed out, stood ankle deep in mud with the rain beating against our faces as we tilted the bottles toward the zenith.

"Reckon it'll be right good for goosin' in the mawnin'," Lem prophesied with his customary optimism.

We talked shooting a bit, while the rain lashed at us.

Another car came along.

"Merry Christmas! Have one on me!"

A fellow can't be rude, can he?

Finally we got under way once more. Carl's driving was by now inspired. We dove through axle-deep water, bounded from bump to bump, slithered from rut to rut. Sometimes our rear wheels followed the front ones, sometimes they ran abreast of them, once or twice they took the lead. I maintained contact with the car with my head and the seat of may pants—alternately.

"Road's a touch rough in spots," Carl roared as we lunged down an incline, vaulted a creek, and flung ourselves up the slope.

Just as we leveled off Carl slammed on both the footbrake and the emergency, and we came to rest alongside another vehicle.

"Merry Christmas! Try one outa mine!"

Several drinks later, singing Christmas carols, we slewed from the road and came to rest between a low, weather-beaten house and a ram-shackle barn.

"This," said Carl, "is the Hubbard estate. Welcome and Merry Christmas! Have another?"

Finally he slid slowly out from under the wheel and, with one hand firmly on the door, tested his legs. After standing for a moment, he leaned across the door and whispered, "I reckon we'd best have a look at the dee-coys. I 'spect my old lady's still messin' with the cookin'. Might not 'pre-ciate you'n me just now."

For an hour or so we sat in the barn, pitching corn to the geese Carl used for decoys. It was after dark when we finally went in to supper, but we were reasonably steady.

Mrs. Hubbard's table was heaped with food—goose, yams, hominy, scrapple, hot biscuits, pie, and heaven knows what. We talked some—about Santa Claus, the kids' presents, goose shooting—but mostly we just ate. Carl had been right. Riding in Cyclone had the effect of walking twice the distance, and, of course, there was the little matter of the corn.

After we had pushed back our chairs, let our belts out a couple of notches, and had a long smoke, Carl and I took a look at the weather. It was no longer raining, and it was much colder, for the wind was definite-ly going around to the north.

" 'Spect we better get some sleep," Carl declared when we reentered the house. "I aim to be out of here come five o'clock. Case you're inter-

Canada Geese 73

ested," he added with a smile, "I aim for us to kill some geese tomorrow."

He took a candle, led me up steep, narrow stairs to a tiny room under the eaves filled to the brim by a huge bed. I pulled off my clothes, climbed into the bed, and sank into goose down and oblivion.

Seven hours later we were pushing a two-wheeled cart loaded with goose crates toward the landing. It was blowing hard from the northwest. As we stumbled aboard Carl's boat and coaxed an encouraging cough out of the icy motor, a gray dawn was spreading over the sound.

We ran a couple of miles along the western shore and then, after crossing choppy open water, threaded our way through the labyrinth of marshland that lies along the sand dunes. As we rounded an island Carl let out an oath. Ahead of us I saw geese on the water—the live decoys of the fellow who had beaten us to Carl's favorite point.

We set out on a point five hundred yards away, put twenty-one of our decoys in the water, and left one—the goose of a mated pair—in a coop which we hid back in the rushes. Before we had finished our blind, poled the power boat around to the other side of the island, and hidden the skiff near at hand, the fellow across the bay had killed a goose. We were putting the final touches on our blind when a bunch of five headed for our stand. They saw us and pitched for our neighbor's decoys. We saw the flash of spray as two birds hit the water.

Far away, geese were moving over the marsh, and, though our location was a second choice, Carl was optimistic about our chances. I am always optimistic, so my opinion was of no value.

The sky darkened until in the west and north it was almost black, and snow squalls drove across the marsh. Then from the south, moving up the sound across the black sky, came a wavering line of white—whistling swans, thousands of them. For many minutes they kept streaming by, far to the west of us. We estimated the flock to be over two miles long.

The last of them were not yet out of sight when Carl pulled me down into the blind. From off to the east came the cry of a Canada.

"Big bunch! Heading our way!" Carl whispered tensely, and began "talking" to our decoys. The goose in the crate back of us let out a questioning *"errunk."* Out front her mate answered. By now the birds coming in from the east were fairly clamoring, and our decoys began shouting invitations. Through the rushes I could see the flock now. Would they really come?

Our decoys fell silent, and I could hear the other fellow's decoys swearing that over there across the channel the feed was better. Carl called madly, coaxing, imploring, goading our decoys into a splendid outburst. But the flock swept past—all fourteen of them. We watched them go straight for the other stand, heard wild greetings flung back and forth, saw that fine bunch swing once, then coast down on set wings, until suddenly we saw them flare, saw two birds start to fold, then heard the shots.

Carl was cursing immoderately. I joined him, and we ran through our repertoire several times before we got relief.

We had occasion to run through it again before long, for another flock headed our way, then went to "that other fellow."

After that bunch Carl had a happy thought. "He can't shoot but two more before he'll have his limit. After he gets out of there, them birds will come to us."

Carl's prophecy was only partially correct.

Another flock swept by us and drove straight on the other fellow. He killed his seventh and eighth goose, and we all but cheered as we watched him retrieve them and commence picking up his decoys.

But when the next flock came, an hour later, they passed us with the cool contempt the others had displayed. Two more flocks did the same thing.

Carl honked his head off at them, then ran through the repertoire until I knew it by heart. Finally, almost breathless, he stopped and drew out his watch. "One o'clock," he said after a long look. "One o'clock, and we ain't killed one goose yet." He held the watch in his hand for a bit, then tucked it away. "If we don't kill a goose by half past the hour we'll move over to that — — point."

It was one twenty-five, and Carl had just put away the watch, when above the howl of the wind we heard them. They came from south of us, straight into the wind—nine of them. As they spotted our decoys the air was filled with goose talk. I buried my face in the side of the blind, afraid to watch them lest they see me move. I could hear them off to my right. Then the sound of them grew fainter, and I knew they too were leaving us behind. But Carl and the decoys were still pleading with them, and suddenly their voices grew louder again and still louder. The decoys were fairly shouting, and overhead was bedlam. Why the devil didn't Carl tell me what to do? Then Carl's fist was in my ribs, and he whispered hoarsely, "Straight over you! Give 'em hell!"

They looked tremendous, hanging there above us. I squeezed the trigger, and they flared, honking wildly. I fired again. Good God, how can you miss *them!"*

Carl was shouting, "Lead 'em! Lead 'em!"

It was incredible how fast they could get away! I swung on a laggard climbing furiously—and fired. The long black neck snapped back as the great bird plunged down to throw water high in the air.

Carl was muttering something about how geese fool you, about how they fly faster than you think. What of it? Hadn't I finally killed my first goose?

A little later three birds pitched toward the decoys, then changed their minds, but before long eight slid by to the east of us, swung back, and sailed in.

How they did climb as we came up on them! Carl cut loose with me, and we folded up four. It seemed as though the whole sky were coming down around us.

Just two hours after I killed my first bird we were in the power boat. Behind us the skiff with its slat coops full of decoys was swinging back and forth as we turned and twisted, searching for the deepest channel. The wind was blowing the water down the sound, and we were in very real danger of getting hung up for the night. Carl, I think, was truly concerned about our situation, for every time we scraped bottom he looked worried.

I refused to be troubled about anything—not even about the prospect of a night in the marshes. What the devil, Carl? Isn't that heap of gray and black in the bottom of the boat a double limit of geese? Sixteen whopping big honkers for Henry to marvel at?

All the way down the sound in the dark of night with snow driving against our backs and white-topped rollers chasing us, I thought of how they had looked—those great, long-necked beauties beating up against the wind, swinging wide around the decoys, then floating in over our heads. Above the fury of the wind I seemed still to hear their wild cries growing louder and the answering chorus of the live decoys.

I did not then realize that I would never again enjoy so fine a goose shoot, but I did appreciate that Carl had given me a tremendous Christmas present. As our boat rubbed gently against the side of the wharf at the lodge, and we began tossing our geese at Henry's feet, I tried to tell him so.

Confessions of a Duck Hunter

BY SIGURD OLSON

1930

I T WAS TWO O'CLOCK IN THE MORNING ON THE OPENING DAY OF DUCK season and for once in my life I was undecided whether to go or not. Never before had there been any ifs and ands, merely a case of being on my way, but this year it was different. Here was the situation and I think you will agree that it was one requiring tact and delicacy. Within the hour, I had become the proud father of a first born son and heir. Now don't misunderstand and accuse me of the slightest disloyalty.

To tell the truth, I was thrilled to the marrow and if I do say so myself, I had experienced to the nth degree all of the proverbial joys incidental to young fatherhood. Yes, it was wonderful, a son, a hunting partner had been born to me and all of our dreams had come true, but why, why in the name of creation did it have to come on this particular morning. That was the point and I think my duck hunting friends will at least give me the benefit of a doubt before pronouncing final judgment.

You can imagine my predicament. In two short hours the guns would be booming and the first wild flight of the season would be on. Of course it was ridiculous to even think of going and martyr like I dismissed the thought summarily from my mind. This was one opening day at least I would have to miss and I might as well make the best of it. In a way, I was ashamed of being even tempted. My place was here today.

After all, what was duck hunting compared to this. First days were never very good even under the most ideal of conditions and there were many weekends coming. Yes, I might as well forget it entirely and play the man. I believe I could have had I not gone to the window, involuntarily of course, and gotten a whiff of the damp air off the lake. That whiff almost unnerved me and was the beginning of my downfall. There was no good reason why I shouldn't go for just an hour or so. Of course, I couldn't go very far or with the rest of the gang. I didn't expect that, but I did know of a place close by where I might get some shooting and where I wouldn't be out of reach. There was really nothing I could do here, merely the idea of standing by.

Tip toeing into the darkened room, I stole a peek at the little bundle in the corner and wondered if he would ever be a duck hunter. In a way, he would be far better off if he went in for golf instead, a much saner and comfortable sport. Beautiful mop of hair he had. His mother opened her eyes and smiled at me appreciatively. It was half past two and I would have to leave soon in order to be there for the first racket. I made one final effort to dismiss the idea from my mind, but it would have been as easy to have stopped breathing.

In my set that sort of thing was simply not done and yet why not. I could go home to rest and not a word would be said but going duck hunting was a different matter entirely. I argued the matter from every possible angle until I was weary with the effort. There was no doubt about it. I was a brute for even considering it at all.

The nurse stopped outside the door and for lack of something better to say, I asked her if everything was all right.

"Yes, everything was as well as could be expected."

"Could I be spared," did she suppose, "for just a few hours?"

"Oh, yes," if I didn't care any more than that sort of an answer.

Out in the hall, I met the doctor and tried to explain in a jovial sort of way just how things stood. All I got out of him was a raising of the eyebrows and a peculiar smile, as much as though he had said outright, "so that's the sort of a dub you are." I could have killed him but he probably played golf and there was naturally no sympathy there. I stole another peek into the bedroom. Junior was sleeping soundly and so was his mother. The nurse put a finger to her lips, and I backed out quickly.

Within an hour, I was at the shore of Shagwa Lake, loading my gun and shells into the canoe. From far out over the water came a sleepy quack and a faint splash. It was dark, peaceful and quiet, the sort of sedative I needed. It was good to be alive and I was filled with a sensation of well being and accomplishment. Wasn't I the father of a son and wasn't this the hour I had been waiting for for almost a year. Everything was as it should be and I might have been perfectly happy, had not the faintest tinge of remorse crept in upon me. I shook it off and stepped into the canoe. Just for the first flight and no more.

The first paddle stroke cleared the air and I set my course for the mouth of the Burntside River, four miles away. Thousands of stars were out and as I pushed along, I had the sensation of floating through the sky itself. Finally I could distinguish the dark mass of the opposite shore and I turned my course slightly to the left. The east was already turning grey and tinged along the rim of the horizon with just the faintest indication of pink and orange. It would not be long now. Suddenly right in front of the canoe loomed a clump of cattails. They seemed to pop right out of the blackness toward me. As I swerved, I was startled by a loud quack and a beating of wings. It was too dark to see a thing but I heard a whistle of wings heading toward the mouth of the river and then a splash. Perhaps a jump shot later on. It would be better to wait for daylight before pushing ahead.

I smoked a cigarette and relaxed or rather tried to. An owl hooted mournfully over in the timber and from Little Long over the ridge came the wild call of a loon. A white mist was rising over the river, hard shooting if it didn't lift. The air was good enough to eat, rich and sweet, with just enough of the smell of turning leaves to give it pungence. I opened a new box of shells and smelled them too. They always are a treat, particularly on damp mornings. About fifteen minutes to go. I wondered how Junior was getting along, probably sound asleep by now.

Bang—Bang—Bang—came from far up stream, someone shooting ahead of time and I cursed inwardly all law breakers in general although I admitted the temptation. Another two minutes. Perhaps my watch was slow and time already up. The cattails rustled softly in a sudden breeze. That would clear the fog in a hurry. Placing my gun against the thwart before me, I pushed toward the mouth of the river and my adventure had begun.

A beaver swam across my path carrying a green poplar branch. When he saw me, he dove whacking his tail with a report like the cracking of a blacksnake. A little further on a pair of rats chased each other merrily through the rushes. Dead ahead was where the mallards had settled. I would have to watch myself. From up stream came a nervous quack and dropping my paddle, I got set. Nothing happened, still too far away. A few short swift strokes and as the canoe glided through the rice, I got ready once more. Suddenly with a wild beating of wings, the biggest and blackest mallard I'd ever seen climbed out of the water. Straight up for thirty feet he went and that was where I caught him before he straightened out for his getaway. First blood and I pushed forward joyously to where he had dropped. One long brown wing was raised upward still quivering. I took the top of it and lifted into my canoe my first mallard well colored and large.

Boom-boom-boom-boom came from Burntside Lake, five miles away. That should start something down the river. I pushed hurriedly into cover and no sooner had I done so than from up river came the whistle of wings. Then I saw them, two black dots tearing like mad down the center of the stream, dodging and twisting to allow for every curve. Off went my safety, eighty yards, sixty and now they were directly opposite. In that first split second of waiting, I was repaid as I am on the opening day of every year for all of the waiting and freezing, all the loss of sleep and discomfort that every season brings with it. My first shot was a clean miss but the second was different. The lead bird crumpled, continued for fifty feet on its own momentum and dropped breast downward with that all-gone limpness that betokens a dead hit. Full three feet in the air it bounced with a splash that could be heard for half a mile. In that splash was also compensation for a duck hunter knows no sweeter sound unless it be the whistle of wings after sundown when they're coming in to feed.

The drake I had missed flew up towards the river's mouth, doubled back looking frantically for his mate. If my luck held there might be another chance. Once more I slipped into the rice, pulled out my caller and gave one of the most seductive quacks I knew. High in the air he circled and circled and then satisfied that everything was as it should be, began to drop. This luck couldn't possibly hold and it didn't, for just at the limit of range, he swerved, set his wings and fluttered into the river a quarter of a mile away.

Now it was a case of stalking and to me there was no greater sport in the world, far more thrilling than shivering in a blind waiting for them to come over. This was real hunting, beating them at their own game. Waiting a few minutes for my bird to get accustomed to his new surroundings, I then pushed cautiously forward. Every paddle stroke sounded as though it could be easily heard a mile away and the noise of the rice against the sides of the canoe was abominable. The first two hundred feet was the worst, then came a stretch of smooth open water through which the canoe glided with scarcely a ripple. The sun was just beginning to peep over the tops of the spruces and the dew on the rice glittered with light. A big spider web strung with pearls draped itself over the bow of the canoe. Another hundred feet or so and I'd be within range. Dropping my paddle, I decided to eliminate part of the racket by pulling myself through the rice. Besides it would leave my hands freer when the big moment came. Too often had the fraction of a second necessary to change from paddle to gun spelled disaster.

For a moment, I stopped dead to get my bearings and to allow my heart to resume its normal functioning. Twenty feet more I pulled my way. This was far better than paddling. If discovered now my duck would be out like a bomb and it would be a case of sheer speed if I'd get in a shot at all. This was about as far as I dared to go and I carefully reached for my gun. For perhaps thirty seconds I waited all tense with excitement. What was the trouble? Had I misjudged the distance or had the mallard sneaked away, warned by my clumsy approach? Perhaps right now he was swimming away up stream far out of range. Finally in desperation, I did one of the many foolish things all duck hunters are guilty of on opening days. Not able to wait another second, I gave a long powerful shove with my paddle. I might have known what would happen for just as I was finishing my stroke and in the most awkward position imaginable, the rice exploded with mallards rising in all directions. Panicky quacks, wild beating of wings and confusion. It was glorious and for once I had duck fever and that badly. My first shot went off in no particular direction which was to be expected but the second held true on a lone bird going dead away. Reloading frantically, I dropped another spiraling high above me. Two wasn't so bad as it might have been under the circumstance and I thought of the many other times similar emergencies had left me empty handed.

Now I knew why the lone drake came back and why he swerved.

The flock reformed its line and disappeared in the wavering line of black dots far over the eastern horizon. Now I had four, two greys and two blacks and I laid them side by side before me in the canoe where I could feast my eyes on their color. It was now about six o'clock and the flight was about over what there would be of it. All that was left was jump shooting to which I didn't object in the least. For the first mile, I saw nothing but blackbirds and there were literally hundreds and hundreds of them, flock after flock, warbling and chattering, drifting gaily from one clump of rice to the other, making merry before their long jaunt to the southland. They too have their place and any marsh in the fall would seem barren and desolate without their cheerful diverting music.

I was seriously considering starting home, when I saw something big and black move in the rice ahead of me, ducks again sure enough. Then I saw two more, the three of them bunched closely together, pushing farther and farther into shelter. A great covey of blackbirds now came to my rescue, flew directly overhead and lit in the very patch of rice I was going to enter. What could be better than stalking under cover of their racket. This time I would hold my fire until I had a bird in line. No more stage fright this season. Another twenty feet and still they didn't move. Finally my curiosity got the better of me and I stood up to look around. No sooner had I gotten off balance than the three flew into action. It never fails, and in spite of my good resolve the first shot went wild. It was just as well however for before I got in my second, I saw in a flash that my three mallards had degenerated into mudhens, half grown ones at that, skittering through the rice dragging their long yellow legs after them. All my excitement had been for nothing.

Then came an anticlimax totally unexpected for just out of range a couple of big mallards beat their way heavily into the air, quacked a couple of times in loud derision and were off. Another minute if I had used my eyes and I'd have had some real shooting. There was no use even cussing. It was bound to happen at least once in every well rounded season and perhaps more. I stood up to watch the sky. Not a thing in sight, clear blue with a few patches of fleecy white clouds and the air warming up. I would have to be going soon.

Then far over the western horizon drifted a long uneven line of ducks, by their slow measured flight mallards without a doubt. Down stream they came, directly toward me and I pushed into the best cover that I could find. On they came in perfect formation, growing bigger and blacker with every wing beat, flying high and far out of range but slowly enough to indicate that they were looking for a feeding ground. The first quack of my caller and they turned ever so slightly, new ducks and innocent. At the second, the leader hesitated, swung my way and began to flutter downward in the falling leaf tumble all duck hunters know so well. The rest of the flock followed suit. Then they straightened out and began to circle still hundreds of yards away. Once they swung almost within range and I clutched my gun nervously. If I'd only take twos and threes instead of sixes, I would be sitting pretty. Once more they came around just at the limit of range and the sun shone on green and bronze as they turned. Then for no good reason whatever they set their wings and headed for a patch of rice a short ways up stream and settled to the accompaniment of much quacking and splashing. I couldn't help but wonder at the time why it is that the other rice bed always looks the best to them even though the one you are in has better feed and you yourself are perfectly hidden. I would have to be more careful this time for those mallards evidently knew more than I gave them credit for at first sight. Perhaps an old seasoned drake in the lead.

At the edge of a clump of brush near shore, I stood up for one final survey before starting. I could see the birds plainly diving and feeding and just beyond something that all but took the wind out of my sails, something black moving through the rice toward them, a man's hat. If this wasn't awful luck but there was no use bemoaning the fact. We were both as far away and would stand an even chance of getting shooting.

I saw my rival was paddling as swiftly as he could. He had already seen me so throwing caution to the winds, I started too. Whoever got there first would get the best shooting. It was now a case of sheer speed and I paddled as I had never paddled before. Suddenly there was a roar of wings followed by the *bang, bang, bang* of my friend's automatic and out of the corner of my eye, I saw two birds drop, pretty shots just as they were climbing into the air for elevation. One lone single came over me so close that

I could see its eyes and I almost fell out of the canoe getting in line for a shot. Another circled high above me, swung out and came back and at my shot dropped like a pinwheel, wings outspread. It wasn't a clean kill and I had to fire again to put it out of its misery. By the time that was over the rest of the flock was dropping over the ridge to more peaceful feeding grounds to the northward.

The black hat paddled away without so much as a greeting. It was a rotten break for him too and I did not much blame him, but what of it. I sat for a moment looking at my ducks and drinking in the warm freshness of the morning air. It was duck season and the world was young. Of a sudden, I came to earth with a crash. What was I doing out here in the marsh with a brand new son waiting for me back home? I had almost forgotten. He would in all probability be awake by now and they would be wondering where on earth I was. Over on the opposite shore was a bunch of maple leaves turned by the first frost. They would brighten up that room considerably. I paddled over, picked the prettiest bouquet I could find, then turned the bow of the canoe toward home. This first morning had been perfect.

I made the trip back in record time. The first person to greet me was the nurse. The speech I had prepared failed me utterly and the brace of beautiful greys I handed her were taken without so much as a word. I had done the unspeakable and no matter how hard I tried to make amends, I could see plainly that I was not to be forgiven. Junior was sleeping soundly and as I kissed his small red forehead, I knew that at least he bore me no grudge. His mother took the red leaves and greeted me with a smile. That helped.

"Did I have any shooting?"

"Yes, I had had a little." I couldn't really tell the truth without hurting her and that I wouldn't have done for the world and a year of opening days. I was sure of her forbearance at least and that was something. For understanding, I would have to wait until I could confess the whole affair to my duck hunting brethren. They would know and sympathize.

Junior is now quite a big lad. He has already sat beside me for hours at a time in a blind and though he hasn't as yet handled a gun, I know it is gradually working under his skin and some day when we are together watching a couple coming in over the rise, he will listen to my story and understand. If he doesn't, I will have to admit that I was wrong, but way down in my heart, I have a feeling that he will come across with a knowing grin. After all, he should be the one to decide, because it was his party and the first day of season for him as well as for me. It was just his hard luck that he couldn't go too.

The Belated Neighbor

BY GORDON MACQUARRIE

1935

T HE DUST ON THE ROAD WAS SO THICK THAT THE PRESIDENT OF THE Old Duck Hunters' Association, Inc., was sorry for the dog and almost sorry for me.

Speeding cars raced across that gravel road because it was a connecting link between two concrete highways, and it was a joy rider's October Sunday.

"If I could afford an automobile," said Mister President, wiping his begrimed face, "I would not monkey around driving this road. I would get on one that went to Mississippi or Manitoba, depending on the season."

At the moment Hizzoner was burdened financially and morally with some 60 automobiles including a half dozen super-supers, priced F.O.B. Detroit. Or was it Flint? Memory weakens in the face of the irrelevant. Thank heaven it holds up otherwise.

The Old Duck Hunters', Inc., was trudging back from a fruitless quest for partridge. It had been a fourteen-mile thrust on foot into the southern hinterland of Douglas County, Wisconsin. Rumor, via a helpful neighbor, had spread the word of a partridge plenitude. We found naught but popple and hazel brush.

Well, there we were, we and the poor dog, a springer of excellent coat excepting the ears which never looked any better than grandpa's buffalo cutter robe. About once in so often a car would honk us into the ditch where we would cower until the dust cleared.

"Dang yuh," the old master accused once, "you have picked the leeward side of the ditch three times hand running."

Jerry the springer was smarter than both of us. At the first faint whine of a hill-leaping car he would fling himself deep into the roadside bush. It

---

The Belated Neighbor **89**

had been a dry year. It was fierce.

"I often wish I were a dog," the president said wistfully.

We went on. I had a heel blister. He contended I ought to be in better shape because I had drunk the most water at the farmhouse, five miles back. His good spirits buoyed me. Also was I cheered when he summoned me to the center of the road. Pointing to a gravelly, dusty rut he demanded:

"You know what made that track?"

"No sir."

"That's where my tail has been dragging."

A speeder from the rear started us for cover again. As we hit the hazel brush the oncomer slowed and Mister President yelled from his ditch, "Heaven help us, here comes a gentleman! Here's luck!"

The car drew up slowly and dustlessly. The driver was a lone hunting man with a long cheerful nose and a hunting jacket white as sailcloth from many washings. He hailed Mister President.

He was of course a neighbor and brother of the chase. He was also the brother of the chase who had sent the O.D.H.A. on its hideous partridge hunt. The President emerged to make palaver with his great and good neighbor. As in a dream I heard Hizzoner in flagrant fabrication.

"Never saw anything like it...Woods alive with partridge...Killed a limit apiece...Pshaw, we don't want a ride...The walk'll do us good..."

As the car vanished over a hill I thought of the big bottle of sparkling water I had seen in the back seat.

"I wouldn't ask that scoundrel for the morning dew on his decoys," Mister President snorted. "Did you see him leer at me when I told him about those eight birds we didn't get? He seemed greatly surprised. All I was doing was lying like a gentleman."

Doubtless, I agreed, but insisted I would rather accept one big cool swig out of his water bottle than all the partridge in the North.

This respondent is not one to quibble with our peerless leader. This respondent knows all about the standing feud between this neighbor and Mister President. This respondent recalls the moribund mouse which this neighbor carried in his pocket to a dance. And the itching powder that went with it. And who done it.

The respondent also knows of the time when this suffering neighbor sat for two days on a Washburn County pothole that never saw a duck land in it from one year to the next. And of the slightly turpentined pointer dog, owned by this same victim, and how said pointer embarrassed him before a gallery of the grandest sharptail hunters that ever put down a dog on O'Connor's potato field.

"If you ask me," I said, "you are just making trouble."

"Who asked you?"

And now let us forget that partridge chapter and by the license granted to the Old Duck Hunters begin right away with the plot, the day of reckoning, the Old Man's Method and the ceaseless turning of the spheres in their courses.

It is three weeks later and the Old Duck Hunters are snugly billeted in a familiar cabin on the shore of a big lake shaped like a rubber boot.

The curtain rises on a scene of ineffable peace. The supper dishes are done. Tomorrow's gear is sorted and laid in the boathouse on the beach, including the stable lantern and horse blanket for warming Mister President's shins.

The morrow is one we have marked for our very own. Bluebills fetching through northwest Wisconsin by the thousand. A growing wind rattling the oak leaves. A full moon slicing the clouds.

"It'll blow harder tonight," said Mister President. "The moon is full. Ducks'll fly under the full moon. There'll be newcomers by morning."

"And we'll have the bay all to ourselves."

"Perchance...perchance..." He was dozing.

And now, music. Music of the foreboding kind, like just before the dagger fight in "Gypsy Love." The back door of the cabin is thumped with tremendous vigor. I hurry to open it and admit the man with the long, cheerful nose—the same who had lured the Old Duck Hunters to the Place of No Partridge.

Now, I say to myself, the Old Boy will let him have it. He will tell him to his long, cheerful nose what he thinks of him. Now he will walk up one side of him and down the other wearing nothing but a pair of river boots with double naught corks.

Quickly and often painfully are the illusions of younger men broken.

Those two friendly foes fell on each other like long lost brothers. Mister President made the visitor comfortable in his own chair. He offered him extra socks! He commanded me to man the coffee pot for he was a way-farer in the night and a friend of long standing.

The long-nosed one explained that he was quartered down the lake shore in a neighbor's cabin. He was alone. He had just arrived. He had to get back and put his boat in, fill the motor, look over the decoys. No thanks, no supper, but a cup of steaming coffee...well now!

Felicitations flowed like hot fudge. Mister President laid the campaign for Cheerful Long Nose.

"Pshaw, I know these waters like a book. Only place for you to go in the morning is two miles down the shore to the Hole in the Wall."

I wondered if Mister President had lost his mind. The Hole in the Wall is where we were going! I listened to him saying—

"You get right up there first thing and grab that blind before someone else does."

Long Nose was formally grateful, but it did seem to me that I could detect he had, hours before, decided to appropriate the Hole in the Wall at all cost. He did not say as much. He merely smiled. What you might call the alarm clock smile which says, "O.K. brother. If you set the alarm for 5, mine'll be set for 4!"

He went away and Mister President wound his watch. I protested the division of the Old Duck Hunter's hunting grounds without a vote of the lodge. He merely yawned and set the alarm clock carefully by the faithful hands of the thick gold watch.

Under the covers in the other room I knew what to expect next day— Cheerful Long Nose in the Hole in the Wall Blind and the Old Duck Hunters making the best of things on the boggy shore a half mile away. The bog sinks under a man. It is a mere emergency blind. Not a fit place at all for the O.D.H. to carry out the rites in comfort.

We had built that Hole in the Wall Blind. It was ours. Everyone knew it was ours. And he had willed it away without the blink of an eyelash!

The wind was picking up as I fell to sleep. It was crying high in the pine trees. It would be a blustery daybreak. A squirrel scuttered over the roof...or was it a chipmunk?...mebbe a handful of scrub oak leaves. Then, soon...I slept.

"Oyez, oyez! The Duck Hunters' Association is now assembled in due form!"

He was leaning over me, a sharp brown eye looking down and a lean brown hand grasping the red blankets. There is no choice at such times. I got up. Better that than to lie there blanketless and shivering.

Breakfast was ready. He looked as if he had been up for hours. There were red spots in his cheeks. They might have been put three by the wind that was fairly tearing the ridge pole off but he said they were "just from leaning over that hot stove frying you four eggs." He was exceedingly happy for a man who had recently given away the best bluebill blind in north Wisconsin.

Down at the boathouse we rolled out the sinews of war and clamped on the motor in a tossing sea. Heaven bless that motor. Not once on the coldest mornings has it failed. Once it spat defiance to a November that came upon us with six below zero in the night.

Half way out of our bay I stopped the motor to listen. The sound of no other motor was heard. There was only the long hissing waves and the wind roaring outside my earlaps. I suggested to Mister President that Cheerful Long Nose was already up there, in our blind. He replied—

"What the hell you worried about that blind for? That guy has got an alarm clock that never goes off until it's too late. Head for the Hole in the Wall. If he shows up we'll move out."

In twenty minutes we had made the Old Duck Hunters' favorite setup of bluebill stool. Outside of the fact that I could write a book about it, it is simple: a long narrow horseshoe of decoys, lopsided where one arm of the layout stretches far and inviting into the bay.

"I believe in being neighborly," said the President as we put gear ashore and tucked the boat beneath over-hanging bank willows. "If he comes along we've got to shove over to that bog. Hope you brought your boots."

There was a good twenty minutes to wait before the hands on the thick gold watch declared the legal moment. Long before the moment the bluebills were dive-bombing the decoys. He waited, watch in hand.

Something was certainly doing. Wings were cutting the air to pieces.

The light grew and the 'bills increased. Beyond in the tossing bay we saw ragged lines of black. Hundreds of bluebills sat there, over the densest growths of coontail I knew about.

When Mister President said "Now!" it was mere routine lodge work for the association to rise and knock four bluebills to the water from the bundle of six that smashed by.

It is an elegant thing to perform such duties with coordinated dispatch. Among the Old Duck Hunters there is no such foolish: "I'll tell you when," or "You tell me when." Duck hunting men of the veterans' stripe know when, where and how. It is a kind of synchronization with each man taking his allotted side of the bluebill bundle as it swoops at the decoys. It is best done by two who know each other well.

Picking them up fell to the least membership and while I was at it a dozen tried to sit in the decoys.

The bluebill seeker outside of the northern states knows nothing of this; he is inclined not to believe it. His ducks are educated. But let him once see the scaups lesser and greater as they glide into wooden decoys in northern Minnesota and Wisconsin and he will know. Too bad so few know. Too bad, too, that brother bluebill takes to eating fishy foods once he gets down a way into the United States. Up there in the northern tier of states he is just a bundle of jam-packed rice and coontail.

Some of them were big birds. Some of them sat among the decoys. Some of them, shot at, would fly 200 yards away, sit down again and look around to say: "What the hell is this anyway?" Which prompted Mister President to declare—

"One of these days when you're scribbling something just put down that anybody shooting at a bluebill on the water is not only a bum sport but a fool. Anybody who can't hit 'em when they get up hadn't ought to have gone hunting in the first place."

They came from the north and from the west. From Minnesota's northern wilderness, and also from Lake Superior, sixty miles straight north of us, where ducks sit by the tens of thousands until the wind gets at them. As I retrieved them the President speculated:

"One of these here experts told me once that if a bluebill's black head is shot with purple he's a lesser scaup; if it's shot with green he's a greater scaup. Now you just show me any 'bill in that pile, big or little, that hasn't got BOTH green and purple in his black head feathers."

I did not show him. I have gone through it all too many times with the President of the Old Duck Hunters. All I know is what I read in the books and what the Old Man says. Both can't be right. And I have too much affection for the book writers to incite them to battle with the Old Man.

The faithful outboard roared forth many times that morning for the pick-up. Once it was to pick up three canvasback, remnants from a big flock that just cut the edge of our decoys.

"Just what we needed," he observed. "There's nothing like a little color to improve the looks of a bag."

By eleven o'clock of that blasty morning we were counting ducks pretty carefully. When the bluebills hit Northern Wisconsin in their big years a man with a gun will do well to watch his arithmetic. There is a great difference between ten apiece and twelve apiece. That difference can happen in a five-second flurry. Hence the mathematics, as fixed and certain with Mister President as the hands of his thick gold watch.

The time came for Hizzoner to make a final count and give the signal. He assembled the gear on the shore and I wound in the decoys. Only on the return, facing the bitter northwest wind did I think of Cheerful Long Nose. He had gone completely out of mind in the robust zest of a grand lodge session. Over the motor's roar I asked, "Where'd you suppose he went?"

Mister President shrugged and yelled back, "He ain't got a good alarm clock!"

Battling waves back into our own bay, where it was calmer, I saw on the north shore a tall man leaning over a beached boat. The waves were beating in there hard for the wind had hauled from west to southwest. The tall man was swooping a pail into the boat. I aimed our boat toward him.

The obvious had happened. The boat he was bailing had drifted away in the night. He was a duck hunter and all such require help. Decoys sloshed in the boat bottom. It was spang up on shore. The wind had been so severe that it had shoved sand up around the boat's bottom and sides. A long green shell case was covered with water.

The man with the pail was Cheerful Long Nose and he was in a Bad Way. Every time he heaved a pailful of water overside to lighten the boat two pailfuls came inboard.

The President was the first to leap ashore and help. He waded in water to his knees, above the tops of his old gum rubbers. He lugged decoys. He grabbed the shellbox and emptied the water. He just took charge of things and eventually we towed the belated neighbor back to his landing.

"Darned if I know how it happened," Cheerful Long Nose explained. "When I left you last night I loaded the boat and then hauled 'er up on the beach far as I could. Put the motor handy. Had every darned thing ready."

The President of the Old Duck Hunters offered him a bundle of blue-bill, which he accepted.

"If it hadn't been for you two I never could have budged that boat," he went on. "I've always been careful about hauling boats up high on windy nights."

"Yep...?" said Mister President, more sympathetic than ever.

"But I see now what happened. The stern two feet was in water. The wind rose and sloshed water overside. It got heavy and the boat slid off the beach. I hadn't tied 'er."

"I'll be damned," said Mister President.

We saw him off for the Hole in the Wall. It was full noon with the wind still roaring. He would finish out his bag there, we knew. We gave him hot coffee. We took over six boxes of dampish shells and give him six boxes of dried ones. He darted out of the bay a happy and grateful man.

The Old Duck Hunters climbed the hill.

"I suppose," said the President of the Old Duck Hunters, "that you think I pushed his boat off the beach."

"Certainly."

He heaved a sigh. He pushed on up the hill burdened with gun and shellcase.

"All I did," he said, "was give 'er a little nudge."

Sport Among the Canvasbacks
BY W. B. HAYNES
1936

J UST HOW FAR DOES THE ELEMENT OF LUCK ENTER INTO THE SUCCESS or failure of a hunting expedition. Well, often to a considerable extent, as many hunters can testify. What duck hunter has not seen his carefully laid plans dashed to pieces by a shift of the wind! If bad luck fastens on you at the beginning of a trip, the chances are it will continue. But so also sometimes good luck can follow you. It worked out so with me on a trip to the North Carolina ducking grounds when everything seemed to come my way even in new, unfamiliar shooting grounds. My best shoot on canvasbacks came to me as a direct result of my guides forgetting the lunch bucket in the hurry of getting away early one morning.

We were two miles out from shore when they discovered this interesting bit of knowledge, and the boat was almost across the big, lumpy waves and into the quieter canvasback grounds.

Who would go back after a lunch with a thousand canvasbacks in the air ahead of him?

"Forget all about it," I said, when they gave me the bad news about the lunch.

So we took a blind and put out 50 canvasback decoys and proceeded to forget all about the lunch, which it is entirely possible to do at 9 o'clock in the morning when canvasbacks are buzzing overhead.

It was a bad day and it blew a wicked north wind that drove a little whisper of fine, hard snow with it—truly a canvasback day if there ever was one, and out of the north came flock after flock of canvasbacks.

They came, swooping down out of the northeast, swinging into the quieter waters of the sound. If they came our way they would decoy, but all they wanted to do was to get somewhere that was quiet—anywhere, to get out of these stinging blasts.

The ocean had been a safe resting place for the big birds, a veritable haven of refuge, for though the canvasback wants his feeding grounds to be in fresh water, he knows that sink boxes do not carry the broad bosom of the Atlantic Ocean, and he can gather his food in the sound at night safely.

But this day there was to be no resting on the ocean, as any canvasback that has looked on the Atlantic Ocean in one of its tantrums could have told us.

"Sort of wish I had 'tied out' the sink box for you," said Ben Jones, "only, when we came out the birds were not 'using' in any particular place, and it would have been guess work."

"I've sent Albert after our lunch with the launch," he added.

A Great Flight of Canvasbacks

Albert came back with the lunch about 2 o'clock, and the canvasbacks had been roaring into the sound in a continuous stream for several hours.

"You won't to able to do much with them today, but tomorrow will be a great day on the sound. There are over three thousand canvasbacks rafted up just south of that big grassy island. I chased them out when I went for the lunch, and when I came back they were in the same place again, only more of them," was Albert's report.

"Sort of south and east a bit from the island?" inquired Ben. "I guess I know what they found in there to feed on."

"It is too late to try for them today," he added, "we won't disturb them today, but there is a tomorrow and if someone else don't beat us to it you will have the chance of a lifetime—yes, better than I've seen for years."

So we shot a fair kill of canvasbacks from the blind, but every flock that cut to westward did not come back. The big raft of birds under the lee of the marshy island soaked them up as a sponge gathers water, and as the great bunch of wildfowl grew, it showed farther through the storm, until there rested there most of the flocks of canvasbacks and our decoys were left there alone to the writhing gale.

"It is lucky I sent Albert after that lunch or we would have known nothing about those canvasbacks."

"Just imagine 3,000 canvasbacks sitting there hour after hour. It could happen only on this kind of a day," and Ben swung his arms to warm up in the bitter blast.

And so the grey day drew through to its chilly close and we pulled up our decoys. On the homeward run Albert steered the boat a bit out of her course to see if the canvasbacks were still rafted up.

They were—to the probable extent of 5,000—the seething mass of ducks tossed in the gale and the white backs of the drakes shifted, a speckled blur, like a kaleidoscope, as they fed.

"Keep to looard," growled Ben, then he turned to me. "I don't know who we've got to race for this plum tomorrow, but if we get it for you, you're due for a shoot you'll never forget."

My shooting companion who was down here with me on this trip had been on the sick list for a few days, but he had been watching the canvasbacks through field glasses and he told me no flesh and blood could stand such a sight.

"If you get that place today," he said to me early in the morning, before we started out, "you will kill your limit early; then, when the day warms up, send the boys over for me and I will try for a while, doctor's orders or no doctor's orders, for it's the chance of a lifetime."

"There is, then, some chance that we may not win out to those canvasbacks ahead of others?" I asked, incredulous. "Why, not a sink box was out on that side of the sound; not a hunter bothered those canvasbacks; no one but us saw them come in."

"You forget," he reminded, "that this driving gale and snow means canvas to every old timer on the sound. When it comes in late December they know the canvas will be here, and they know within a mile or two of where they will be rafted up. This much is in your favor; they also know that the redheads will be swarming in the North Sound, and will race for it early.

"Knowing as you do, just where the birds are located, will give you the inside track over the outfits from this side of the sound. But, some guide will remember that his father had a great shoot on canvas over there on just such a day, at just this time of the year, and his sharp eyes will see that raft, and, as you know, there is only one best place." This from Ben, who had been hunting the sound for years, made me see it was to be a race. When men, sons of wildfowlers, living by wildfowling, set out to do their best for the hunters who hire them, rest assured no tricks will be forgotten, no knowledge is thrown aside.

Pride of profession is nowhere more evident than in the great business of guiding, and no guide wants to play second fiddle to his rival.

The Start Next Morning

In the grey of the morning we loaded up the sink-box skiff, but we did not leave the shore. The law on the sound is that the boats do not run out into the open sound until sun up, although they may cruise up along the shore.

This big raft of canvasbacks, however, lay directly opposite us, east across the open water, so we lay quietly in shore, for this and the additional very good reason that we did not want to head for the raft until the other sink boxes were past us, out of sight to the north.

Soon there passed us in the grey, the sink-box outfits we had been racing every morning. They held past us, driving for the North Sound headed for the redheads while we lay in shore.

When they were clear and signal came from the house "Sun up," we cut out into the waves and struck out across the sound in the wintry north wind.

Then, when the place neared, with the wind at our backs, we rode down long, easy swells toward a black, squirming dot, acres big, on the water, while Dewey and Ben grinned at another sink-box outfit, struggling a mile off to the south against the gale.

"We got it for you," said Ben. "We can beat the world to them now. Wait till you see 'em fly up!"

The great black blot shifted uneasily at our approach.

It was indeed a sight. Not far from 7,000 canvasbacks were feeding in the raft; they rose in a smoky blur, and, as the boys put down the sink box, they streaked athwart the low clouds in all directions.

The sink box that had raced us stopped when the birds raised and took the next best place to the south, but we knew it would do them no good, for although the canvasbacks passed over them and around them, their only wish was to get back, promptly, to the place they had been disturbed from, for such is the way of ducks; they go back to the place they've been using.

Ben and Dewey dumped the sink box overboard, unfolded its wooden wings, then anchored it in the shallow water and put around it 200 decoys. Then I took my double-barreled Parker and a hundred shells and possession of the sink box.

Even as the boat moved away a pair of canvasbacks headed in and I missed them, as they went to the right side of the box and I tried to cover them from my right shoulder instead of taking them left-handed, which by the way, is a trick every sink-box shooter should learn to do. Anyway I missed them, but I didn't miss the next bird that skirted the foot of the sink box.

Far out, off to the south, I sunk lower in the box, when—swish! and from the right came a single bird.

I raised, covered him and dropped him kicking into the decoys, while shot-scared canvasbacks were headed at me from three different angles. A minute later six more set their wings above me and two big drakes fell from the flock at my first shot. I raised to my feet and finished one cripple, then sank back, for it was as if the heavens had opened and started to throw canvasbacks at me. They came up the sound in a wave after wave, and in wave after wave the feathered avalanche flung itself against the steady wind at my sink box.

Again I dropped two at one shot to my left, as they slid together, wing almost touching wing, over the big set of decoys.

Now I settled down and took toll of the decoying flocks carefully, and with all certainty that I could kill the limit. For almost an hour the heavy flight kept up, white-backed birds every few minutes, and I shot well and steadily.

Then the boat came to pick up the fallen birds.

Picking Up the Birds
"How many down?" Dewey called.

It had happened so swiftly I hadn't kept track, so I have to make a guess, as I was ashamed to say I didn't know.

"You ought to pick up ten or eleven," was my hazard. "They look mostly like canvasbacks," I added

Off downwind they scoured the sound, while, of course, the birds stopped coming, due to their boat being so plainly in sight.

They soon returned to the sink box.

"We're going over for the sick man," they yelled to me over the roar of the high wind. "He's out in front of the house tramping in a circle, and he'll be a raving maniac if we don't go and get him pretty soon."

"How many did you pick up?" I shouted.

"Even twelve birds." And when I yelled, "What kind?" they answered, "All canvas."

The boat drew away and I clutched the old Parker and sunk back in the box as I was entitled to a few more.

A pair with set wings raced in to me. I raised to a sitting position and the great drakes flared. One wilted to the right barrel and I swung ahead of the other and dropped him also. A single big drake came over me and I centered him fairly and in falling he almost struck me as he crashed into the battery wing. It was a fitting final, the prettiest shot of a great day.

My Companion Does Some Shooting

Now the boat was returning with my companion who was to have his turn in the box.

"Doctor's orders were that you were to stay in the house," I yelled to my friend, who was so eager the boys had to hold him to keep him in the boat.

"Doctor says I've got the grippe," he barked at me. "Says I must stay off the sound. Says I must let these flutter around all day." He waved his arms at the string of canvasbacks that sheered out wide, then he crossed to the sink box and settled down in my place, shaky but satisfied.

So I gave him a little prescription, namely, that he must stay in the sink box until he had his limit of straight canvasbacks, which he had no trouble in taking, for there was so stopping them.

On returning to the house I took a good look at the great bunch of ducks I had killed, canvasbacks all, no blackheads, not even a redhead in the lot, for the raft of canvasbacks had been located off the beaten track of their lesser neighbors. Twenty five years of wildfowling had not brought me such a chance, and it was not likely of encore. Verily, as Ben said, it had been the chance of a lifetime.

But even as I looked over the superb bunch of fowl I could see that there was a loser's end to such a lucky day, because, when you have done this, when you have killed the limit in three-pound celery-fed canvasbacks, you have reached the top of the wildfowling mountain.

What greater prize has the wildfowling game to offer you, than can be legally attained?

Hudson Bay Geese

BY JIMMY ROBINSON

1936

I T WAS A SIGHT TO CHILL THE MARROW IN A MAN'S BONES AND CONGEAL his blood. The Eskimo boy called Dennis Okatiark stood as if transformed, his next step frozen in the air. A few remaining wisps of sea fog rose from the water's edge and crossed my vision like white wraiths, so that I could not be sure I had seen aright, but the boy's stark immobility at once told me I had.

My startled eye followed his gaze, and now I plainly saw the big, yellowish-white bear ambling along the mud and rocks of the treeless river bank. He was distinctly yellower than the white patch of fog that floated along the bank above him.

Another patch of yellow, this one motionless, caught my eye. A second bear sat comically on its haunches, staring after the first one. The ludicrous posture broke the spell.

"Nanug!" Dennis whispered. "Polar bear!"

Gradually the Eskimo's uplifted foot came down and made noiseless contact with the barren earth. Then, ever so carefully, he let the three Canadian geese he was carrying slip to the ground. Without so much as swaying in my tracks, I reached slowly into a pocket and brought up three BB loads for the 12-gauge shotgun I was carrying. Then I dug up three more and pressed them into the Eskimo boy's limp hand. Somehow I took assurance from the fact that his fingers closed over the shells.

The morning fog was dissipating rapidly now, fragmenting away in ghostly wisps; and the rocks, the water's edge and the bears gave the illusion of being closer than ever.

I wished mightily that I had brought my camera, then realized that there was no remedy for this. My camera was back at the tent on the high bank above the Little Seal River. And we dared not move, lest we alarm these bears or perhaps even provoke them to attack. Slowly we squatted on our haunches, heads sucked into our parka hoods so that, motionless, we would resemble the huge boulders scattered all around us.

I remembered the Alaska brown bear hunt I had made with George Hart the previous April and the stories Dick Johnston, our Alaskan guide, had told us about the critters. "Polar bears are worse," he had said. "You never know what a polar bear will do. He may run—or he may mistake you for a seal and try to make a meal of you."

It wasn't funny. But there was a funny story about a polar bear that crossed my mind now. It had been told to me by Tony Sabanski, owner of the Hudson Hotel in Churchill, the day of our arrival on this subarctic goose hunt.

"Only yesterday I heard all this shooting and laughing outside the hotel," Tony had said. "I went out and there were about twenty kids pursuing a big polar bear right down the main street. They were throwing empty Coke bottles and stones at the bear. You know what it did? It just kept right on going and when it got to the Churchill River, it jumped right in. But I wonder what would have happened if that bear had decided to turn around and chase the kids."

Remembering the story made me feel a little safer. I was no longer conscious of the rasp in my breathing. Actually, I was beginning to get a kick out of watching the bears. But I was brought back to reality with a start when the big sow who had been sitting on her haunches slowly rose and started walking in the direction of our tent.

Now what should I do? Wait and let her make a shambles of our camp and devour our dwindling grub supply, or try to chase her away? Without reason, I suddenly stood up and let out a yelp that would have frightened a banshee. Then I fired a shot over the head of the sow.

Both bears halted abruptly in their tracks. They saw us instantly. Before I had time to assay their intent, one leaped over the river with a huge splash. The other wheeled and broke into a gallop that quickly carried it out of sight along the bank. Only then did I realize how foolhardy I'd been, how rapidly the bears could have covered the distance between them and us. The realization numbed me.

"That was close." Dennis looked around at me and grinned.

"Phew! Too close! What if they hadn't run?"

"We wouldn't be here now." The Eskimos are a stoic breed.

As we walked more easily toward the tent, I thought, this has to be the highlight of this goose-hunting trip. How little did I know what lay in store for us. In fact, at the June Jamboree Trapshoot in Winnipeg, where Bert Fraser had introduced me to Tony Sabanski from Churchill, I had been eager to accept Tony's proposal that I fly up North this fall and have a goose hunt with him.

"I can show you some pretty good goose hunting," Tony had said.

When anybody talks goose hunting, he talks my language. I was ready to talk. "I'll be there for the opening," I said.

After the Grand American Trapshoot at Vandalia, Ohio, I headed back home to Minneapolis and greeted my wife, Clara, with the words, "Start packing right now. I'm going to Churchill to hunt geese. We'll drive to our duck camp in Saint Ambroise, and I'll fly up from there."

Joined by Ed Stow, who had flown in from Minneapolis to accompany me to Churchill; we slept in our Delta Marsh duck camp the next night. The following morning Ed and I were heading north from Winnipeg in a big, four-engine Viscount over prairie pothole, marshy lakeshore and spruce bog I had hunted in most of my life. The Pas-Flin Flon-Lynn Lake. These were but interruptions in my train of thought that already had me in Churchill!

Churchill! What history this 300-year-old fur-trading post on the west coast of Hudson Bay has made! Now it is an air and radar center amid a cluster of shacks on the bleak, rocky property facing the wide inland sea that is Hudson Bay.

Tony was waiting at the airstrip and, with him, Don Kileen, from Winnipeg. We had left Winnipeg in a mid-forty-degree temperature, but here it was windy, cold, and even freezing.

"Hope you brought plenty of warm clothes," Tony said. "Snowed here last night" Snow—in the first week of September!

We skidded more than we walked over the frozen puddles on the airstrip to pick up our baggage. I sorted my luggage from the mountain of stuff disgorged by the plane.

"What's those things in the bag?" Tony asked.

"Goose decoys," I said. "Best you can buy."

"Leave 'em right here at the airport. We'll not be needing 'em. They'll only scare geese. We use newspapers and napkins up here. Then when we've shot a few geese, we prop 'em up for decoys. That really brings them in."

In the Trans-Air hangar I saw a familiar face, Gregg Lamb who operates a fleet of planes out of Churchill. More than 25 years before, on the Saskatchewan River, I had hunted geese with Gregg's dad, Tommy Lamb of the Pas. It was like Old Home Week.

Gregg had flown in from the Arctic the day before. "I saw geese all the way down," he said. "They've just started to move south."

Before I could open my mouth, he was talking again. "You may think you had good goose hunting in California, but wait'll you hunt the Seal River. It's the greatest. Be sure you take your fishing tackle. Plenty of Arctic char and grayling in the Seal. Good time for speckled trout, too."

I was in a fog, too confused to protest that I wasn't the least bit interested in fish. In my mind, those big flocks of geese were coming right at me across the airport runway.

At Tony's Hudson Hotel, I got briefed. "We were all set to take off today," he said, "but this weather is too rough for small planes.

"So two of my friends, who'll be hunting with us, left yesterday to get everything ready. They went up yesterday in a 20-foot freighter canoe with an 18-horse outboard. Got our tents and most of the equipment. Everything'll be set when we get there."

Rain continued to slant in from the northeast all day, and I could sympathize with Joe Hickes and Gene Hermanson, the Churchill natives who were toting our gear in a canoe to the mouth of the Seal. By midnight, the rain ceased; skies cleared; and the next morning we were ready to go.

There was a touch of winter in the air. Rocky Parsons, the pilot of our Norseman, was a veteran of the North who had the reputation of being able to fly through any kind of weather.

Soon we were at the mouth of the Seal, where we were to meet Hickes and Hermanson at the camp they had set up. Rocky let down to 200 feet and started looking for the tents. There was nothing in sight so the Norseman headed upriver for several miles. Still no sign of the tents...

There was nothing in sight. So the Norseman headed upriver several miles. Still no sign of tents.

"Maybe they camped on the Little Seal," said Tony. "Let's go over there. It's a cinch they ain't here."

Rocky headed the plane south to the Little Seal River, and from the mouth, we followed it upstream about three miles. On the south bank, we saw a single tent.

"Must be them," said Rocky. He hurriedly wrote a note, tied it in a white handkerchief, weighted it with a bolt, swung low over the tent and dropped it. The note asked the boys to take the canoe and run down to the mouth of the river to meet us, for both the Seal and Little Seal are shallow in spots, with fast water rushing over acres of stones.

Our landing was accomplished smoothly, about a half mile out in Hudson Bay from the mouth of the Little Seal. We figured that with the swiftness of the river current, it should take our advance party no longer than fifteen minutes to reach the open bay. But we waited and waited and waited—and no sign of the canoe.

The moment of decision arrived. Should we fly back to Churchill before we were marooned by low tide on the mud flats? "I'm for walking up the river to see who those people are," Tony said. "Anybody want to come along?"

We all tumbled out of the plane, which now stood in three feet of fast-dwindling water. Ed decided he'd stay and watch the plane. The rest of us waded ashore. Soon Rocky and Tony were far ahead of Don and me. Perhaps we had walked upstream two miles, the toughest two miles I had ever experienced. Exhausted, I dropped to a convenient rock and said, "Let's build a blind, Don, and shoot a few geese. That's what we came for, isn't it?"

It was now about three o'clock, and geese by the thousands were flying overhead. Don and I built makeshift blinds about fifty yards apart and sat there for several minutes watching the geese coming and going. It was a thrilling, unbelievable sight.

Presently, a big gaggle of geese headed over Don's blind, quail-high. He gun spoke twice, and a big snow tumbled to the quivering earth, I saw him run out and seize the bird, hold it up admiringly and then running breathlessly over to show me his kill. "First goose I ever killed," he said. "Jimmy, this alone is worth the trip."

I could find it in my heart to bestow praise for this singular feat. "And it's the first goose taken by our party. Probably it's the goose killed farthest north this year."

Within the hour we had bagged six geese. I examined their crops and found them full of a small blueberry, the bilberry, or Arctic blueberry. Then we spotted Tony and Rocky coming back down the river. Tony had four geese hanging from his shoulder.

"Eskimos," he said. "That camp was Eskimos. Three of 'em. Been hunting and fishing. Know one of 'em—Peter Bruce, from Churchill. Nice guy." The three Eskimos, one a 15-year-old boy, lived in Churchill. They had been out seven days, on a hunting holiday. "They've got a good canoe, and they'll come down and pick you up," Rocky said.

So the four of us started the long, arduous trek back to the Norseman, which by now was sitting like a lighthouse on a pile of bare stones, half a mile from the river mouth. The tide was at ebb, and now there was no question of Rocky's getting away for Churchill that night.

Back at the plane, we found Ed had bagged two geese while standing beside a pontoon. So that made twelve, and we hadn't even started to hunt yet. Presently we heard the chug of the Eskimos' motor. They pulled their canoe up on the mud flats and pitched in to help us transfer our guns and food from the plane. The canoe was loaded to the gunwales with the seven of us, plus all our baggage. We bade Rocky goodby and left him high and dry, waiting for the tide to come in so he could return to Churchill.

The Eskimos, with native intuition, had picked a proper spot for their small tent. They had placed it at the top of a 30-foot bank, which was covered with small bushes and weeds. But they had nothing to eat—no bread, no coffee—nothing!

"Plenty of geese and fish to eat," said Jack. "We not starve. Been here seven days." But now they were low on gas, and they were completely out of shells. They had two more days to go before they had to start back for Churchill. But, with typical Eskimo fatalism, they were unworried. What would come would come.

It was fortunate we had happened along. We had plenty of shells and food; they had a canoe. What could be better? Luckily, Rocky had brought a small tent along and had left it with us to cover our equipment. We had no tent poles, but the Eskimos lent us a spare paddle, crudely carved out of a black spruce log, to use as an outside ridgepole. We set up the tent between two large bushes on top of the bank near the Eskimo tent. It was small and full of holes, with but one opening for a door and no flap over it. When we piled in all our equipment and crawled on top of it, there was scarcely room for any of us to take a deep breath.

The Eskimos were very friendly, and Peter excitedly told us about two polar bears that had been hanging around their camp. Each time they went hunting, they had been forced to leave one of their group to guard the tent. Polar bears! Hadn't the two Mounties I met at the Hudson Hotel, the night before, warned us to be careful of the bears? They told us about a polar bear that had attacked two hunters, near Churchill, a few days before.

Exhausted, we bedded down early. I was dreaming of polar bears entering our tent when I awoke to find that the wind had risen during the night and that rain was trickling into my face through the holes in the tent. I tried to shift my position in my sleeping bag, but Tony was barring the way. I pulled the bag over my head and tried to ignore the drips of water. But the wind was persistent and steadily increasing. When it acquired a velocity I estimated at 50 miles an hour, our little tent started to sway.

Finally, the canoe paddle caught a gust and turned sideways. The tent collapsed in one swoosh and tumbled down over us. Luckily we had been sleeping with all our clothes on. We crawled out from beneath the tent, into a driving rain. Somehow we got the tent up again, but by this time we were as wet as fish in their watery world. But then daylight arrived. Over breakfast, we wondered what had happened to Hickes and Hermanson. Not until we returned to Churchill did we learn that they had run into nothing but trouble and had nearly lost their lives in the bargain. And everything would have been fine had not a big storm arisen over Hudson Bay the first night out. Sixty-mile winds from the northeast had quickly whipped up waves much higher than the normal 14-foot tide, and the little island on which they were camped had been inundated. The storm had blown down their tents, and they had lost all their equipment. Waist-deep in water, they had somehow clung to their canoe all the rest of the night. When the storm abated in the morning, they had managed to salvage one tent and their sleeping bags. They had immediately set out for Churchill. We had passed them Friday morning on the way out.

Now, on this sodden morning, a heavy fog hung over our makeshift camp near the Eskimos. A light mist soaked into our clothing, and we were all chilled to the bone. "Let's get going and bag some geese," Tony suggested. "That'll warm us up."

Nothing, I felt, could warm me up. I volunteered to stand guard over the camp with the Eskimo boy, Dennis Okatiark. The rest of the party loaded up and headed downstream to the goose pass.

After sitting in the doorway of the tent for a few minutes, I decided to take a walk and loosen up. Perhaps a good walk would warm me up, too. There were geese passing within easy gun range of the tent, but I had no desire for this kind of shooting. Anyway, they might drop into the river, and we had no canoe with which to retrieve them. I beckoned to Dennis. "Let's walk over in that meadow beyond this hill."

Anything was acceptable to the boy, and I could see that he, too, was cold. But he was used to it. I handed him a gun and some shells, and we started off over the hill. We had walked perhaps a hundred yards and could see geese everywhere—to our right, to our left, in front and in back of us. It didn't really make much difference where we stopped. Finally, we came to the edge of a small pothole, where we flushed a bunch of mallards.

Dennis and I, new confirmed friends, had said we'd watch the camp. In a few minutes, the Eskimo and I decided to walk over to the blind we'd built by the edge of the pothole. We had scarcely finished setting out new decoys of white napkins when a huge flock of at least 100 blues and snows came tumbling in from the sky. They circled once, then headed in against the wind, directly in front of us. "Hold your fire!" I whispered to Dennis. He smiled and nodded. "Plenty snow geese. Lots of blue geese, too."

The big flock alighted on the pothole and started walking to the muddy shore to feed on bilberries and goose grass. Some of the geese were within twenty yards of our blind. We watched in amazement for at least half an hour. The sight reminded me of the times, more than 40 years ago, when my dog, Chum, and I lay for hours watching prairie chickens dance on my grandfather's farm in southern Manitoba.

But these geese were so close you could see their bright, beady eyes. Although I have hunted geese since I was a small boy, I had never had an experience like this. The birds ate continuously. Occasionally one would snap at another like a dog defending a bone. I longed for a camera. Presently, a big snow goose walked right up to our blind. By the inquisitive turnings of his head and neck, I judged he was as puzzled as we were.

Without provocation, the big snow gave the alarm. His wings extended to their fullest, and he clawed for the sky. At once, the rest of the flock took alarm and clamored into the air, squawking. I can't imagine how many geese we could have taken had we shot while they were bunched in the air. We never fired our guns. Later, we tumbled three geese. I emptied my gun, and we called it a day—a great day! I could have shot a dozen more geese during the next hour, as we sat watching the flocks. But I was content to look at them coming into the decoys. Occasionally we'd stand up, and they'd chatter excitedly as they scrambled upward and away, only to circle and try to land among the decoys.

By now, I was chilled to the bone again. So we returned to camp and the coffee pot. The rest of our boys came back at dusk, with enough geese to fill our limits for this trip. "It was fabulous," said Ed. "I'd never believe it if I hadn't been here to see it for myself." Even Tony, a goose hunter since he was in knee pants, was enthusiastic. "Had some great shoots at The Pas, where I guided for many years. But these two days were the greatest I've ever seen."

Coming from Tony, a veteran goose hunter, this was quite a tribute to the Little Seal River and to the Eskimos who had picked this spot.

The next morning, the four of us, with Jack and Peter, loaded our scant equipment into the canoe, leaving our remaining group at the Eskimo camp. At 11 A.M. we shoved off in the canoe for our rendezvous with Rocky on the bleak Hudson Bay coast. We'd have plenty of time to meet him at the noon deadline, when the tide would be at its peak.

When we reached the mouth of the river, we tied up to shore and waited in dismal weather. By one o'clock, the tide had started to move out. Fifteen minutes later—only 15—and the tide was so low we had to move our canoe closer to the bay. Then we heard the roar of a plane. It was Rocky.

By this time, the tide was going out so fast that rocks and huge boulders were sticking up everywhere. Now the problem was getting out across the mud flats to the plane. Could we make it? Six in a canoe, loaded to the gunwales, bucking waves ten feet high on the rugged northeast wind. It didn't look feasible.

It was the longest mile any of us had ever traveled, but it was just another mile as far as Jack and Peter were concerned. Jack handled the canoe as though he had been born in it. His actions were as smooth as velvet, riding the canoe up one big wave, sailing it through the foam at its crest, then plunging it at dizzying speed down the windward slope to the trough at the bottom. At long last, we reached the plane.

I climbed into the cockpit with Rocky. He wasn't sure he could get the ship off the water. "We may have to stay here all night," he said. "Don't want to smash the pontoons." But a trial was essential. He poured coal to the engine, and the plane leaped ahead in a blinding shower of spray. We plunged through the first few breakers, then smoothed off as we began hitting only their tops. My heart was in my mouth. But suddenly the spray and the roughness were gone. We were airborne, our plane a white-winged bird of the north wind, like a snow goose riding down from Arctic breeding grounds beyond the wind.

Mattock Bay Mallards

BY NASH BUCKINGHAM

1936

Ben remarked, turning out the gas lamp and side slipping into a capacious bunk, "If the rice fields flight stages dress parade, I'll show you a sight for sore eyes in the mawnin'."

As my particular job meant observing wildfowl and shooting conditions nationally, I naturally voted in favor of any "wow" thereunto appertaining. We now chatted awhile across the "cat-walk." I tried to describe the White River bottoms of years agone; the magnificent fishing lakes, monumental timber resources, and vast adjoining rich prairies lush with stupendously varied game resources. Pauses lengthened, and Ben purred softly. Drowsing, too, I rolled toward a window and stared into jet, pin-pricked with star gleam. Ruffled water lapped the houseboat's hull. How swift our transition from business to Wintered wilds and the joys of duck shooting.

Easing into my office after lunch, Ben had bewailed complete breakdown in his transportation system. "The old story, my bus in the shop and the Madame needing hers for school taxi." Husbands will grouch when gunning rides can't be hooked.

"Where's your outfit tied up?" I queried.

"At old man Hazleton's," Ben replied gloomily, "and the weather man says get set for one grand duck day tomorrow." He sighed heavily.

Somehow I, too, grew suddenly tired of slugging a typewriter for "bread and drippings." "If it's a matter of life or death, and you crave company," I commented, "maybe I can negotiate the 'borry' of my youngster's tenth cousin to a Rolls-Royally—she's a good sport."

"Cr-crave-company," stammered Ben, "why—why—heck—you're prac—practically—ab—abducted." Thereafter, duck business dropped it into high and stepped on the gas. In an hour a packed rumble chased us westward. Grub for a two-day city fade-out, gunning duds, Ben's Winchester pump and my ten-pound twelve-bore Magnum with a stock of three-inch cases carrying No. 4 copper-coated pellets. Flying across a strip of Eastern Arkansas topped Crowley's ridge. Then a long hem of old Grand Prairie's rice belt. Thence onto southbound gravel and gumbo that tended against shadowy sunset across cold, darkening Mattock Bay. Light, left, nevertheless, to net and coop Ben's six live callers, put the roomy Johnboat shipshape, and then gas, tune and carefully hood its powerful outboard.

The Cook Goes into Action

A class AA cook flies on the job like a high-grade file clerk fanning his card index. An experienced observer can watch a real cook go into action and tell whether the chuck's going to pan out toe-curling or punk. There isn't any middle ground if culinary fundamentals slip. So, thoroughly satisfied, I accept a kitchen vice-presidency, which, around camp, means setting the table and acting as trained nurse and in an advisory capacity to the main operator. But, compared to camps of the good old days (and getting to them, too), modern "K.P.," with its protein labor saving and vitaminic short cuts, is a mortal cinch. Cellophaned loaves, already sliced; prepared dough and self-starting pancakes! It wasn't long before we sat over a pair of thick, juicy steaks, baked Idahos, steamy green peas and a pan of hot, flaky biscuits.

Dishes washed and table set for an early "up and away," Ben sacked half a dozen wooden mallards and tested his long-range spotlight. Into my faithful rucksack went camera, water bottle, shells, binoculars and those other personal sworn-by odds and ends, lack of which, at some critical moment, hangs, like the sword of Damocles, over every wilderness hunter's noggin. Hefting that pack, I thought back upon its years of mileage atop my spine; salvaging everything from Canadian pelts and Rocky Mountain tid-bits to prairie chickens and Dixie's teal, geese and Bob Whites. Once, when Neal and I thoughtlessly tramped the shins off his littlest shaver, rabbit hunting, the lad fagged badly. So, knees to chin, and to the child's infinite comfort and delight, I rode him home in the smelly leather and canvas berth.

For a while Ben and I tuned our duck calls. Blew 'em loud as we pleased, with no women folks around to plug their ears, roll their eyes and shake their heads, as much as to say "Screwy—scram." Like the Old Master of Duck Lingo, Perry Hooker, Ben and I are "two-call" men. For, frontier-like, hard hombre Perry, instead of whipping our "six-guns," practices quick draws with a pair of sixty-caliber, leather-lunged "mallard tooters."

We Prepare for the Next Day

Ben set the clock's jigger for 3:30 A.M. Then we saved the nation awhile until Ben pulled a couple of Joe E. Brown's. Such green light to the hay was what brought on my star gazing, until, as the old darky said, "De fus' thing I knowed, I didn't know nuthin'"!

"Haven't heard but one motor start and it went north." Ben balanced half a soft fried egg delicately mouthward. We had outsmarted "first call" accidentally. Up bay apiece, some wildcatter's juicing a big engine had bounced us both afoot. I pitched a match into the coal-oiled wood stove and Ben tickled the cookers. A few moments later, soapy about the ears, we groped for opposite ends of the face towel. "Heavy frost," grasped Ben, combing his hair and doing a fraction of his daily dozen to keep up circulation. We'd even gotten the Java to perking before the alarm went into its dance. Camp to rights, we trimmed the water sled, donned life preservers that quilted frost sting, and I nosed a stubby prow channelward. Ben heaved a deep breath and yanked the motor's pullrope. "Atta-boy an' glory be!" Away we hummer. This immediate sector was new territory to me. Beyond knowing we were to gun "Lower Forked," I was still "in the dark."

The "Bay" pinched in ere long and heavy bank timber loomed. Across our now winding course burning watch stars swung like lanterns. At intervals Ben slowed, whipping his powerful ray onto some well remembered but dangerous snag or treacherous shoal. Old head and cool pilot, Ben profits by many a close shave and never gambles with "Ole Miss" or her temperamental tributaries. No shooting competition was, as yet, within sight or sound.

Twenty minutes later Ben's prying beam whipped and centered a steep bank. "I'm going in," he warned; "yonder's the mouth of Lower Forked's drain." Making snug, we split the duffle and Ben's flash spotted the trail. Two hundred yards crunchy-footing through spectral timber and blackwater, criss-crossed with reflections, swam ahead. Opposite a towering cypress, dubbed "The Point," Forked broadened slightly, ending at the throat of a douthed inlet 200 yards away. Typical woods slash, one of many such, when freshets hoist the volatile White and turgid current guzzles hungrily through a web of interlacing "dreens." Knowing every foot of the terrain, Ben parked our loads at the "Point" and hunted up the pond's one boat. Quickly we lined out the callers, sprinkled out our wooden counterparts, and beached the leaky tub. Then we put the blind all hunky-dory and sat by for customers.

Six o'clock and day in the humor to come clean and clear. Six-fifteen! The jade flap over our lakelet paled perceptibly. Came a winged siren of zig-zagging silhouettes. Etched for an instant against faintly starred damask, Ben grinned and lit another cigarette. "A hundred in that mob," he hazarded. "Watch carefully now—notice how the main flight will work steadily from the same direction for an hour or more—then reverse—and our shooting'll come from down river. But tomorrow, depending on how it first takes off, the 'big parade' may switch—if I could fly you over those bottoms in an aeroplane, you would understand after studying the water and bottoms curve and gentle layout."

Ben's observations checked. Far too high to risk a poke even in good light, smear after smear of clucking mallards barraged the heavens. I sat spellbound. No wildfowl flight could surpass this for sustained volume and brilliancy. By now it was legally time to bang away, but still a trifle vague for deadly measuring off.

Above a cove to our left a burst of mallards suddenly clapped on wing emergencies and parachuted delicately waterward. But an unsuspected ambush in our rear banged these early birds away from their worms. Ben swore roundly. "What th' Heck!" he shouted. "What's th' big idea of busting into our circle—you knew we were put out here." No answer, only vague forms flitting through the woods. A second gun crashed. "If you stop a hide full of shot it's your own fault," warned Ben. "Tack heads," he scoffed, "they must have swell guides or be pretty darn hard-boiled or dumb. There's ample room down yon way—they could get good shooting and not bother us—if they'd only move in time."

About then it literally rained mallards around our "Point." Dainty shapes splashing among our decoys like pelting gusts of Spring thunder shower. We had to "shoo" them off water, high enough against skyline to gaff a pair of drakes.

From Ben, as we reloaded: "Well, that's that."

Drawing our calls, we now settled to the morning's chief interest in duck acquisition. One man's blowing can be wholly effective, or course, but put two fellows to work who know their notes on well-tuned instruments and some added "come hither" gets into circulation. Mallard lingo varies in timbre and modulation. The more alluring these voices, sounding from below, the more frequently and readily Drakes and Susies investigate. Each hunter thus puts his own sales talk into effect. Properly conducted, such "two timing" system will beat a singletone all hollow. We had mapped our campaign. Ben, with his improved cylinder and "Trap Loads," was to have "first crack" at the call-downs. My job was to pick off side-climbers, flatten swimming "crips" and, in case of dry spells, to make myself as useful as possible with the "tree-top talls." Ben, about that time, worked in a gorgeous drake. The cautious fox swung three circles, but figuring an incoming bunch was about to toll him off and make a sucker out of hardworking Ben, I took a chance with the big gun and whanged the fellow to dry land.

Ben scratched his head, whistled softly, and set his own weapon against the cypress bole. "Lem'me peg a time or two with that bloomin' cannon," he demanded. "I still don't believe it." His chance came apace.

Frankly curious at my call, a compact flock of eight or ten black mallards filtered gingerly out above Forked. "Swing well ahead and cut loose a one-two," I advised. Ben is away above the average duck puncturer, but he's never intensively investigated wildfowling in the ballistic stratosphere. Just the same, at his salvo, two of those dusky fliers plugged through with hefty punching coppered "4's," tumbled dead as canned herrings. Ben's ears were almost engulfed in a splitting grin. "I don't believe it even yet," he soliloquized, whiffing smoke from the yawning tubes, and then, reflectively, "but I'm sold or hooked, I dunno which!"

Few reasonable chances escaping our combination, I and Ben, ere long, had "boom-banged" practically through a pair of fifteen-bird limits.

We Now Have a Visitor

Just as my companion spider had persuaded a brace of beauties to "walk into the parlor" the big birds got a great break. For a dapper little man in a wasp-waisted overcoat and rather startling white Fedora hat, walked into our blind. "Gentlemen," he announced, "I'm afraid duck shooting inexperience has annoyed you. My friend over yonder, and I, left this hunt to our guides, but even a novice can tell when he's imposing on good nature. One of our guides has walked himself off anyhow, but when he returns we'll get right out of your way."

Well, when a shooter puts up a fair line of talk like that, why bygones are best bygones, and there's only one comeback. "Why," laughed good-natured Ben, "no harm done, Buddy, we're about through shooting anyhow. Move your pal over; we'll be glad to stick around awhile and call 'em in for you." As he spoke we had to freeze and wangle in our last pair of victims.

"You see," Ben insisted, "we're over and done with; you get your Boy Friend."

The visitor's eyes sparkled, and, trotting off, he soon returned, leading a youngish redhead, half suffocated with joyful inexperience. Posting our neophytes, we fell to calling, and soon hove in a bunch. When their autoloaders were empty, our valiants had one dead bird and two "crips" to show for their water rake. "Next time," Ben suggested tactfully, "try not letting them all light."

But now a chap sauntered through the forest and beckoned away our little visitor in the white Fedora. He returned after a lengthy conference, stating as how their paid chaperon had located a wonderful flight not far distant. So, if we'd excuse them, maybe they'd best move. But redheaded friend objected. "Why," he yelped, "we're fixed for life right here—let's stay—these gentlemen will help us. They can shoot on our credit. Let's get us some ducks; what we want is meat."

Ben and I exchanged glances. "No," we told him, "we guessed we couldn't shoot any more, but we'd get them in plenty of birds and enjoy seeing them shoot." But after another private conference, redhead was overruled. Our late disturbers gathered bag and baggage and were herded off by their somewhat disgruntled boatmen.

They left at half-past eight, trooping toward what Ben called "Beaver." "Something odd'll turn up about all this," he mused, loading his duck strap with rice fat mallards. Then: "I didn't hear more than eight or ten shots from Beaver way since daylight. There must have been thousands of birds banked in there, and there were four fellows in that party, but," he added, "you recall one of them left and came back with some good news?"

Now for our portage. Across bright, leafy carpets danced mallard shadows, reflected from skies of sheerest blue. Tree tops flashed and thrummed with bird life. Through flood-stained hardwoods, glistening with sun drench, we were soon at the boat. Around the first bend we spotted a good-sized gas boat tied ashore. "There's their oil can," muttered Ben. "Let's look the shebang over."

Under an oilcloth forward we turned up quite a cache of mallards. Interesting, if true, because our visitors left Forked less than twenty minutes before, with only three ducks to their credit. This, of course, might be another outfit; but suspicion grew. Quietly we threaded inland until Beaver, considerably larger than Forked, came into view. A heavy-set chap I recognized as their "returning guide" stepped suddenly from behind a tree.

"Their luck," he replied in answer to a question, "had been pretty good."

"Where'd you put your sports?" Ben asked; "we haven't heard any shooting since you pulled out."

"Down the bank a ways," the fellow replied furtively.

"Judging from the load of ducks in your boat you sure have had fine sport," went on Ben. The chunky sap grinned and winked knowingly.

Just then his partner came up and broke in with: "Oh, hello, you're the same two fellows that did all that shooting over to Forked awhile ago?"

Ben Does Some Sherlock Holmes Stuff

"Yep," Ben allowed, "we're the very self-same pair."

Chatting awhile to get a good look for identification purposes later, if need be, we turned away.

Ben reconstructed that crime. "When that fat guy saw we had those two freshmen in dutch with us over at Forked, he slipped on over here just about daylight and unraveled that autoloader of his into a duck raft. Those were the five quick shots I heard, and the others cripple stoppers. He knocked off that pair of mallards in that gas boat all by himself. To cover the deed he then had to hurry to Forked to his sports and hustle them over here. That's why he wouldn't let 'em stay and why the little punk tipped the redhead when he wanted us to stay and 'shoot on their credit.'"

We hoofed it along in silence awhile, then Ben blurted out: "That pint-size cuss meant well enough, apologizing to us for butting in, but he and his running-mate, and particularly those two rats allegedly guiding them, are just the types dutching duck shooting faster than governmental neglect and conservational 'blah-blah' can save it. Their performance is typical of a tinhorn breed that tries to snitch more than its money's worth of meat, not giving a damn, either, how, where or with what they get it—just so it's butchered. No wonder we have to have shorter seasons and lower bag limits—and thank God for them, too, because I've got a boy and he likes to ramble these woods and ponds just as well as I do." We reached the Bay, and Ben, rocking the motor, added: "That gang will keep right on shooting until the last duck is gone and be back after some more tomorrow. But I'm glad we didn't flush the covey. We'll leave word at the landing, and I'll bet a buck to a bust in the 'schozzle' that Tom Mull picks up their trail in jig time."

We Now Head Our Boat for Home

Droning home we soon raised Broad Bay and a rolling sea off the spanking tail breeze. Tied to the houseboat, we hung our ducks to a chilling wind and set about such delightful chores as shaving and changing to woods footgear. Then we worked gradually around to pea soup, scrambled eggs, toasted biscuits and a brew of potent Java. Dish peace restored, ensued forty-five minutes of highly satisfactory bunk fatigue.

"Now," suggested Ben, "what say we rubberneck the country?" So, all afternoon, we boated miles of bay and bayou. We tramped timber sections, peered into hidden lagoons and waterholes working with mallard life. Along castaway water-courses, we visited with houseboat gunners, tucked away and, like ourselves, resting after a morning's magnificent flight. We penetrated to a lake along which timber moguls, owning much of this region, had built a spur track, backing their palatial private cars to within gunshot of perfect wildfowling. About dusk we drifted against the home dock. In honor of the day Ben put flourishes to the evening's menu, and I dents therein. Attempts at war debt settlement and tariff revision lost a quick decision to Morpheus. "There'll be a race to Lower Forked in the morning," Ben opined.

Sure enough, we were headed off at the "dreen's" chute. A light flickered around the "Point." The winners proved to be a resident commercial fisherman and his wife, out for a "sailor's holiday." A pair of good sports they proved to be, too. Knowing them, Ben stopped for a chat, before passing on down the bank to stake out at Forked's lower end. Our decoy line spanned it there, and for "blinds" we sat quietly on chunks backed against lofty oaks. Not versed in calling, our up-slough friend was at a disadvantage with only live decoys out front. But he refused to fire while ducks worked our way, and we, in reciprocation, laid off his prospects. As a result, both stands enjoyed ample shooting.

During a lull we sighted a tall, stalwart, hip-booted figure threading the underbrush our way. "Tom Mull," whispered Ben. "You know Tom, of course—the game warden—that was his lovely old home we passed this side of Holly Grove comin' in. He's sighted, but doesn't 'savy' us yet; but he's sure puttin' up a neat stalk, isn't he?"

Seein' as how I'd coached Tom in his "prep school" days and abetted his development into Alaskan big game hunter, expert with pistol or revolver, and champion bow and arrow shot, I 'lowed as how I ought to know Thomas. Ducking from our cover, arms elevated, we raised a howl of "Kamerad!" The ducks could wait. Tom was heading west just now, toward a lake in whose vicinity he suspected some sort of conversational skullduggery. About to unlimber his long Luger at a distantly perched marsh hawk, a cartwheel of mallards now swished into Forked, erupted when our calls blasted invitations, and, splitting, patronized both stands. When the smoke cleared away Ben and I were through for the day and so was our fisherman friend up the way. Time to reload the duck straps and stagger Bayward.

The Game Warden Investigates a Little

Tom checked our license numbers. Even with old friends he is just that thorough, tactful and active. Then, squinting his compass: "By the way, fellows, what about those sapsuckers shooting the 'Point' yesterday—met 'em, didn't you?"

"Yeah," replied Ben, flashing me an "I-told-you-so," "why?"

"Oh! nothing much," continued Tom. "Just got something along the 'grapevine' yesterday and headed them off before they could skip the country—got 'em just in time, too. Got to talkin' with 'em after I ran 'em in. They mentioned meeting two fellows—I suspected whom—after I heard you two birds were in the country. At that I guess those greenhorns were victims of those two hard eggs with them. They're in bad now, too, on their guide licenses, to say nothing of having too many mallards." Remembering now the little fellow's apology for having "muscled in," Ben and I put out a note of sympathy in his behalf.

"I asked them," Tom explained, "to describe the two fellows who had offered to call for them."

"Did they mention about asking us to 'shoot on their credit?'" remarked Ben.

"Yes," said Tom Mull, "they told me about that, too. It should have been a 'tip off' if nothing else." Tom smiled as he handed out chewing gum and helped himself to a guzzle from our water bottle. Then he grinned. "I sorter had you figured out, Ben, but it's been a good while since I've seen Buck, and at first I couldn't dope a 'heavy-set fellow with a big gun and a hawk's feather stuck in the back of his hat.' I suggested to those birds that in future they'd better lay off offering 'shooting credit' to strangers. The runty guy with the city slicker overcoat and hat asked me, 'how come?' I asked him if the 'heavy-set fellow' with the Yankee Doodle in his hat shot great long shells and blew a fancy carved duck call. He sorter perked up at that and said, 'yes.' So I said, 'How come? Well, he's a Federal game protector, that's all.'"

"How did they take that sad news?" laughed Ben.

"The young redheaded one said, 'Well, I'll be diddlely damned,' and the one in the white hat soter wilted."

"Didn't he crack anything?" asked Ben.

Tom Mull smiled infectiously and hitched up his gun belt. "He said something worse than that," chuckling. "So long, boys, I'll drop in for coffee on my way home."

The Wheat Fields of Alberta

BY VAN CAMPEN HEILNER

1936

T HE GEESE ARE SOUTH OF THE ATHABASKA! LOOKS LIKE AN EARLY FALL and a great one for shooting!"

That's what they greeted us with when we got off the train at Edmonton. We had crossed the Rockies from Vancouver, gem of the Pacific Northwest, through breathtaking Jasper Park, just in order to shoot a few ducks in the Peace River country of Alberta.

Strangely enough I first heard of it from Ward Ames down in Florida the year before. "Never saw anything like it in my life," he assured me. "When ducks get up like smoke from every damp piece of land in the country and from many a dry piece too, you can take it from me there are some ducks there." He hadn't told me the half of it, as it turned out.

I'd been up on the wild northeast coast of Vancouver Island having a go at the great tyee salmon of Campbell River and it seemed a logical thing on the way back to take in those ducks. I wired Julio Sanchez in Los Angeles whose real home is in Cuba but who also does a little wandering on his own hook and he flew up to Vancouver and joined me at the railroad station.

We left Edmonton on the bi-weekly train that stopped, we figured it out, every fifteen minutes night and day. Around sunset that evening we began to see ducks from the car windows and right up until dark there was a constant procession of strings of fowl scared up by the train from every slew and puddle and streaming off into the twilight. It was some introduction to that country, I can tell you.

We didn't sleep much that night. Not so much on account of the ducks but on account of the roadbed. The tracks were laid right across the muskeg with no ballast at all and the train swayed and rolled like a ship at sea. I would just as soon have ridden a camel.

Sometime during the night we passed Lesser Slave Lake and in the morning we were in the wheat country. Miles and miles of wheat stretching away into the horizon like the brown dunes of the Sahara. Rippling, waving wheat standing in the fields, shocked wheat standing row on row in "stooks" like regiments of soldiers, wheat and more wheat.

By the early afternoon we had reached our destination and it was good to be off the train. Dan Wishart met us and took us to our lodgings where after a wash-up and rest we spent the afternoon buying shells and equipment that we'd forgotten. The next morning was the opening day of the season and we turned in early with hopes high. "More ducks than for seven years," were the last words we heard before hitting the hay. Well, we hoped so.

The country is rolling and in between the wheat are little clumps of trees. Scattered here and there are small lakes, ponds and slews. The ducks leave the lakes and slews twice a day, morning and evening, and fly into the wheat fields to gorge themselves. It was still dark the next morning when we took up our positions on a high hill some distance from town.

As it grew lighter we could look down across country and see the lakes black with ducks, hundreds of thousands of them. Soon they commenced moving around and getting up in small bunches and leaving for the fields. We marked down one particular heavy flight going into a big field about two miles away.

Closer by, however, there was a neck of land between Hermit Lake and Bear Lake and across this a great many ducks were passing. We decided to hide in the stooks in the intervening field and get a crack at them as they flew from one lake to the other.

We took up our positions across the field, making blinds out of piled up wheat stooks, and awaited developments. They were not long in coming. Ducks were constantly getting up off of Hermit and making a bee line across the hill for Bear. As they neared the Bear side they'd start to pitch and by shifting our position we managed to get approximately under the spot where they started to coast down.

Western gunners don't have to be told that pass shooting is the sportiest duck shooting in the world. In the east it's practically unknown.

There's a place on Cape Cod known as Shoot Flying Hill where at certain seasons the coots pass over into Buzzards Bay and here pass shooting of a sort may be had, but it's in the western states that it reaches its highest state of perfection. No decoys, no nuthin'. Just you and your gun and a goood eye. What greater thrill exists in the world when one of those high babies passes over, to fold up suddenly in mid-air and come hurtling down with a terrific thud!

As long as the flight lasted we were at it hot and heavy, and by nine-thirty were all through for the day.

The next morning we went out to the field where we had seen the big flight going the day before but although it was just getting light when we arrived there it was too late as the ducks were already leaving the field and returning to the lake. A wild dash across country in the car got us near the lake for which they were heading and by running across fields and scrambling under fences we got in the direct line of the flight.

I was standing behind some small bushes and could see endless bunches of ducks heading straight for me. Sighting the water of Spring Lake which lay behind me they would start to lower. Some would pass directly overhead, others to the side, the prettiest kind of shooting. Every once in a while one would come crashing down through the trees breaking off branches in his fall. Our Chesapeake, Jerry, one of the grandest dogs I ever hunted with, and at this writing the property of my friend Winston Guest, would go dashing off into the thicket and never failed to return with the duck in his mouth.

Off to my left Julio was shooting like a machine. I could see the ducks falling in one's and two's. He was the most beautiful duck shot I had ever seen. He never hurried, never seemed to miss. I had shot with him in Cuba where his shooting was a byword and here he was three thousand miles away from his native land still picking them off with that deadly accuracy that was a joy to behold. You can't tell people how to shoot, all the books to the contrary notwithstanding. It's a gift. Good shots are born, not made, and practice keeps them perfect. Perfect timing is the answer to the whole business.

When we got back that evening there was a message for us. A lady living about ten miles out of town had sent in word to Robbie, our guide, that she was having "duck trouble" and would we please come out the next day and try and cure her of it! It appeared that about five thousand ducks came into her wheat fields every afternoon around four o'clock and what they were doing to her crop was nobody's business.

When we got out there the next day we found her almost in tears. She took us out in her fields and showed us. Where the wheat was in stooks, practically every sheaf had been denuded of grain. "I don't know what I'm going to do." She said, "If this keeps up I won't have any crop left at all. I thought perhaps if you gave them a good scare, they might leave and go elsewhere. I expect to start threshing next week but maybe there won't be anything left to thresh. If you can do anything I'll be grateful."

Needless to say we were the ones that were grateful and we assured her we would do our very best to see that those trouble makers got the scaring of their lives.

About three-thirty we went out and built blinds in the wheat, heaping the stooks up around us until we were completely hidden. It was a pretty big field and we tried to station ourselves so that we could cover it as best we could, although once the flight started it might be necessary to change and take up new positions in a hurry, depending on to which part of the field the ducks went.

It was Julio who first called my attention to it and I looked at my watch and saw it was just five after four.

At first it looked like a thin wisp of cloud way in the north and then it grew larger, widening and billowing like the distant smoke of a train. For a moment I dimly wondered if it could be a swarm of locusts and then I saw what it really was. Ducks! Thousands of ducks! And coming our way! They seemed strung out all across the northern sky and there didn't seem to be any end to them. As the vanguard of that great host neared our field I could look way behind in the distance and see them still coming, flock after flock, bunch after bunch, companies and regiments advancing to the battle line!

The first flock passed over the field and then started to swing it in a wide circle. On their first turn they passed me fairly close but not close enough. On the second round they swung directly over Julio, flared high in the air, and three fell out to hit among the stooks with sickening thuds.

The second flock also swung over Julio and again more fell out. The third flock was an enormous one, must have contained three or four hundred birds. They only circled the field once and then all lit down among the stooks about a hundred and fifty yards from me. I knew I'd have to get them out of there or everything else would go to them.

I commenced an elaborate stalk, crawling across the stubble and dodging from stook to stook but they saw me and arose with a deafening roar of wings. I managed to knock down one and cripple another which set its wings and sailed off behind the rise of a little hill. I ran as hard as I could and got to the top of the rise just in time to see him fall dead some distance off.

More ducks were circling the field at this point so I lay low to give Julio a chance. He repeated with his usual regularity and I went back to my blind.

It was one of the greatest flights of ducks I have ever seen. They came on steadily for an hour and a half. While one flock would be swinging our field there would be three or four others in sight at the same time. When we finally picked up and started in, both we and the owner of the field were satisfied.

It was lonely in the wheat country. The miles of waving grain or stacked stooks seemed to stretch away into infinity. Here and there the gleam of a far away lake or scattered clumps of trees broke the sweep of the wheat fields. On very clear days away to the southward you could see the distant peaks of the mountains in Jasper Park.

But this country cared nothing for mountains. It was wheat, wheat, wheat, first, last and always. On Saturday nights the farmers drove into town from forty miles around and you couldn't get a bed at the local hotel or a seat in the picture show for love or money. The dance palace was jammed and everybody was happy and spent money freely. Occasionally a drunk would stagger out of a beer parlour and attempt an argument but there was always a Mountie at hand to lead him quietly but firmly away.

As we'd come back from the evening shoot, the sky would be ablaze with dying color and the distant tonkle of a cow bell would be wafted across the wheat from some little homestead perched on a knoll. But always there were ducks, endless strings of them flighting across the sunset, wings that whispered softly overhead in the gathering dusk or the soft quank of a mallard drake leading his flock to its nightly roost.

One day we took a picnic lunch and went far out of town on a sort of free-lance shoot. No particular place in mind, no particular ideas. Just scouting out the country and taking what pot-shots we could. We'd drive along the muddy roads and suddenly pass a little slew hard by the road literally swarming with mallards. We wouldn't stop, for as long as the car was moving they paid no attention to us. We'd drive about a quarter of a mile past it, then stop and get out. Julio and I would walk back and take up our stations on the road opposite the slew while Robbie went around behind it and walked through it, driving the ducks over us.

It was the sportiest shooting imaginable. Fast and furious while it lasted. The ducks came across high in order to clear the trees at our backs and the trick was to drop them on the road or before they crossed it; otherwise they would gain too much altitude or fall in the woods behind us where only the dog could find them.

The main body of birds came first and then as Robbie got nearer to us he kept routing out pairs and singles that were hiding in the long grass of the slew and these came rocketing over us with the speed of arrows. It reminded me of a pheasant drive and we really should have had gun bearers as we could not load fast enough.

The best shoot of all, however, was reserved for nearly the last day of our trip. Dan Wishart and Robbie had been doing some scouting around and making inquiries from the various farmers during that part of the day when we were generally doing a little concentrated sleeping, and reported that they had located what looked like a honey of a water shoot. They had found a big marsh at the head of one of the lakes where the ducks were coming in to roost in the evening by the tens of thousands. It was hard to reach and tough going when you got there but it looked like money in the bank from a duck standpoint.

It didn't get dark until around nine or a little after, so about five that afternoon we started out and got as near to the marsh as we could in the car and walked the rest of the way; Julio took the dog and walked around to the head of it near the edge of the trees while I waded with great difficulty out to the center of it and took up my position on top of a muskrat house alongside of a little opening in the reeds. This opening formed a sort of little pond about forty feet in diameter and the edges of it were drifted thick with feathers. It looked like the genuine article all right and I sat down to wait developments.

For a long while nothing happened. An occasional bunch of teal zipped in fast over the grass, twisting and diving with cupped wings, but that was all. Then a lone pair of mallards was sighted coming over a hill from the direction of the lake, then two more, then three, and the flight was on.

That first pair made straight for my pond hole, set their wings and came right in. Then ducks started coming from all directions and settling all over the marsh indiscriminately. A big flight was coming in from directly behind Julio and as they topped the trees and pitched in for the marsh he was ready for them. I could hear them falling, *thump, thump, splash,* and hear the excited whine of Jerry as he bounded here and there retrieving the fallen.

Meanwhile I was having my hands full. I was shooting my .410 and while the range is practically the same as heavier guns, you have to hold very close. It was generally either a clean miss or a dead bird. But every once in a while you'd pick off one of those high babies and what a thrill that was! He seemed to be coming down for ages. Just as if he'd fallen off the top of the Eiffel Tower. Once one just missed me by inches but I was so excited I never noticed it until he struck almost at my feet and splashed water all over me.

It was one of those red letter evenings that you never forget. I write these lines in the Bahama Islands with the blue of the Gulf Stream and the turquoise and jade of the reef glimpsed through the waving palms but I can turn away and live again that twilight in far off Alberta. I can see the winged hosts topping the hills and the timber and pitching down to the ever deepening dusk of that marsh, where Death, in the person of Julio and myself, stood ready and waiting.

But most of all do I see the wheat. Endless miles of it stretching away to the horizon. Rippling like golden waves in the early autumn wind or standing in regiment-like stooks awaiting the coming of the threshing teams. I see the ducks, millions of them, preparing for their great migration southward, southward across the plains and down the flyways of the great rivers, fanning and spreading outwards through lake and pond and slew until they reach the Gulf Coast and the *bahias* and *lagunas* of Mexico. But behind them they leave the place to which they'll always return, the lonely vistas of one of the greatest duck hatcheries in the world,—the wheat fields of Alberta!

Dodie's Duck

BY WALTER CLARE MARTIN

1936

T HIS MORNING I RECEIVED A COPY OF S.R.A.—B.S. 83, ISSUED BY THE Bureau of Biological Survey, a promulgation of the national duck law.

In this important booklet I find innumerable rules, regulations, statistics, etc., etc., but I note one deplorable omission. Nothing is said about the duck-hunting activities of Coyne McCreagh of Coon Ridge, whose experience, I think, throws more light on the federal conservation program than all the leaflets you could set a match to.

It was not jealousy, I am sure, which inspired the Bureau of Biological Survey to ignore Mr. McCreagh so effectively. More likely they considered him outside their scope, because, that hazy dawning of November, he did not set out to hunt ducks.

The truth is, he set out to hunt rabbits.

He set out with three rocks, having no civilized arms except an erratic muzzle-fed musket. And for the musket he had no munitions.

He talked some of borrowing a Twenty-two from the Flints; but they lived a right smart down the holler. The Flints' shotgun had been reduced to historic scrap-iron when Bud fired it with snow in the snout.

So Coyne equipped himself with three rocks, round and cold, about the size of baseballs.

It is a matter of record that such missiles, addressing a rabbit broadside, may detail him with catastrophic effects.

So Coyne McCreagh, crunching the frosted leaves, stalked from one brush-pile to another. Into each pile he peered, and each pile he kicked hard with the heel of his home-soled boots.

Coyne was no Houdini, however, and the rabbits failed to appear. Two rocks chunked heavily into his skunk-perfumed coat, and the third chilled his throwing hand until it stiffened.

Coyne shifted this rock to his right perfumed pocket and rubbed his hands between his legs with much vigor. He then put his hand inside his pants pocket to warm it against his thigh.

A rabbit some thirty-odd feet away, blurring into a background of buck brush, sat watching these human maneuvers. With the infernal perversity which animates all cottontails he waited until Coyne's throwing hand was tightly tucked into his pants, then he jumped like a guilty conscience.

Coyne caught the insulting white flick of his tail as he scooted between the rough legs of the forest.

With a startled "gawd blast!" Coyne wrenched free his hand and fumbled a rock from his coat. He hurled it with desperate violence.

The beast was too far, and the total effect of the throw was to increase his ambition to travel.

Coyne McCreagh's body sagged as he watched the meat disappear.

"I'm sure sorry, Dodie," he said.

This Dodie, as the Biological Survey should know, was Coyne's young faithful wife, very expectant. She expected a baby, in three or four months, and today she expected a rabbit.

Budgetty matrons whose caloric adventures begin with the telephone, who year-round visit smiling vendors of T-bones and sidewalks piled high with fresh spinach, can but weakly conceive what that rabbit meant in the life of young Mrs. McCreagh.

Six weeks she had rationed on salt sowbelly and corn-pone, with slippery-elm bark to chew, when too hungry. Dodie needed no Johns Hopkins guide-book to tell her she was not doing right by Coyne's baby. Her stomach, without publicity, turned upside down and the mountain bloom began to fade from her cheek.

It had reached such a crisis, Dodie had said to her man:

"If you don't get some fresh meat, I'll take fits."

That was why Coyne said he was sorry. He did not want his young mate to take fits. He did not want his heir to be born chicken-breasted or too crooked to swing a man's ax.

He was sorry, but he tightened his rawhide belt and trudged farther on, down the hollow. He probed and kicked every brushpile. He thrust twistin' poles into old secret logs. He circled patches of briarbrush and peeped under bunch-grass, and the one thing he did not find was a rabbit.

"Taint no use," he muttered. "They clubbed 'em too close."

Just to keep the Biological records straight, the "clubbed 'em too close" referred to the winter before, when a fifteen-inch snow smothered the Ozarks. A vaste horde of pot-hunters, with clubs and with dogs, waded out and enjoyed a snow massacre.

From Coyne's county alone, 50,000 dead bunnies were piled upon trucks going east.

A great week! Kettles simmered. Coins clinked in surprised pockets. But it so happened that not one of those 50,000 dead bunnies laid an egg to be hatched the next Easter.

Great sport for the pot-hunters; but now Coyne tramped the hard hills without sighting a living creature. He began to doubt the one flicker of fur he had seen was anything more than a ghost. A rabbit ghost haunting the scene of the massacre.

Hungry, chilled, disillusioned, he paused on a bald knob to take bearings. He could see his home smoke, miles across bristling gulches, and told himself he should be there, chopping firewood.

But Dodie was expecting a rabbit.

Off south lay the river, smeared with fog like whipped cream. Some ten or twelve miles, by the tumbling road half a mile to a crow, or an airplane.

An automobile horn sounded along the ridge road, across the still vale from Coyne's knob. Sportsmen, probably, bound for the duck blinds. Lordy, lord, couldn't Coyne eat a duck! Dodie could eat a duck, too, he reckoned. How her anxious brown eyes would light and dance if he came swinging a fat duck by the neck.

It burst over Coyne, then, that despite war, flood, and damnation he was going to get Dodie a duck.

Furiously he plunged into the hollow. Through bramble and briar, through sassafras and blackjack he made for the nearest arm of the river. If he could get to the blind before the sportsmen arrived, he could offer to work—for a duck.

The car beat him, by a couple of minutes. The hunters were dragging out guns. Automatics, pump-actions, double-barrels, all sizes and chokes—Coyne never had beheld such an arsenal of shotguns.

Three men in the party and three guns to each man: short range, middle range and long distance.

The financier of the party was Lawrence Bogart, husky-voiced, impatient, red-shaven, meat-fed; a man who had inherited much and made more. He operated an overall factory.

The other two were physicians—Doc Pyne and Doc Smith. One lean and sardonic as a wolf at the door; his fellow thick, swarthy, coarse, friendly.

They were transferring luggage from the car to the blind. Coyne McCreagh hurried up, half winded.

"I reckon I could help you unload," he said.

Bogart sized him up.

"How much?"

"I'd do it for one mallard duck," said Coyne.

The thick friendly Doc laughed:

"You like 'em better than I do."

Bogart said:

"Can you keep your mouth shut?"

"A feller can't talk with his mouth full o' duck," said Coyne.

"Very shrewd, indeed," said the wolf.

"You're hired," said Bogart. "Just do what we want, and you'll eat duck till you quack for a week. There's a bonus, also, at the end of the day, if everything goes off smoothly. All right, pitch in. We'll unpack the car and run it into the willows. Then lug all the stuff to the blind."

Coyne McCreagh pitched in, his heart singing. He was quite willing to quack for a week.

The junk was unloaded; the big car concealed; and the four men laddered into the blind. It was half sunk in lush slumps at the shore of the stream, warm and roomy, finer far than Coyne's cabin.

There were shelves for tall bottles; built-in boxes, bug-proof; fold-up couches; wall lights, operated by electric dry cells.

Coyne asked several questions about these smart lights, resolving to buy one for Dodie's Christmas.

As the program progressed, the men talked and drank. Coyne inferred that Doc Pyne was a novice. He was an expert skeet shooter, and office partner to Smith, who was striving to outdoorize him.

"When do you put out the decoys?" Pyne said to Bogart.

"Not legal this year," said Bogart.

"What about your phonograph records?"

"They're legal if made from mechanical quacks; but not legal if made from live fowl."

"Which are these?" inquired Pyne.

Bogart spun a phonograph disk with his thumb.

"I didn't ask when I bought them," he said.

They tried out the records. Quack, quack, quack, quack—a lively medley of friendly duck voices. Coyne would have sworn, had he not been standing there staring at it, that the river was swarming with mallards.

"Guess I'll plug my guns now," said Bogart.

"Plug?" said Doc Pyne, puzzled.

"Sure thing, that's the law. Repeating shotguns must have their magazines plugged to three shells. A damned silly thing, if you ask me. We have a bag limit of ten. Since we can take only ten what the hell does it matter if the gun shoots five loads or three?"

"Five loads would be better, I reckon," said Coyne.

"Why?" all the hunters looked at him.

"Cause the more shots in a gun the less number of flocks would be banged at to fetch down the limit of ten. That means fewer bunches is disturbed from their feed. It's breakin' rest and feed that hurts most."

"The man is right, Bogart," said Smith.

"Maybe so," said Bogart, "but it's no hair off my neck. I know how to beat the law—legal. Three loads in three guns are nine loads, as I figure. Here, McCreagh, you take charge of these two guns, and when I reach, hand 'em to me—like this."

He practiced Coyne in the art of gun-passing.

Smith was boring the sky with a hand telescope.

"Mallards!" he cried. "Drop the roof."

Bogart pulled a lever which let down the grassed roof. The men snapped to their shooting positions. Through the sloping glass panes, camouflaged with tall reeds, they could scan the smoking face of the river.

Smith set the phonograph calling. Coyne held the gun ready to pass.

A triangle of mallards dipped down through the haze to discover the source of the quacking.

Disappointed, they rose and circled the woods, their hollow wing-bones whistling, "Follow."

"They're gone," complained Pyne. The others signalled him "Hush." Soon the birds reappeared, dipping lower.

"They're tired," whispered Bogart. "Next time they'll drop."

The air in the room seemed to stiffen.

Around came the ducks, stretching, eager, convinced that no foe lingered near. They supposed the friendly ducks, whose voices they heard, were concealed somewhere in the weeds.

The shrill whistling ceased as by signal. Nervous wings relaxed in midair.

Tail rudders snapped down to check landing speed. One instant they hung in suspended power as if a still camera had caught them. The instant hunters rave about in their sleep.

Up sprang the camouflaged roof of the blind. Fire and thunder shattered the picture. Scatter loads, choked loads, and long range charges of shot ripped to pieces the gallant formation.

Surprised by the furious cannonade, the ducks climbed away from the death trap. Courageously they re-formed their torn ranks. Leaving wounded and dead whom they were unable to help, they cut a swift path through the ghostly haze and steered for less sinister waters.

The dead mallards and wounded, of all degrees, floated on the white water like lilies. The boat lay concealed at the weedy shore of the stream; but the men made no attempt to retrieve.

One by one the fine dinners for which Coyne would have given his cornfield headed into the strong flow and shot down. He stared at the ducks and the boat and men. When he could endure it no longer, he blurted;

"Ain't you aimin' to fetch in them ducks?"

"Hell no," said Bogart.

Coyne hesitated a moment. To him the idea was incredible. Enough dinners to support him and Dodie for two weeks were drifting away, for the turtles.

It must be a mistake. He persisted.

"Don't none of you fellers enjoy to eat duck?"

The men were annoyed, and showed it.

"Sure we like duck" said Bogart, "but we like shooting a damned sight better. If we picked up all the ducks, we would about have our bag limits and be heading home before we got started. We won't have our bag limits until sundown."

Coyne's hungry jaw stiffened, indignant. "It don't rest my mind none," he retorted. "That's the way it went with the rabbits. Last year they were growin' on every bush and nobody showed 'em no mercy. This year you can tramp till your tongue hangs out and not get enough hair for your eyebrow."

Bogart growled irritably:

"There's plenty of ducks."

"They ain't," said Coyne, "and if they was, this kind of business would soon blot 'em out."

"Take a drink and forget it," suggested Smith. Pyne added:

"It's strictly our business; and strictly within the law."

"Lawful or not," said Coyne, "it' ain't right. Wild game to you fellers is just something to bust; but it's serious meat to us here in the hills. It ain't right to waste meat and it ain't right to let cripples float off and die slow."

"We can't get 'em," said Bogart, "they are too far out."

"Loan me your boat," said Coyne, "I'll fetch em."

"Like hell! and get us all in a jam. This river is patrolled by state and federal men. One might chance along any moment."

"Let 'em come," said Coyne, "I ain't breakin' no law."

"Then for your information," said Bogart, "it is unlawful to use any kind of boat more than one hundred feet from the shore."

Coyne gaped: "Is that the law?"

"Yes, that's the law," they all nodded.

"It's a damned funny law, I reckon," said Coyne, "if a man can't pick up shot birds."

"There's a lot of damned funny laws," said Bogart, "but we manage to have our fun. And this particular law suits us just fine; it's an excuse for not picking up birds."

"I don't like it," said Coyne, "it ain't right."

"And I don't like lectures," said Bogart. "We won't need you any more today. Here"—he held out a one dollar bill.

Deliberately Coyne turned and climbed from the blind; ignoring the proffered pay.

Again Coyne found himself on a ridge; alone, cold, rabbitless, duckless.

Instinct urged him to go back home; eat cornbread; chop wood; get warm. Pride told him to keep on trudging.

His eyes toured the hills for suggestions. The nearest smoke flew from the roof of the Flints, two or three hours across hollows; tough going.

The Flints, he recalled, had a rifle. They might have a cartridge or two. Coyne knew a place, down the river, where frogweeds grew on mud flats. There often fed ducks; which a man could approach, if he used enough patience and cunning.

Resolutely he scraped down the hillside and worked across the oak deeps toward the Flints. It was mid-afternoon when he sat astride their worn fence and shouted at the clay-clinked log cabin.

It was bad manners to approach without shouting.

At his voice, mongrel dogs set up a fierce brawl. In the doorway a sockless woman appeared. She turned and spoke to Squirrel Flint—patching boots by his fire—and Squirrel Flint shuffled out to meet Coyne.

Squirrel Flint, tall, fibrous, bald, weather-warped, hard, made Coyne think of his old hickory ax-handle.

Coyne skipped the weather and all the usual small chat, and told Flint why he had come. He wanted a gun to hunt ducks.

"I'm plumb sorry," said Squirrel, "but my shotgun is broke. Buddy stodged some snow in the muzzle."

"I reckon you don't have no ca'tridges for your twenty-two target," said Coyne.

"I mought," said Flint, "but you would be wasting your time. You can't fetch no ducks with a rifle."

"I mought fetch down one," said Coyne.

"With a heap o'luck maybe," said Flint. "We shore wouldn't need no bag limit for ducks if everybody used a single-shot rifle. I won't say a feller can't do it; but you shore need to take plenty of pains."

"I aim to take pains," said Coyne.

Flint got the rifle and six twenty-two shots; of which Coyne borrowed three. He declined an invitation to cider. Flint's cider was ripe and went to a man's eye. Dodie's duck required him to shoot straight.

Coyne warmed his raw hands at Flint's fireplace; and looked briefly at Flint's 'possum pelts. He then struck with gaunt strides through Flint's turnip patch, on the last leg of his march to the river.

Almost to the river, keeping close under shade, he saw a flock circling the fog.

He listened: the mud flats were quacking. He crouched until the flying birds settled from sight beyond the tangle of high weeds and willows.

His heart bounced. Dodie's dinner was waiting. Indian-like he moved forward, half crawl, half run, toward the thick dank vegetation below.

He made it without being seen. In the willows and poison white sumacs he paused and held open his ears.

No ducks jabbered now. His hopes trembled. A dog, a loose rock, a fishing boat on the stream would fill the fog with a wild hurry of feathers.

He had borrowed a cord from Flint's rafters. He tied a loose loop and slung the gun on his back, to avoid jabbing mud into the muzzle.

Belly-flat in the herbage he wriggled along like a crocodile with a man's head. Inch by inch his muddy track lengthened. The closer he wormed to the edge of his cover, the more pains he took to be noiseless.

Light broke, at last, his screen thinning. He could see the frog-flats just ahead. Half a hundred gay waterfowl disported themselves—mallards, blue-wings, mergansers, and sprig-tails.

Wet and shivering, Coyne huddled behind a drift-log and studied the situation. A single-shot rifle—one chance. The nearest duck was a teal, a bright blue-wing cock, wrestling with a live fish in the puddle.

About fifty yards to the teal, Coyne figured. If the gun was any good, he could hit it. But a teal was a small profit; just one tempting bite, and beyond that teal, ten yards, sat a mallard.

Desperate, like any gambler who stakes his world on one throw, Coyne decided to try for the mallard.

"Now gawd damn you, little rifle, shoot straight!" He nosed the sly weapon across the drift-log and laid his right eye in the sights. The front bead appeared to blur slightly. Slowly, cautiously, holding his breath, he withdrew the gun from the log. With a bandanna, he wiped off the fine web.

Again the determined muzzle crept over the concealed log. Again Coyne rose into the sights. He pinned the head on the sheen of the lusty drake's wing, on the whistling bone that carries mallards to safety.

Tenderly he tightened his finger. The rifle let go its canned death. Powder smoke stung his eyes as the flat roared into air and the sycamore tops sprouted feathers.

Coyne jerked his breech bolt, forced in the fresh load, and fired his farewell at the mallards. His slug punched a harmless hole in the zenith. He shoved in his third cartridge and turned his mind to the flat.

There lumped his duck, dead as a doorknob.

A fine human pride caroused in his chest as he hurried to take up his bird. The muddy sop was adhesive.

He squished. Ankle deep in frog-pudding he retrieved the big drake and imagined what Dodie would say.

A motor-boat came rippin up-river. Two men in warm clothes scanned the shores. When they glimpsed Coyne, they swerved, swung the boat up a slough, and split the weeds within a stone's throw of the hunter.

They stepped from the boat with a business-like air, their legs sheathed in high boots. They came over.

"Did you kill that duck with that gun?" said one.

"Sure did," said Coyne, "plumb center."

The spokesman showed his credentials.

"You're under arrest," he said.

"Get into the boat," said the other.

"Hey! Hold on!" said Coyne, "you fellers got the wrong hunch. I bought my license last June. I got it here, in my shirt pocket."

"License or no license," the first officer said, "you killed a duck with a rifle. That's a violation of the federal law."

Coyne gawked.

"Crazy or not, that's the law." The man reached into a pocket. He brought forth a soiled copy of S.R.A.—B.S. 83 and read pointedly:

"...migratory game birds may be taken during the open season with a shotgun only."

"Get into the boat," the other man said.

Coyne stood, staring queerly at the duck he had shot. Then he blurted:

"I tell you what, warden. Let me take this duck home to Dodie, my wife, then I'll cheerful go with you to jail."

"Can't be done," said the spokesman. "That bird is evidence now. It is proof you have violated Regulation Three which provides for the protection of wildfowl."

"Get into the boat," said the other one.

Coyne walked to the boat, his face tightening. The mud pulled with a loud sucking sob. The men took his duck and his rifle and seated him in the bow end of the boat.

They pulled from the flat, towards the current.

Up the river a sudden noisy bombardment gave Coyne his farewell salute.

Rockets of the North

BY JIMMY ROBINSON

1937

I NTO THIS ROCKET-MINDED WORLD THE SPEEDY BLUEBILL FITS MOST admirably. If there is jet propulsion among birds it all started with him. As he rides the northern gales he comes with the speed of a bullet, and he is gone before the slow-minded hunter can get his gun to his shoulder.

For those who love duck hunting the time of the bluebill is the high mark of the year.

Few birds are speedier, few offer a more sporting target. And, above all, few are more obliging in responding to decoys. For the bluebill, "scaups" to the hunters on the eastern shore, is a gregarious little bundle of energy. He loves company and he will arrow into your stool with the greatest of confidence, even eagerness. Another high recommendation for him is his edibility. There are fewer tastier birds than these Delta Marsh jets.

As the great Delta Marsh at the southern shores of Lake Manitoba begins to freeze for the winter, a great wave of bluebills comes hurtling down from the north. They pile in. They bore in. They zoom over. They are like bullets. They are like slugs from a multi-machinegun nest singing over your head. The air in the more concentrated migrations of gray and blackish dots is darkened like a blackbird invasion.

The French-Canadian natives of the Delta region, who trace back their ancestry to the long-gone days of the fur voyageurs, and know well all the prairie ducks from long and close association, wait impatiently for this bluebill flight. Yes, the canvasback is a fine duck, they say, and the mallard, and others. But they'll take the little bluebill. They always have. Barring a local dropping of an atomic bomb, they probably always will.

Picturesque and apt of speech, especially in English, which for them remains a second tongue, the Delta French Canadians have a word for bluebills. They call them "nordern" bluebills. Not bluebills. Never. They are always "nordern" bluebills. And this is as fine a tribute—remember, it is a totally subconscious one—as I could write to the little bluebill in a thousand times as many words.

For the real north is a place of superlatives to the Delta natives, as it is, in a sense, to all of us who live in more clement climes. It stretches there before them, vast, primal, elemental, to the Arctic Sea. It is "down north" to them, and it rifles down the savage arctic gales, the fierce prairie blizzards. They know, and many of their ancestors helped to make, its glorious traditions. From the north come the great local flights of waterfowl, the big Canada geese, the outsize mallard drakes with the curl in their tails, the heavy canvasbacks, and others. And from there come these spectacular bluebill flights, racing the arctic gales that bring the final freeze-up, providing, as they have for centuries, a portion of the natives' winter provender.

The beloved, inevitable "nordern" is not a plagiarized Scandinavian accent, lifted bodily from the Swede settlers scattered thereabouts. It is completely indigenous. The "nord," or nor', is the French for English north, which the Delta people have never recognized, or rather, pronounced. The apt English adjectival ending has been adopted, but with small concession to the unfamiliar and difficult digraph "th."

The Manitoba Delta Marsh is one of the great waterfowl breeding and resting places of the continent. Some sixty miles west of Winnipeg, it is a vast expanse of marsh cane, bulrush and cattail islands in a sea of shallow, food-rich water. Twenty miles long and several miles wide, it attracts most of the waterfowl species of the continental interior, both as breeders and as migrators. In the spring, as soon as the first slivers of open water appear along the island borders, the first ducks make their appearance (not the bluebills). In the fall, the marsh is frozen tight and hard before the last ducks leave. The great bulk of the tag-end migrants are the little bluebills. When the last open water in the marsh glazes over, there always are diehard bluebills that raft up in great Manitoba Lake.

The "nordern" bluebill exodus at the freeze-up always is the most spectacular duck flight of the year. One day the weather turns, and suddenly the chilling bite of deep winter is in the air. The film of ice creeps out over the marsh. The open water contracts steadily. The teeming bluebills on the marsh, a good percentage of which rode down the last lusty north wind, are nervous, restless, as a disturbing, age-old instinct stirs within them. Presently, the restlessness may take on the look of approaching panic. The birds seem in a quandary of indecision. They fly up quickly in little bunches, settle down in another part of the marsh, only to find that is not to their liking, and they are on the wing again, and again they settle down. The bunches get larger and larger. Phone calls to Tom Nelson at Fergus Falls—to Dick Bonnycastle at Winnipeg—to Ed Chesley at Petersfield in Manitoba—would reveal that a brisk northwest wind had sprung up, more likely than not an incipient blizzard. In the afternoon the northwest blow has reached the marsh. A few bluebills ride before it. Just before twilight a flock of marsh "bills" rise into the wind. Others join them. They swing around over the marsh in a great majestic circle until they feel the wind's hard push behind them. Then they straighten out and head southeast, pin-pointed for their next stop and their wintering grounds. Big flock after big flock takes off after them.

Now great flights of birds from the north begin to come over the marsh, sometimes when weather abnormally compresses the flight, in tier on tier, reaching high, high in the air. When light fails the sky is full of ducks, most of them "nordern" bluebills, as far to the north and the west, and the east, and the south, and as high, as the eye can see. Far into the night the birds can be heard—*brrrr, brrrr, brrrr*—passing overhead, the purring murmur of tens of thousands of "bills" blended by the distance, sounding like a distant roaring waterfall.

In the morning, if the storm has been a bad one, most of the great flocks have gone from the marsh. Practically, the season's shooting is over. If any open water remains, these patches will have their bluebills. Out on the great lake, bluebills will still be rafted. If the storm petered out during the night, the open water oasis of the marsh, and especially the lake, may still hold great numbers of die-hard bluebills, northern birds which swooped in during the night. But even these will be an anticlimax.

This is the time the typical bluebill hunter, who can sit in a freezing blind, battered by the elements, and not only live through it but like it, lives for the rest of the year. In the cities and small towns to the south, as the duck season draws to a close, these counterparts of the Delta natives have restlessly marked time, impatiently scanning the weather reports, waiting for news of the beginning of this flight. When it comes, there is an exodus to the shooting lodges similar to that of opening day. The "nordern" bluebill flight over its main route is the most dependable of all the species'.

For the little bluebill, more than any other interior species as a whole, flies by the weather. An experienced, observant gunner to the south by keeping tab on the weather to the north, can forecast pretty closely when the bluebills will come piling over his favorite sloughs and passes, usual-ly eager to be lured down to a rest and feed by inviting stools. Out of the north sweep the bullet flights, often in single file like great black pencil lines against the sky. Riding their favorite blasting wind, they may be zooming at sixty or seventy or even more, miles an hour. Then there is pass shooting at its very best. Or, scudding before the wind, they may sud-denly shoot into the decoys. Normally, perhaps, most flights will arrive at night. Then, still nervous, erratic, jumpy, moving in short, quick flights about the marsh, the bluebill will provide some memorable shooting in the morning.

This medium-sized, handsome, black and white duck (the drake) is the swashbuckler of the airways. He's the hot fighter pilot of the duck family. He's the aerial acrobat, the daring young drake on the flying trapeze. Riding the high north wind across a pass, he laughs at all but the most instinctive shooters. The sky may be empty, the next moment he is overhead. In high, rough weather, which he loves, he likes to hedgehop. He comes from nowhere. The good bluebill shooter at these times has to be on his toes. He would be much happier if he had eyes like a fly—every-where. Apparently drunk as a lord on the wine of the north wind and the mysterious call of the season, the bluebills may come in from all sides, at all levels, now skimming over the surface of the water, now swooping down from above. Stand up suddenly in your blind or your boat and you're likely to get your cap knocked off—if not your head.

I was hunting once with Jack Price at the Delta, and it was that kind of a day. We were in a boat in some scant rushes. The bluebills were zooming over before the wind like bullets. Jack saw a few coming and stood up to make them flare. He was a little slow. The lead bird, sizzling up so fast that Price afterward swore he saw him smoke, smacked him on the head. Jack sailed overboard in a flat curve like he had been hit by a 75mm shell. He cleaved the water neatly with his head, about ten feet way, but unfortunately his spread-eagled legs and arms, not to mention the gun, detracted from the effect of his dive considerably.

Jack had a little trouble extricating his head from the marsh bottom and I was about to go in after him when he stood up groggily in about four feet of water, pond weeds draped like a milliner's latest exclusive model about his noggin. He was occupied for a while clearing mud out of his nose and mouth and eyes, sputtering for breath. Then he muttered, "Why didn't you tell me were shooting jet fighters this morning?"

Another time I was with Emil Lamirande, ace French-Canadian guide, on a narrow point extending to the Delta Marsh, and the bills had again been drinking deep in the north wind and the season. I put Jack McKeag and Joe Hochevar on Jimmy's pass, between the big lake and Cadham's Bay, and I was on a point extended across a flyway, 200 yards away, and the birds, riding a gale, were passing it hell-bent, like black and white and brown meteors, virtually just above the shore growth. Emil and I were crouched in it. It limited our lateral field of vision. Lamirande's job was to watch for incoming ducks and give me the signal when to jump up for a shot. Then the birds would flare and my pump would speak. That was the theory. The trouble was, it wasn't working. Emil would give his signal, I would bounce up like a spring-steel jumping jack. And I would have my gun practically knocked out of my hands by feathered projectiles that shot past so fast the swish of their wings and bodies reminded me of an express train. Several flocks went by in this manner, with no more damage than a momentary fright occasioned by an apparition that suddenly sprang out of the ground into their midst and then as suddenly subsided again. They couldn't hear me barking at Emil after I hit the dirt when the last flight passed.

"For Pete's sake," I pleaded with Emil, "can't you give me a decent lead on those berserk bluebills?"

Emil shook his head humbly. "In twenty years, Jimmy," he said, "I never seen anything like this. I look up, but this blessed grass, I cannot see. It wave like mad, it bothers me. Before I see, there they are. I do my best."

Emil maneuvered to where he could catch the birds a little sooner. He lengthened his "lead." Now he gave his signal when the oncoming "bills" were still at least sixty yards out. I would pop up as though I had suddenly sat down hard on a tack. We finally got the thing coordinated so I had those boiling birds flaring at about forty yards, and I was able to pick out my "bills" at a decent shooting distance. Those sizzling bluebills that day gave me some shooting I will long remember.

I saw my first little "nordern" bluebills on the Delta Marsh in 1903, a good many years before I would be eligible to discard my short britches. I didn't know a bluebill from a whooping crane. My Grandfather Cruikshank, who lived in Winnipeg at the time and loved duck shooting as well as he loved his race horses, which was a great deal, took me with him on a hunting trip to the Marsh. I was too young to shoot, but my love for duck shooting dates from that time. It has been a rare year since when I haven't returned—some say like a bad penny—to the Delta Marsh in the fall for a duck hunt. And every year I have never failed to treat myself to at least one real shoot on those late-flying torpedoes, the "nordern" bluebills. Of course, the flights, as those of other ducks, are not what they used to be. I do not want to give the impression that bluebills have not suffered from the same causes that have decimated other species, because emphatically they have. With the necessary modern limits, the old-time bluebill shoots are a thing of the past. But the little bluebill, ornery, erratic, complacent, persistent little devil that he is, will probably be with us as long as any duck. Let us hope that will be forever.

There is a lot to be said for our old way of hunting. Naturally, it will never come back. There always were plenty of ducks, and plenty of places to shoot. About our only worry was shells, and we loaded these ourselves. There were no city hunters in those days, and the farmers, with the tractor and the combine still over the horizon, were all too busy to shoot. The roads during the autumns would have been impassable to automobiles, but so far as I know there was only one gas buggy in the county, and it wasn't ours. Gumbo mud, though, was no barrier to our youthful shanks.

On a red-letter day we were able to borrow a buggy from Granddad Robinson, a lumber man in central Minnesota.

My youthful duck bags were usually heaviest with bluebills. No day was too cold or blustery if a bluebill flight was on. If a good flight happened to coincide with a school day, my intake of formal knowledge would be apt to undergo a hiatus on that day. Numerous were the lickings for which the bluebills were responsible. I was singularly unsuccessful in my efforts to impress the proper authorities with the soundness of my conception of the relative importance of the bluebills and school.

Bluebills coming down with a hard wind provide just about the sportiest shooting you will find. I had several good bluebill shoots one fall, but the sportiest came, strangely enough, the day after the Delta Marsh began to freeze tight. It was due solely to herculean icebreaking efforts on the part of the late Freddie Miller of Milwaukee, the Notre Dame football all-American of some years back.

Freddy flew up late on October 22, with Walt Taylor, Pat McClain, Mike Droney, and Chuck Murphy. I had been telling him about the tag-end bluebill, and bull canvasback, shooting on the Marsh for years. Now here he was at last, and the Marsh was freezing up. In addition, snow had started to fall. Only that afternoon, my wife, Clara, who is the major-domo of the camp, had been insisting it was time to close up our Sports Afield lodge. The shooting season, so far as the weather was concerned, was over. I was in a quandary. There still would be plenty of bluebills left in the morning—barring an old-fashioned blizzard—both on the big lake and on any open water remaining in the Marsh. I wanted Fred to get the "nordern" bluebill and can shooting (assuming any cans remained) he had set his heart on. But the only place to get it was out in the Marsh. And the Marsh was freezing over.

I took Fred to one side and tried to explain the situation.

"With this near-zero weather and no wind," I said, "the Marsh is going to be frozen tight in the morning. We can't get out there. I'm afraid you'll have to forget the bluebills. But how about a stubble shoot on big northern mallards? They've been working over Bill McCowan's field over there the last few days."

I went to the window and pointed. The barley field was half a mile away, but we could see the mallards swarming over it. Freddie nodded. Sure. It was O.K. But I could see the deep disappointment in his eyes.

After supper that evening we sat around the lodge. Another season was coming to an end. Walt Taylor and Chuck (Rip Van Winkle) Murphy, who had shot in the barley stubble that afternoon, described their field shoot in glowing terms. Young Mike and Henry Mulder, who also had arrived that afternoon, could not wait to get out to the field in the morning. I looked at Freddie Miller. He was listening attentively, but it was plain it was not mallards he wanted on the morrow; he wanted die-hard bluebills drunk with the north wind, bluebills riding on a gale, scudding over a pass, such as I had described to him.

Mike Droney, a reincarnated Baron von Manchausen with a bottomless fund of tall duck stories, had been dozing by the fire. Now, refreshed, he ambushed the conversation. He took us down to Iowa of the early 20's, and sketched a graphic picture of long-gone days, of mammoth duck migrations that would never be again, and shoots that could never again be duplicated. A spell of nostalgia gripped me and I forgot about Freddie Miller.

At length Rip Murphy, the old blind-snoozer, roused, looked around and asked, "Where is Fred?"

"All he's talked about for a month is late bluebills and cans," observed Irvin O'Connor, who had made the air trip to the camp will Miller and Joe Laird, the pilot. "He's probably snooping around the marsh."

I slipped outside, and a buzz of talk, mostly excited French, led me to the guide shack. There was Mr. Miller, trying hard to slip a calm Anglo-Saxon word edgewise now and then into a spate of Gallic-English from Frank and Ed Lavallee, two of our French-Canadian guides.

"The boys tell me, I think, they can break through the ice and we can get a bluebill shoot in the morning," Fred greeted me with an apologetic grin. The Lavallee boys nodded vigorously.

I was dubious. I argued the new ice would be pretty solid by morning, that it was a job for an icebreaker to get through the mile or so to the island that we would have to reach to get across the flyway—the path the birds would use between the lake and what would probably be the only open water remaining in the Marsh, Cadham's Bay. But I consented to make the try. I dragged Fred away from the guides, who would have jabbered "nordern" bluebills all night, and we went to bed.

Five minutes later (it seemed) Big George Rennie, former Mountie, our chief cook, who never can get it through his skull he can't beat me at gin rummy, had me by the legs and was dragging me out of my bunk, in a last-ditch effort to awaken me. I almost froze before I got into my clothes. The lodge shivered in a virtual gale from the northwest. I went into the dining room to cross to Freddie's room to awaken him and found him halfway through his breakfast of Rennie Special Canadian bacon and wheat cakes.

Ed and Frank, the two Lavallee boys, came in and we went down to the Marsh shore. Freddie greeted the wind with a glad eye. As far as we could see, the island and beyond the Marsh was frozen. I walked out a little way on the shore ice, and it seemed as solid as concrete.

"Freddie, Ed and Frank," I said, "you have your work cut out for you. If you think you can break that ice all the way out to the island, you're welcome to try. But kindly include me out!"

Freddie, an assistant football coach at Notre Dame, who frequently scrimmaged with the boys, was not daunted. "Come along, Ed," he said. Grabbing a heavy handmade oar which was like a war club, he pushed a boat on the ice and began belaboring it. Slowly he and Ed opened a channel. Frank and I followed in the other boat.

Dawn broke, gray and overcast. The wind howled. The cold was bitter. I worked up a mild sweat, however, just watching the herculean labors of Fred and Ed. Bluebills scooted past to the west, headed for Cadham's Bay. In order to look busy, I picked up my gun and assiduously did some dry shooting, which, as any honest hunter knows, is a back-breaking, man-killing exercise. Occasionally Fred would seize a second or two from his labors to contemplate the darting bluebills. He reminded me of a famished far-north explorer sighting, at long last, a herd of meaty caribou. Then he would return to his beloved toil with quadrupled vigor.

Yard by yard the stubborn channel lengthened. I was bundled up like an Eskimo infant, but the wind was driving the cold into my bones. Freddie and Ed had long since removed their outer coats.

It was two hours before we reached the island. The bluebills were still scooting by, trading between the lake and the bay. Stamping my feet, which were like ice blocks, I stationed Freddie on the island's south shore, in bulrushes, and I took a place seventy-five yards away. We shoved our cork and balsa decoys out on the ice in front of us. The wind was now terrific, an occasional gust practically lifting us off our feet. It was coming from an angle, behind us.

The bluebills—and a few late bull cans—coming from the lake were skidding before it. Now and then a mighty gust would catch them and the would hurtle by like miniature rockets. We would pick up a flock in the distance, small and black, boring toward us. Quickly they grew larger. Then in a moment they were over us and past. Fred's double would blast. My pump might blast, or it might not. To my surprise, I was hopelessly slow on these rocketing birds. My heavy clothes were catching my gun butt.

There was a lull in the flight, and I noticed that the wind had dropped. Then it began blowing again, from the opposite direction. Birds were in the air again. The wind picked up soon, it seemed, and was blasting by with even more ferocity than a short time before from the other way. I started to shed my coat, but decided against it. It was too cold. A few bluebills torpedoed by. I had just four ducks down when Fred's Labrador picked up his tenth duck, his limit. Fred came over, crouching in the wind, with his ducks, eight "bills" and two bull cans, and asked me what I thought of the shooting.

"Some character must have put baking powder in my shells," I grunted. "Duck down, here comes a flight!"

A flock of "bills" was riding a hurricane gust, highballing up at an incredible velocity. One moment they were half a mile off, the next they were hurtling by overhead, off to the side. I led the lead bird instinctively and let fly. The leader and two other birds dropped out of the flock. They skidded like ricocheting shot along the shore ice, all three dead.

"Can you get me some of that baking powder, Jimmy?" said Fred, slowly. "I, too, would like to make a bluebill triple in a 70-mile wind."

In the Presence of Mine Enemies

BY GORDON MACQUARRIE

1937

THE DUSK OF LATE DUCK SEASON WAS HURRYING WESTWARD ACROSS THE sky and slanting snow was whitening the street gutters as I turned into the automotive emporium of the President of the Old Duck Hunters' Association, Inc. The man in the parts department explained that Hizzoner was out on the used-car lot. There I found him, thoughtfully kicking a tire on an august and monstrous second-hand car, soon to be taking the Association on its final expedition of the season.

"We could try Libby Bay again," he reflected. "But the Hole in the Wall will be frozen. Jens says every bluebill on Dig Devil's has hauled his freight. Shallow Bay'd be open at the narrows, but I s'pose Joe's hauled in all his boats. Phoned Hank. He said there's an inch of ice on Mud Lake and she's making fast."

He went over other possibilities. The situation was urgent, for only a few days remained of the season. The widespread below the Copper Dam of the St. Croix? "Might not see a thing 'cept sawbills." The grassy island in the open water of the St. Louis River? "Too much big water to buck in this wind." Taylor's Point on the Big Eau Claire? "Wind's wrong for it and she's gonna stay in that quarter."

Street lights came on and home-going city toilers bent into the grow-ing storm with collars turned up. One of them crossed the street and tried the showroom door which the parts man had just locked. Mister President called from the lot, "Something I can do for you?"

"Ye're dern tootin!" came the reply. "Open this dump and let a man get warm."

Mister President grinned. "It's Chad," he said, making haste to unlock the showroom door.

Anyone in the community on reasonable terms with the way of the duck, the trout, the partridge and the white-tailed deer knows Chad just as he knows Mister President. Before the days when I cut myself in as an apprentice, the ODHA had consisted almost solely of Mister President and Chad. In recent years they get together only a couple of times per year on outdoor missions which can be anything from looking up old trout holes to picking blueberries.

But they meet regularly in church, except during the duck season and possibly two or three Sundays in late May or early June when the shad-flies hatch. Chad is an especially stout pillar of the church, and passes the collection plate with a stern and challenging eye on the brethren he considers too thrifty.

The belligerent affection which Hizzoner and Chad reciprocate was once amply demonstrated at the Men's Club meeting in the church basement when suggestions were called for.

"Get a one-armed guy to take Chad's job passing the plate," volunteered Mister President.

Chad, who came upon holiness late in life and became so enchanted with Biblical wisdom that he quotes verses every chance, snorted back, "Let him who is without sin cast the first stone..."

"The time," Chad announced, "is short."

"There'll be no 14-year-old touring car with California top repaired here this night," declared Mister President. "Tell you what, though—bring it down to the lot and I'll give you $7.50 for it on a new job."

"My son, attend unto my wisdom," said Chad sagely. "Last deer season I was on a drive in back of Little Bass Lake. Found a spring-hole at the edge of a big marsh." His eyes gleamed with what is recognized in church as religious fervor. "No map shows it. Everything else in the country was froze up, and this little spring-hole was open. There's a point of high, dry land poking into it. There's smartweed in there and watercress, and the day I saw it mallards jumped out of it."

"How about the road in?"

"We'll have to walk a mile."

Mister President frowned briefly, but Chad's mustache became a reasonable straight line as he intoned, "If thou faint in the day of adversity, thy strength is small."

"Let's at it, then," decided Mister President.

Quick getaways are no problem for the ODHA in the critical times of the season. At such times decoys are always sorted and sacked, shell boxes full and thermos bottles yawning for their soup and coffee. Against emergency conditions, Mister President also sets the old horse blanket and barn lantern conveniently at hand in the garage, for it is by these implements that he keeps warm in late-season blinds.

A mere accessory to the reunion, I drove the big car while the two cronies smoked and remembered. They agreed I'd come in handy toting gear and that I could be put to use if ice had to be broken. Objections on my part were swept away as Chad patted me on the back and said piously, "The righteous shall flourish like the palm tree."

Fine slanting snow darted across the path of the headlights. With that northwest wind I knew it would not snow much; but should the wind veer to the northeast, then we would be very happy at having the heavy, high-wheeled monster of a car for bucking drifts. It was a little after 9 P.M. when we disembarked beneath the high oaks which spread over Norm's place on the north shore of Big Yellow Lake, Burnett County, Wisconsin. Norm appeared with a flashlight.

"Might have known it'd be no one but you out on a night like this."

He lit an air-tight stove in an overnight cabin. Chad, police suspenders drooping as he readied for bed, set his old alarm clock with the bell on top for 5 A.M. A few minutes were allowed for final smokes and for further recollection of past delights. Chad had started to recall "the night we slept on the depot floor at Winnebojou" when a car entered the yard.

Again Norm emerged, prepared a cabin, and went back to sleep. As is always the way in duck camps, the newcomers pounded on our door for a pre-dawn investigation. As the two men entered, somewhat suspiciously I thought, Chad's face fell for a brief instant, but he made a quick recovery and fell upon the two hunters with vast friendship.

Where were they going to hunt in the morning? Weren't we all crazy for being out in such weather? How's the missus and the children?

Chad volunteered with bare-faced frankness that we were "going down the Yellow River a piece to that widespread just this side of

Eastman's." Our visitors alleged they had it in mind to try the deep point in the cane grass across Big Yellow. Mister President and Chad solemnly agreed that sounded like a promising spot—"mighty promising."

The two departed for bed, and Chad cried after them cheerfully, "See you in church, boys!" The moment they were gone Chad seized his alarm clock and set it to ring an hour earlier. "Those fakers aren't fooling me," he snorted.

"Me, either," said Mister President. "Somebody knows something."

"They were with me on that deer drive last fall. Gentlemen, say your prayers well tonight. There's only one spot on that marsh that's really any good, and that's the little spring-hole." He rolled in with a final muttering: "Deliver me from the workers of iniquity."

Within a few minutes the cabin resounded with the devout snores of Mister President and Chad. I lay awake a bit longer, listening to the wind in the oaks, weighing our chances for the morrow and marveling at the hypocritical poise of my comrades in the face of emergency. I knew those two adversaries of ours better than well. One was a piano tuner who, by some transference of vocational talent, cold play a tune on a Model '97 that was strictly lethal so far as ducks are concerned. The other was a butcher likewise noted for his wing-shooting and his stoutness in going anywhere after ducks.

Mister President and Chad snored. The snow tapped on the window like fine sand, and then suddenly someone was shaking me in the dark. It was Mister President.

"Get up quietly," he hissed. "We beat the alarm clock so they wouldn't hear it. Don't turn on the light. Don't even strike a match!"

Like burglars we groped in the dark getting dressed and gathering up gear. "How about breakfast?" I asked. Mister President snickered, and Chad's voice came as from a sepulcher in the pitch dark: "Trust in the Lord and do good."

Softly we closed the door behind us and climbed into the car. Mister President got behind the wheel with Chad beside him and me alone in the back seat. The motor roared, headlights blazed and almost simultaneously a light went on in the cabin of our neighbors.

"Step on 'er!" Chad shouted, and the old crate made the snow fly as it leaped out of Norm's yard.

"We've got the jump on 'em," Chad exulted, but did not forget to add: "The righteous shall inherit the land and dwell forever."

It was a wild ride on a wild morning. The snow had stopped when two to three inches lay on the level. That was enough to make for skidding turns on the sharp corners where Mister President kept to maximum speed. We roared up steep hills and kept the power on going down. We passed white barns ghostly and cold-looking in the dark, and at the field fronting a farmstead owned by one honorary member of the ODHA, Gus Blomberg, Chad ordered the car halted. He got out, took something from Gus's front yard that rattled like tin and stuffed it into the car trunk.

"What was it, Chad?" I asked.

"Out of the mouths of babes and fools," he retaliated, poked Mister President in the ribs and roared: "Step on 'er some more! He shall deliver thee from the snare of the fowler!"

I knew part of the road. But after they skirted the base of the long point jutting into Little Bass Lake and took up pulp trails through the jack-pine barrens I was lost. Chad ordered "right," or "left," or sometimes, "Don't forget to turn out for that big scrub-oak."

We labored up a hilltop on a barely discernible pair of ruts, and the big car came to a stop, practically buried in low scrub-oak. Instantly the lights were switched off, and Mister President and Chad listened for sound of the enemy's motor. They heard nothing, but nevertheless hurried with the job of loading up with the sinews of war and heading for the spring-hole.

Only you who have been there know how a 60-pound sack of decoys in a Duluth pack-sack can cut into the shoulders when hands are occupied with gun and shellbox. Chad led the way in the dark and took us miraculously through the better parts of that oak and pine tangle. A half mile along the way we stopped to listen again, and this time we heard the motor of another car laboring up the hill through the scrub.

"Step on 'er again," counseled Chad, shouldering his burdens. "They haven't forgotten the way in, and the piano tuner can run like a deer!"

Chad permitted the use of lights now. We stumbled for what seemed miles until he led us down a gentle slope, and there before us was black, open water, about an acre of it. The omens were good. Mallards took off as a flashlight slit across the water.

"Keep the dang lights on all you want," said Mister President. "Let 'em know we're here fustest with the mostest."

Mister President and I spread his ancient decoys while Chad busied himself on a mysterious errand some distance away. As I uncoiled decoy strings I saw that the hole was a mere open dot in what must have been a large, flat marsh. Tall flaggers hemmed in the open water and stretched far beyond the range of the flashlight.

Mister President and I dug a pit in soft sand on fairly high ground and embroidered the edges of it with jack-pine and scrub-oak. We heard the piano tuner and the butcher push through the cover on the hill at our back, heard them panting and talking in low voices. Chad returned and boomed for all to hear: "Ain't a thing open but this one little patch. Betcha we don't see a feather here today!"

He fooled no one. The piano tuner and the butcher made a wide circle around us. We could hear them crashing through brush and Chad grudgingly allowed, "That butcher can hit the bush like a bull moose." Then we heard them walking across the marsh ice among the raspy flaggers and soon, five hundred yards across the marsh from us, came the sound of chopping as they readied a blind. Chad was worried.

"No open water there, but that's the place where the mallards come in here from the St. Croix River. Those muzzlers are right in front of a low pass through the hills. Them mallards come through there like you opened a door for 'em."

There was at least an hour's wait to shooting time. The two old hands puttered with the blind. They rigged crotched sticks to keep their shotgun breeches away from the dribbling sand of the blind's wall. They made comfortable seats for themselves, and finally, as was their right by seniority, they wrapped the old horse blanket about their knees, with the lantern beneath, and toasted their shins in stinking comfort.

Long before there was any real light, ducks returned to our open water, and the ODHA, waiting nervously, sipped coffee and made a career out of not clinking the aluminum cups. In that blind with Mister President it was almost worth a man's life to kick a shell-box accidentally in the dark.

Chad briefed us: "When the time comes, don't nobody miss on them first ones, 'cause our friends over there are situated to scare out incomers. That is, in case they get a shot. Praise be, neither one of them are cloud-busters."

As the zero hour approached Mister President produced his gold watch and chain, and the two of them followed the snail's pace of the minute hand.

"Good idea not to jump the gun," said Chad. "No use to break the law."

To which Mister President added: "Might be a game warden hanging around, too."

"Now!"

As Mister President gave the word Chad kicked his shell-box and stood up. The air was full of flailing wings. I missed one, got it with the second barrel and heard three calculated shots from Mister President's automatic. I also heard Chad's cussing. He had forgotten to load his corn-sheller. The air was a bright cerulean blue until his city conscience smote him and he said remorsefully, "Wash me and I shall be whiter than snow."

With daylight the wind shifted from northwest to northeast and the snow began again, from Lake Superior this time. That kind of snow at that season is not to be trifled with, for northeasters can blow for three days and fetch mighty drifts. I picked up the drake mallard I had downed and the three birds Mister President had collected in his methodical way. The two old hands agreed that none of the mallards were locals, but "Redlegs down from Canada—feel the heft of that one!"

There was a long wait after that first burst of shooting. Obviously there were not many ducks left in the country. The original ODHA comforted themselves with hot coffee and thick sandwiches. From time to time one of them ascended the little knob at our rear to look across the snowy marsh and observe operations over there.

Chad came back from a reconnaissance and exclaimed, "She's workin', glory be."

The words were hardly out of his mouth when five mallards materialized out of the smother, circled the open water and cupped wings to drop in. As they zoomed in Mister President and Chad picked off a drake apiece, and when the wind had blown them to the edge of the ice I picked them up.

"You got him broke pretty well," Chad observed.

"Fair, just fair," grunted Mister President, squinting through the snow. "He's steady to wing and shot, but a mite nervous on incomers. Needs more field work."

Shortly before noon I climbed the hill myself for a look across the marsh. Through the snow over the high flaggers I could make out the dark green blob that was the jack-pine blind of the butcher and piano tuner. We had not heard a shot from the place. As I watched six mallards, mere specks at first, approached the marsh from the direction of the St. Croix River. They were coming through the low hill pass just as Chad had said they would. Normally they would have flown almost directly over the distant blind.

Some distance from the blind I saw them flare and climb, then swing wide around the edge of the marsh and sail straight into our open hole. From my vantage-point I saw the two old hands rise and fire, and three ducks fell.

Mister President called up to me: "Pick up that one that dropped in the scrub, will yuh?"

"We'd better keep careful count," Chad suggested. In a few minutes he dropped two more that tried to sneak into the water-hole.

"I'm through," he announced. He acknowledged his limit with a thankful verse: "Thou hast turned for me my mourning into dancing."

The afternoon moved along. The snow increased, and when limits were had all around we finished the last of the soup, washed it down with the now luke-warm coffee and picked up. It was high time we were moving. A good six inches of snow was on the ground. There were steep, slippery hills between us and the main road.

Back at the car, we turned the behemoth around. Parked just to the rear of us was the conveyance of the piano tuner and the butcher. It was a modern job with the low-slung build of a dachshund, but in maneuvering out of the place Mister President's locomotive-like contraption broke out a good trail.

Mister President and Chad were jubilant as the big car tooled carefully over the crooked road to Norm's where we picked up gear left behind in the unlighted cabin hours before and said goodby to Norm—"until the smallmouth take a notion to hit in the St. Croix."

Homeward-bound. Chad's best Sunday basso profundo broke into a sincere rendition of an old hymn which emphasizes that "He will carry you through," and Mister President joined him with a happy, off-key baritone. We halted at the curb in front of Chad's house, and he emerged from the car laden with mallards and gear smelling of horse blanket and kerosene.

"We sure fooled 'em," said Mister President.

"Thou preparest a table for me in the presence of mine enemies," Chad intoned, and went up his walk to the door.

At Mister President's back door I helped him with the unloading. What, I demanded, was the thing Chad had removed from Gus Blomberg's front yard?

"Well, sir," said Mister President. "It was a device calculated to do the undoable and solve the unsolvable. I couldn't have done better myself."

He sat down on a shell-box on his back steps the better to laugh at his partner's cunning.

"You know," he said, "when he stuck that thing out there just in the right place, he came back to the blind and told me, 'Mine enemies are lively and they are strong.'"

"What was it?" I insisted. "All I know is there was something out there that made those mallards flare."

Hizzoner picked up the shell-box, his hand on the door knob, and said, "It was Gus Blomberg's scarecrow, and I'm surprised you haven't figured it out."

"All I could guess was that it was something made of tin cans. I heard 'em rattle."

"Gus Blomberg," said Mister President, "always drapes tin cans on his scarecrows soste they'll rattle in the wind. Good night to you, sir—and don't forget to come over tomorrow night and help me pick these ducks."

How Come?

BY NASH BUCKINGHAM

1937

URR, LEM AND I WENT TO LAKE ARTHUR AS MY COUSIN EVELYN'S guests. The memory of it is a full spectrum of wildfowling emotions. An overnight ride from our homes in Memphis; several hours convivial gadding about in picturesque New Orleans with old friends, and a near-dusk detrainment far westward at Jennings, Louisiana. Thirty minutes via automobile landed us at Port Arthur, point of embarkation for the Club's palatial houseboat. Other arriving members and guests swelled our company to nine. Licenses were issued and baggage holed. After our captain-helmsman and his crew of two were aboard, twelve of us were sardined into the low-roofed cabin of a high-speed gasboat.

Booming thunder, jagged lightning and a high wind added nothing to that situation and by now, most of us realized that with thirty-five miles to voyage, we were facing an "out yonder" capable of maturing into an extremely sloppy business. Nineteen miles of tortuous channel until the storm's fury forced anchorage in the lee of a last lighthouse mainland. Sixteen miles of tossing lake ahead.

Then, abruptly, the lashing rain drew off. Puffy whorls sent fog scuds scurrying. Friendly stars twinkled apology. A timorous moon rose over the ribbonlike shore line, and suddenly we were off like a greyhound across untroubled waters. Winding lagoons eventually led us toward a glowing patch on the horizon. The clubhouse! Two hours overdue, we docked to relieve considerable apprehension. Welcoming hands! An open fireplace! Bright lights! Food and more of it! Drink and what of it! We were safe and whole again. To the duck hunter, danger passed comes under the head of "old business."

Lake Arthur's clubhouse boat is moored to a small island cast away amid an apparently limitless vista of sere coastal marshland. What with the guides' home, boat sheds and servants' quarters, the beautifully landscaped outfit is a community for sport royal. At most duck clubs the "draw" for stands and pushers is an event. At Lake Arthur it is ceremony. Each guide rules an individual domain. Assignments of each day and "bags of species" are recorded in the club's game register. At the season's end their total "kill-by-species," together with all additional observations and data of value, is reported to the United States Bureau of Biological Survey at Washington, D.C. Such information, incidentally, should no longer be *asked for* cooperatively, but *required* from every duck club and commercial shooting resort in the country.

"Your guide tomorrow will be 'Joe,'" my old trapshooting friend, manager Bob Worsham, tells me after the draw, "and a fine lad he is, too. Coffee at three-thirty sharp. Buck—your duffel bag is up in the 'dorm'— grab a bed; you can't go wrong, they're all mighty good sleepin'." Rough-weather rubberalls, and other comfortable if odoriferous ducking duds, are piled handy. Alongside are stacked my favorite three-inch shells loaded with copper-coated fours. And towering close by is "Bo-Whoop," as Hal Sheldon dubs my ten-pound, overbored, Burt Becker twelve-bore Magnum.

White floodlights startle me awake. My wrist watch dots three-thirty. Grinning Granville, an ebon study against cook's frills, slippers into view via the stairhead. He offers us cups of stygian Louisiana "drip." Reluctance to desert Morpheus gets a kick in the pajama pants shortly after the first intakes of that rowdy fluid. The "dorm" becomes vigorously astir with cheerful salutations and matutinal tubbings. Shaved and in utter sartorial discord, we troop to the breakfast board. Jocose black boys thrust fresh "drip" before us; bend attentive ears and scuttle kitchenward flinging advance orders in chaotic patois. These reappear as *fruits en saison*, eggs *au beurre* something or other, girdles of bacon, and relays of thin patties with ribbon cane sweetening.

Finally, we nondescripts of the duck blinds are herded toward the boathouse. To the accompaniment of smoky lanterns, prying flashlights, inevitable "where's-where" and "who's-who," boat quotas are handed into shallow-draft motor craft; while balky engines gulp, Cajun invectives sputter, and caged live decoys writhe and squawk. A stocky, clean-cut chap locates me amid the confusion and grins as we shake hands—my guide, Joe. I hand over part of my equipment (habit forces us old-timers to hold onto gun) and follow him into a boat with two other sports going our general way. Someone spins a wheel; we clear the boathouse, and head out across a choppy bay. In the damp, inky chill a heavy coat is comfortable. The sky brims with stars. Grouped on the motor housing, our Cajun guides patter away in jerky marsh jargon. We gunners appraise the morning's prospects. Twenty minutes eases us into a pocket that narrows rapidly into a ribbon-like canal. Up this a piece we stop at a small planked dam, shutting off a ditch through the marsh wall. Joe bestirs himself. "Eef yu plees, M'sieu, we go obode heah—yu an' me—there—steady, M'sieu—das eet." We call "good luck" as the motor picks up and slips away around a bend.

Lifting our cockle shell of a pirogue across the barrier, we relaunch and effect a delicate entry. Shift your chewing gum or change your mind in a "pee-roog," and see what happens. The slit is not five feet wide and its few inches of water make tough poling for Joe. But we slide along as he puts arms and back into his crutch-ended prod pole. Our whole world is suddenly pulsing with the thrummings and rustlings of nomadic wildfowl life. There are distant roars from duck rafts. Nearby alarm calls are passed seaward and fade into the distance.

"Heah we are, M'sieu," Joe whispers. "We be right dere pretty queek." Joe pushes his pea-hull steadily ahead with his long paddle. A hundred yards of slog through matted growths, and I sense that a clump of "cut" grass showing up dead ahead is Joe's objective. Built into its center is a four-foot platform. Joe quickly arranges the stool to suit himself, stakes out three live callers, and hides his boat in an adjacent grass mat. The sun is about to crash a suffused East. Sinuous lines of ducks weave the horizons; wispy bundles high overhead burst into rocket-chaff. Their subdued chatter comes down to us. I cram a pair of shells into the big gun's breech and estimate yardage to a passing flock. "Too high, M'sieu," whispers Joe, "motch too haut." And Joe is right—this time.

"Almos' too bright t'day, M'sieu, de dox dey see longways—maybe pritty soon som' foolish fellas com' 'long—ah! To de right, M'sieu—

queek—I call dem." I've picked them up by now—eight lugging mallards, five drakes and three tagging hens. Joe slaps his tiny cane call to his pursed lips, grunts a tune-up, and turns loose a hail, than switches abruptly to the "*tuc-atuc-atuc*" feeding chatter. Joe's talk is crudely unlike the almost too-perfect duck lingo of my native ponded tall timber. Sounds odd, but by Jove it works. My own Hooker duck call stays in my pocket while I listen intently to the other follow's racket. From a distance, it must be nigh perfect in quality. Four of the mallards break sharply away and circle toward us. "Down, M'sieu," hisses Joe, "dey comin', sho'." He couldn't have "worked" them more satisfactorily. Letting the two lead birds light, I crumple a right and left above them. Carrying a third shell in the corner of my mouth is an old double-gun reloading trick—providing you can concentrate solely on shoving it into the gun before looking up to locate the third chance. But I manage it, and annex a third drake from the bewildered, leaping pair.

Joe is all smiles and enthusiasm. "Fine beeginnin' we mek, M'sieu, dose shots ver' fas'—pouf-pouf—*pouf.*" He searches the reeds for my three ejected shells. "Deese hulls wid d' extra long brass ends—I ketch dem all when d' gun fly open—we use d' brass f' mek dock-call—yu see?" He shows me his own, fashioned simply but neatly from marsh cane, based with shotgun shell brass, and equipped (most important) with a reed filed from a rubber comb. Joe twigs out our three victims as decoys.

The sky is now rarely void of traveling waterfowl. An occasional goose note drifts our way. One moment our immediate vicinity is bare of ducks, while the next, one scarcely knows which shot to take first. The "limit" means merely making one's choice of species—mallards—teal—or what have you. Now Joe produces a jug of fragrant, hot *café au lait,* and over it we become better acquainted. He is exceptionally intelligent and well informed on regional wildfowl conditions. Comparatively young in years, Joe is an "old head" at the guiding and shooting business; born to it on an old farm down Grand-Chênier way. His eyes light with joy while we discuss respective home lives. There are the *grandpère* and Joe's blue-eyed baby daughter. "Bot," he adds, "eet ees so lon'lee whin I com' heah t' guide in de winter—lon'lee widout dem two, but, M'sieu, work ees work an' mo' monny f' take back—she ees so lov'lee, M'sieu—golden hair—t'ick lak d' moss—an' soch blue eyes—ah, M'sieu—so lov'lee." And I tell Joe I have such a one at home, too.

Before we know it, ten o'clock has drifted around, and ten a.m. at Lake Arthur means quitting time, limit or no limit. We start the long shove to our motorboat rendezvous. Ahead, on the ditch bank I sight a trapped raccoon intently watching our approach. Joe traps "partners" with Gabe D'Aquin on this particular sector. "Now, M'sieu," he grins, "I show yu how we dooes business wid d' coons. Regardez, M'sieu." Stepping gently from the pirogue, Joe snaps open a long-bladed, keen jackknife and approaches "Cooney." "Pauvre p'tit—d' lil garçon in Joe's trap—eh?" The glistening blade is whetted for an instant on Joe's palm. "But d' dollar ees d' monny, mon ami. Maintenant—regardez bien, M'sieu." The raccoon, a roly-poly fellow erect on his haunches, looks upon the proceedings with half-furtive belligerency. Joe fences with him, using a bit of cane switch to gradually elevate the animal's guard. Feint after feint. Black-fingered paws warding off pokes higher and higher! A few low snarls. Then—"Z-i-t." Straight down into Cooney's heart darts Joe's slender blade; an oft-practiced thrust so deft as to almost foil the eye. A look of wondering, agonized surprise leaps into the coon's troubled, stricken eyes. "Why," he seems to gasp, "why, fellows, I wasn't really mad at you—you've—you've got me all wrong—you've—!" In exactly eleven seconds I count there, he is dead from the lethal stroke—and boated. We push along, and Joe whistles. "Mo monny, M'sieu!" And why not? Toll of life in the great marsh, and at that a merciful end, far better than shooting or battering. Just another coonskin coat for some campus waster.

Good luck has attended each of our party's efforts. And such a lunch when we have napped, tubbed and tidied. Peeled duck gizzards with gravy in a sizzling curry; mallard breasts grilled, sauced fish cutlets and fresh vegetables. Then, following renewed siesta, Evelyn and I put in an afternoon of furious sport with fly rods and big-mouth bass. The sun rims the sedge as we paddle from a chain of lakes down to the main canal.

I am drawn next morning with Emory, a husky Cajun, whose shooting is noted for canvasback flights. Our motorboat drives breakneck into and through a long, narrow chute; skidding corners and cutting across wide lakes. Some higher intelligence seems to guide and guard our destinies. Emory deposits me at the very tip of a grassy point, hides the gasboat and returns in the pirogue. I sit in near reverie as another grand day is born.

"Voilà," explodes Emory, "vite, M'sieu!" I wheel to see a bunch of cans flaring off the stools. I catch up with them a bit tardily—for all save a tailender. Emory peeps through the rushy rampart and points a questioning finger waterward. "Heem—daid?" One must converse somehow. "Oui, mon Emory—là bas—bien mort." My towering friend grins widely—"A-h-h-h—s-o-o-o—on parle français—oui?" Torrential Cajun. I've let myself in for it now. "Un peu, mon Emory, très peu!" But I am saved immediate exposure. A mass of birds slithers suddenly among the shadows. Teal—by Jove! Follows a rush of cans, with just enough wait in between shots. I slice down a tall voyageur, and, getting cocky, ingloriously muff an easy decoy shot. Considerable questionable conversational French that somehow gets by on my part. A good scout, Emory.

Again the motor craft reunion and luncheon that overtempts one. A crab gumbo, broiled snipe, and a challenging array of side dishes. After the inevitable nap, we cousins unlimber twenty-bores and fill our pockets with snipe loads. A short run across the bay and we tie up at quite a chênier. With Emory to help retrieve, I go my way and skirt a damp palmetto patch. Distant shots begin mingling with my own. What a bird dog this Emory. Cattle have gashed the soft soil and frequently a double on the long-bills sends the birds headfirst into hoof holes. But the gigantic, black-haired Cajun's eyes dart from bird to bird unhesitatingly. The circle of a mile or so is all that is required for a limit of the snipe. And along with a lowering sun we chug peacefully home to the houseboat.

That evening Evelyn makes the "draw" for which he has been hoping, so, with characteristic generosity on my kinsman's part, I am turned over to Adler, a springy, well-knit Cajun of about my own age. His is a merry smile and happy disposition. His territory is far distant, but noted for its chances at both blue and Canada geese. It is still pitch dark when Adler and I tie his gasboat at the end of a long canal and clamber over into the marsh. Salt air from the sea is almost like vapor in our nostrils. A full mile of "mud-planing" lies ahead, so two push faster than one. The coastal pampas suddenly level off into a series of meandering ponds, and these, in turn, widen into grass-splotched spreads. Distantly disturbed geese swell the chorus of departing ducks. "This," I say to myself, "is just about the finest gunning lay I've clapped my eyes on in many a moon."

We round a grassy point and slosh in among some scattered wooden decoys; this is the set. The boat is lifted into a clump, and shooting preparations oriented. How many hours of my life, I wonder, have I passed in such reedy nooks? A bit of rest while we swig the inevitable *café au lait*— and plenty of it. I load my gun and look about. Plenty of high birds crossing, but why gamble at this stage? Unlimbering his call, Adler does some throat-clearing and note-fingering before cutting loose an alluring overture of the marsh.

Two sailing mallards, well to our left, dip at the hail and sweep toward us just as the rule book says. But one of them suddenly veers and climbs for dear life. Gets away with it, too. As for his buddy, a storm of fours clips him and he lies "tummy up" with his pink toes going gradually out of control. Adler is still offering congratulations when a flash of color slants from above and a wary duck hawk drifts into focus. Evidently he likes the look of our peaceful live decoys. Watch this fellow; he is a killer! He circles cagily; a few lazy turns to satisfy himself that the coast is clear. A bit of a rise and dip to one side for favorable air; then down he knifes with plummeting velocity. Decoys scream and tug at their tethers. Poised for a kill, shins extend, hackles fluff in the sunlight, and razored talons are hair-triggered. The big gun bellows and atop a lily-pond hammock, Mr. Hawk crumples to a well-merited end.

Forty minutes later Adler and I have become buddies; who wouldn't with this infectious, hard-working fellow. "I t'ink now, ol' fren', I mek peek-up, we got mebbe few mo' t' git—not manny do'h—you stay—pretty soon we tek mo' coffee." But I'm hunting exercise by now, and clamber after Adler. Final count shows three ducks needed, but these are soon added. Adler grins as he uncorks the thermos. Meanwhile, far behind us and seaward, gabbling geese have been trading—trading—drifting at times almost within good gunshot. There must be some way to get at them. A wave of talking Canadas rises from the concentration, circles enticingly and resettles something over a quarter mile away. Adler watches them down hungrily.

"Manny ol' goose ovah dere now—by golly—yaas, suh!"

"Adler," I query, "why can't you and I wade over yonder?"

Adler sizes me up about the waistband. "By golly, ol' fren', you tink you kin mebbe pool troo d' mod—meks d' laigs ache—long way—ol' fren'—but you ain't got hardly no belly—no?—an' we needs d' gooses mighty bad—yaas?—so by golly dams yaas—le's go."

The stalk begins. Adler threads a careful lead from clump to clump. "Tek yo' time, ol' fren'," he tosses over stooped shoulders, "go vairee easy—lak meester mink—I ve'y motch lak knock d' socks plum off beeg gooses dees treep." Compared to some wading I've done through Arkansas "no-bottoms" and boggy elbow brush, this stretch isn't half bad. But it'll be no pushover before the final gong, at that. Gradually we near the marked landing sector of that last big bunch. Like a warpath Indian, Adler skulks from vantage to shelter. Every vestige of cover is utilized. Suddenly, stiff as a pointer on quail, his eyes turn to mine as his lips frame an appeal for extra caution. A nod that spells—"just ahead."

Bent double, I twist in front of him and a bit to one side. We can hear them now—wing flaps, "twits" and an occasional gurgle of discord. Adler whistles shrilly and upward leaps a dinning black cloud. Toward its middle and climbing with one certain black neck, swing the big gun's tubes, subconsciously toward the touch-off. Just how many will fall to this pair of shots? I lean into the weapon's recoil—a shade higher—*Now!* Then I all but plunge headlong into the muck, a victim of the most awful realization that can stab a laboring wildfowler to the heart. A sharp, hollow "snap-snap"—both barrels—unloaded!

Oh, shame! Oh, alibis! Where are you now, in this my moment of agony and hour of high need? And to pull one like this on good Adler—there behind me—looking pitifully on! This is bitter—bitter! Fading goose "razzberries" pierce me like red-hot needles. Utter chagrin and one sickly swallow after another. To miss when one's time comes is bad enough; but this other business—this—this! But as my crestfallen eyes meet Adler's, something in them explodes. Face wreathed in smiles, he claps me on the back. "Why—nev' mind, ol' fren'—you know one tame las' wintah I mek moch longer walk—oh! by golly yaas—ver' moch longer—an' den I dooes de same damn t'ing—just too bad do'h—I say t'm'se'f—Adler—I bet ol' fren' ruins dem gooses—an' now—by golly—damn—look at dem fellahs." On pour the fine fellow's consolations during my long, sweaty silence. How intolerably hot the marsh has grown. Or maybe it's my red face? But Adler's merry one brings me to life. "Well—com' on—les' git goin', ol' fren'—by golly—hell dem ain d' onles' gooses in d' worl'—les' mek walk aroun' awhile—we fool dem fellahs som' mo'—but—" (and this time his eyes exploded again) "—dees tame plees load d' gun."

We potter aimlessly about the marsh. Not a goose note in the air. All I can do will be to tell the funny story and go into the routine. Then, just as even stout-hearted Adler is about willing to call it a morning, comes the break. A hiss—"Down—down queek—dey com'—in behin'." I collapse against the base of a friendly grass bunch. There they are—seven of them—low and straight over us if they hold their line. Wait just three beats more—if you slobber this chance, Big Boy, why start running. *Chug! Wham!* One snaky neck sent sprawling. A second down! Then, completely off-balance and overly excited, I let nature take its course and sit down in the mud and water. Feels good, too. Who cares? Adler is rejuvenated as he collects that pair. "By golly-damn, ol' fren'—didn' Adler tell you—didn' he say giv' d' ol' fren' tame—das whut I say—just giv' d' ol' fren' tame— he git 'em."

Catching breath, we plunge along the home stretch. Within a hundred yards a second warning from the alert Adler announces another trading squad of honkers. Determined to make amends, the gun overlaps two long, skinny black necks and then, swinging, downs a badly scared lunker standing practically still in midair. We divide the load and stagger onward. Who cares now for a soupy underfoot and heavy gun? What if it was all *my* fault? It is a good story *now*. What matters anything when Old Man General Average and Lady Luck decide to come on the party—arm in arm? Sweating and garlanded with geese we tumble into the pirogue. Stripped to the buff we bathe and let the wind do towel duty. We toast the finale in drafts of "drip."

"By golly-damn, o' fren'," chortles Adler, gesturing a soggy bandanna flamboyantly at a conquered goose land, "by golly-damn jus' giv' me an' ol' fren' plenny tame—us gits d' gooses." But, somewhere, stretched at ease and grateful for that face-saving break, I know full well that I shall endure many wakeful hours, looking along those empty gun tubes, dying a thousand deaths, while still wondering vaguely—how-th'-*hell*?

Bull Cans of the Delta

BY JIMMY ROBINSON

1938

N O BIRD, AMONG ALL THE DUCKS, FIRES THE IMAGINATION QUITE SO much as the big, silvery bull canvasbacks that tarry on the far reaches of Lake Winnipegosis until most of the other ducks are gone and the booming winds of October come hurtling down with the first bite of the advancing frost.

Then they arrow into the wind-bent canebrakes of the Delta Marsh at the south end of Lake Manitoba and fall on your decoys like fiery meteors. They have come far; and they can dally but a short while for they have far to go across river and mountain in the eastern seaboard.

Lucky is the hunter whose time and convenience can put him on the Delta at the precise instant of the bull can arrivals. Most cans operate on schedule and pull out in mid-October. But these rare, big silver bulls are unpredictable. He who hunts them must be brave, too, and thoughtless of his own comfort because the wind will be bitter and the cold will penetrate to his marrow.

It was on the evening of such a day that I sat in our *Sports Afield* Duck camp on the Delta, playing gin rummy with my old friend Walt Bush. Cec Browne and Hugh McKecknie of Winnipeg were kibitzing. Wife Clara and Edith were busy closing up camp and Walt and I were the only hunters in camp. Outside the clamor of the Arctic wind made us smugly content to be safely inside by a glowing stove and occasionally sampling the aroma of roast canvasback wafted in from the kitchen.

An unearthly medley of rattling and sputtering, climaxed by a terrible screech of brakes, rose above the thundering voice of the storm. Then it ended suddenly as it begun. Even the wind seemed still by comparison with the human juggernaut that burst through the door of our hunting shack. Walt Bush even dropped his gin-rummy hand to stare at the intruder.

It was Rod Ducharme, the giant, black-thatched French-Canadian from nearby St. Ambroise.

"Cheemy, da big bull seelver cans are here!" He had never learned to pronounce "Jimmy" like other people.

I had been getting ready to gin and this eruption threw me completely off my stride. "Will you drop?"

To Rod the game of gin was so much Greek. He probably never even heard me. "Yah, da bull seelver cans, Cheemy! De're here, ya betcha! In da mornin', by golly, we go get 'em, huh?"

I grinned, snatched a quick look at Bush's sour puss (he had been losing steadily), then I wiped the grin off and turned to Rod.

"What's here? I'm sleeping in the morning."

"Seelver cans, Cheemy. Da big bulls, I tol' ya about dem. Ya said t' be sure t' let ya know if dey come or ya break my neck. I come here fast as my truck go."

How Rod expected me to break his neck, set atop a 6-foot 3-inch frame carrying 280 pounds, I wouldn't know. But he seemed impressed. His skill as a Delta Marsh duck guide was as proverbial as his feats of strength, and they were legendary. Once, when my car was stuck in a heavy rain on a Delta dirt road, Rod and his brother Louie had merely carried it to solid footing.

"You call that wreck a truck?" I said. "Sounds more like a wagonload of loose bolts. And the only silver cans I know of are on the dump behind Ernest Lavallee's general store."

But I knew what he meant perfectly.

The year before, Rod had written me after we closed the duck camp. He told of being out on the marsh as it was freezing up and all other ducks were long gone. He saw some big flights coming in from the lake. They were cans—the biggest canvasbacks Rod had ever seen, and the whitest. They flashed in the sun like silver—"seelver cans."

I had at once put in a long-distance call to Bert Cartwright, chief naturalist for Ducks Unlimited at Winnipeg. "What do you know about overgrown canvasbacks that come into the Delta Marsh a week or two after most of the other ducks have gone?"

Bert had heard of them. He believed these outsize cans composed a flight from the most northerly part of the breeding range. Up there the long hours of daylight permitted them to develop more completely in body size and plumage. But few people had seen them. They came only after the big bays were making ice and the hunters had put their guns away. They stayed but briefly, then arrowed eastward for Chesapeake Bay.

"All right," I said to Rod. "Tomorrow it is—if I can get Bush away from this gin-rummy game."

Walt was skeptical. "Never heard of such flights before. I don't think they exist. But you'd have to break my leg to keep me off that marsh tomorrow."

At five the next morning Walt, Frank Lavallee and I were at Rod's house in St. Ambroise, thirty miles around the marsh to the east. Rod's wife, Rose, prepared a hearty breakfast of pancakes and home-smoked bacon.

"We take da truck t' da marsh," Rod announced. "Can't afford t' break down an' lose time gettin' dere dis mornin'."

I shuddered. Here was the world's most sublime optimism. What made this big meatball think his truck would hold together long enough to get us to the marsh?

Five minutes later we were careening madly along in "da truck," charging through an ice-slicked trail of matted cattails and cane. My fine breakfast was back in my mouth, my teeth rattling and I was bouncing like a dowager on her first bronc ride. The morning was jet black and I couldn't see Walt, but at intervals I could hear low moans escape him.

Rod had two boats cached at the end of a narrow channel that extended inland from the Bay. They were frozen solid in ice. He and Frank went to work with axes.

We shivered in temperatures a few degrees below freezing as we waited. The north wind, raw and biting, was still with us, but instead of roaring as it did the day before, it was only muttering. This should be a good day for "da seelver cans."

We pushed the boats out into the channel ice, then settled them through the crust, and Rod, in the lead boat with Frank, started belaboring the ice with a bludgeon of an oar made from a 2 by 6 plank. Hercules, in all his twelve labors, never worked so hard. We made progress. Before I knew it, open water gleamed ahead through the now lightening gloom. While we were still in the ice, Bush changed to Rod's boat, Frank to mine.

We had almost a mile of open water to cross, straight into the bite of the north wind. Our destination was a group of small islands near the northwest shore of the bay. The silver cans should be rafted there, in the lee.

Dawn came as we were making the traverse, and the first ducks began to appear. A few goldeneyes, two or three tight little bunches of bluebills. There were no canvasbacks. The sky was clearing as the north wind pushed the overcast rapidly before it. Though I had on my long-johns, by the time we made the islands my teeth were chattering like a telegraph key, and I was bemoaning the ill-starred day I first met Rod Ducharme. That Jonah, with parka off and hands bare, had worked up a nice sweat.

He assigned Frank and me to a small island with a nice growth of bulrushes and moved on to select another shooting stand. The islands curved away to the southwest and Rod headed in this direction almost downwind. Soon he and Walt were out of sight behind another island.

Forty yards from our blind, Frank tossed out canvasback decoys—big, white-backed blocks for late-season shooting. He mixed a few "bill" stools with them. Then we pulled rushes around us, and I snuggled into a stack of hay with which Rod, in one of his lucid moments, had equipped the boat. The wind couldn't reach us here, and as the red ball of sun began to crawl above the wide marsh, the blood started moving in my veins again.

Still no cans. A few bluebills darted in and one flight of goldeneyes swept past. I thought nostalgically of some canvasback shoots I had known.

Now, the canvasback is the king of ducks in the old hunter's book, and an epicure's delight in the bargain. He is the hardest of them all to hit as he hurtles hell-bent across the sky. The big bulls remind you of a jet fighter with their bullet heads and sharp, small, swept-back wings. Those wings claw air at such a furious clip that they send the big, fat bodies racing along faster than any other duck. They are straightaway speedsters made for a big track, and they never flare or dodge.

One of the wariest of ducks and usually suspicious of decoys, once he has made up his mind, the canvasback just bores right in like a dive bomber on a pin-point mission. His reliance always is on his speed, and he is apt to get so close before you can let off a shot that he makes your 12-gauge pattern look like a rifle slug. When he comes tearing over you quail-high at 70 miles-an-hour air speed (often 90 in relation to you on the ground), you can take a bow if you drop him.

Somebody fetched me a clobber on the back, hard, and I heard Frank's voice shouting. "Cans, Jimmy! Silver cans. North. A big flight heading this way. Wake up, Jimmy! Get set."

I swiveled for a look behind me. A big flock was bearing down, riding the north wind like the tail of a comet. They were over us and past before I could reach for my gun. Then they zoomed up and wide, circled well out and parked in open water. Were they Rod's silver cans? I began scratching in the hay for my glasses.

"They were silver cans," Frank assured me. "I thought they'd never come. I thought they'd probably left the marsh. If you hadn't slept so sound I would have said to leave this spot an hour ago. Now I think we're all right. More goin' to come." He kept his eyes on the northern sky toward Lake Manitoba. The flight had come from there. I began tossing Rod's blasted hay overboard and at last found my Bushnell glasses.

"They're comin'!" Frank said.

I saw a small cloud of dark specks which materialized almost instantly into a flock of cans—big ones—and they were heading straight for our blocks. They swept past, a long-shot high, and their great bodies flashed bright silver in the sun as I caught the quick whistle of their blurred wings. What music!

A few birds dipped a trifle; then they were over the bay. Frank gave them a *brrr, brrr,* and five silver cans sliced off in a tight bank. We hunched and tried to wish them in. Straightened out now, they came plummeting wide open to the blocks. I watched, mouth open. It was a sight to remember. Silver cans...big ones!

Somehow I got on the lead bird and pulled. It dropped, close in. Frank got it and handed it to me. I took it reverently. It was easily the biggest duck I had ever shot. And so white. I thought of Rod's description, flashing "seelver."

"More comin'!" Frank warned, and I hunched down. Three bunches were swooping in. They whooshed past and a dozen birds turned back to Frank's call. I took two big bulls and so did Frank. He marked where they drifted into the rushes.

They kept coming now, a dozen, five, three. They began to peel off regularly to the decoys, diving incredibly fast. We took only the biggest bulls.

"Never have I seen anything like this," Frank said. Nor had I. When he counted out our limit, we just sat there watching them in utter fascination. Several flocks were still slashing through the sky.

"Haven't heard no shootin' from Walt and Rod," Frank said, as we picked up the decoys. Now that I thought of it, I hadn't either. Could those two characters have missed the flight lane? We headed in the direction Rod had taken. The north wind was still blowing, tireless and raw.

Moving around a point, we beheld Walt. He was perched on a muskrat house swinging his arms to keep warm. Decoys were riding in front of his vacant blind, off to the right of the rat house. At intervals his arms would raise above his head and he would turn his face up to the heavens as if in supplication. It was positively mystifying.

As we got closer, I could make out a rapid-fire mumbling, then I was able to recognize a few phrases like "that no good"..."that bug-brain"..."that addlepated son of a ..." This was not like Bush, who is the most mild-mannered of men.

"Is something wrong?" I asked soothingly as we came up. "Where's Rod?"

That did it. Walt seemed to explode like a balloon of bubble gum. "Don't ever mention that name to me again!" he roared. "I'm going to leave him here for crow bait! That's all he's good for."

He stopped to get a new grip on his vocabulary. "I've been sitting here on this ant hill of a muskrat house for hours...and that peabrain's got my gun! He went away with it! I practically had to comb those silver cans out of my hair. I had to watch 'em plying in my decoys."

Another pause. "And what is he doing? Shooting silver cans all by himself. That's what he's doing. I heard a gun blasting all morning off in his direction—to the south. I tell you, it's more than a man can stand. Give me a gun. I'm going after that goat herder!"

I pushed quickly away from the rat house before Walt could climb aboard. My mind visualized a dozen possible contingencies—all bad. Here was a dilemma that had to be solved at once, without gunfire, and I was sure it would be much better if Bush was still enthroned on his muskrat pile when I came up with the doomed Rod. By this time, I reasoned, the rat house must be practically like home to Walt anyway. I closed my ears to his heart-rending cries.

I took an oar with Frank and we humped it downwind. Not far beyond Bush's throne, a considerable expanse of open water appeared with more islands on the far side. At another turn around an island, we saw a second figure on a rat house, also hysterically waving its arms.

"What goes on?" I groaned to Frank. "What is this strange affinity for Manitoba rat houses?"

It was Rod...who else?

"Start talking," I said as we edged into him. "You're in danger of having your hide shot as full of holes as a flour sieve."

Rod swallowed hard and rolled his eyes. His face wore a pitiful, pleading expression.

"Cheemy," he choked. "Cheemy, what have I deed?...Poor Walter...poor Walter! He want t' shoot dose beeg, seelver cans so bad!"

His agony was almost contagious. I think I felt a twinge of sorrow for him.

"I didn't mean it, Cheemy. Ya talk t' Walter. I am as eenocent as da new born babe. All at once, da oar she was gone...like dat! What could I do—sweem?"

Eventually we got his story. He had set Walt on a rat house while he put out decoys. In the process, one of his oars had slipped unnoticed from the boat and drifted out of sight. It was then he had discovered to his total dismay, that he had Walt's gun. He had tried desperately with one oar to buck the north wind back across that stretch of open water, but it was no use. All he had been able to do was wait for the wind to die or for Frank and me to come. He had spent an anguished morning.

As he had crouched dejectedly on his own rat house, screened by rushes, the big silver cans had begun pitching into his blocks. It had come to be more than any mortal could endure. So he had taken an occasional shot as the morning wore on.

Rod pointed in his boat. Ten big silver cans lay there.

We tied his boat behind ours, and he and Frank pulled against the wind toward Bush's rat house. As we came up, Rod suddenly stowed his oar and became extremely busy with the decoys, untangling anchor lines. I looked for Walt's gun and couldn't find it. There was only one place it could be...under the boat's hay pile. If bad came to worse, Rod figured to have time to start swimming anyway.

By now Walt had taken in the situation and greeted us, relaxed, with a grin. He was still balanced safely, with the sure feet of long acquaintance, upon his mud pinnacle. But he must have had a bad moment when the good-hearted Rod raised his eyes for the first time and said:

"Ya look all in, Walter. I got a whole limit o' seelver cans. Why don't ya take dem and den ya won't have t' stay and shoot any more?"

Armistice Day Storm

BY GORDON MACQUARRIE

1940

WINONA, MINNESOTA. THE WINDS OF HELL WERE LOOSE ON THE Mississippi Armistice Day and night.

They came across the prairies, from the south and west, a mighty, freezing, invisible force. They charged down from the river bluffs to the placid stream below and reached with deathly fingers for the life that beat beneath the canvas jackets of thousands of duck hunters.

They will tell you of this for years to come. They will recall how dad and brother were saved, and men who came through it alive together will look at each other with new understanding, as is the way with those who have seen death brush them close.

And eventually they will look back upon it as "the year of the big wind." To such a futile phrase will come what now seems to be the greatest hunting season disaster in Northwest history—and perhaps the greatest in the country's history.

"The dead in this area, 50 miles up and down the river, will likely come to 20 and we know of 16 men," say Winona newspapermen. So much for the statistics, which will be tallied for days as more of the missing are found and more upturned skiffs located.

The winds of hell it was that were abroad that frightful Monday and Tuesday and the winds of hell in high gear with the throttle wide open.

They came, those winds, with little warning of their intensity. After a poor duck hunting season along the Mississippi, duck hunters welcomed the wrath from the west. They liked it in its early stages. They tossed out their decoys and said, "Let 'er blow, that's what we've been waiting for."

They stationed themselves on tiny sand spits and boggy islands and the ducks came. The ducks came with the blast, riding it bewildered and headlong, so many a man, in the first mad hours, took his limit of birds easily. "Bushels of ducks we could have killed," said one survivor. "But we forgot about the ducks..."

Tuesday night on Louis Stantz' boat livery dock, a few miles out of town, 50 skiffs lay at anchor. The dock was snow covered and deserted. Seven dead ducks, frozen stiff, lay there, forgotten. The people who crowded to the dock all day Tuesday had other things to think of. Up the bank from that dock Tuesday came five dead men. The ducks lay there on the dock where the river goes by.

The wind did it. The furious wind that pierced any clothing, that locked outboard engines in sheaths of ice, that froze on faces and hands and clothing, so that even survivors crackled when they got to safety and said their prayers.

The wind did it. The cold was its ally. Mother Nature, sometimes a blue-eyed girl with corn-colored hair, was a murderous mistress Tuesday night on the Mississippi.

She caught thousands of duck hunters on Armistice Day—a holiday. She teased them out to the river and the marshes with her fine, whooping wind and then when she got them there she froze them like muskrats in traps. She promised ducks in the wind. They came all right. The survivors tell that, grimly, but by that time the duck hunters of the Mississippi were playing a bigger game—with their lives at stake.

By that time men along the Mississippi were drowning and freezing.

The ducks came and men died. They died underneath upturned skiffs as the blast sought them out on boggy, unprotected islands. They died trying to light fires and jumping and sparring to keep warm. They died sitting in skiffs. They died standing in river water to their hips, awaiting help.

They died trying to help each other and a hundred tales of heroism will be told, long after funerals are over.

Over in Winona General Hospital tonight lies Gerald Tarras, 17, a survivor. He is a big boy, nearly six feet, and strong. He had to be, to live. He saw his father, his brother and his friend die. He has not yet come to a full realization of what has happened, for grief is sometimes far in the wake of catastrophe.

Gerald Tarras, his head buried in a hospital pillow, his frost-blistered hands clutching nervously at the bedspread, tells part of it. Just a part. No need to ask him exactly where he was. Just out there on the river. Out on that hideous gut of water between the high bluffs near Winona, where the furies came on endlessly. Gerald tells it hazily, in a sort of open-eyed trance.

"We went out about 10 in the morning, the four of us. It was raining and warm. The wind came at noon. We began to worry. My father (Carl Tarras, 43, Winona) said we'd better go back. It got fierce. Then Bill Wernecke (his friend) died. He was cold. We boxed each other to keep warm. Bill died. I was holding him. He went 'O-h-h-h...' and he was gone.

"We were standing in water. We had a black Labrador dog with us. My brother (Ray, 16) died next. Yes, he died. I knew he was dead. He was cold. An airplane flew over and I moved my arm. It saw us. Then my Dad died. They took me off in the government tug and gave me some coffee. They gave me some whisky."

In a Winona restaurant sits Max Conrad, aviator, sipping coffee with Bobby Bean, his assistant. He tells his story very badly, for he is a modest man.

Conrad took a Cub training plane with a top speed of 75 miles an hour and led the government tug *Throckmorton* and other rescue boats to marooned hunters on the river. He flew all day, sometimes with Bean, sometimes alone.

He would fly his plane repeatedly over a spot where hunters were caught and the rescue boats would know where to go. He would toss out packages containing sandwiches, whisky, cigarettes and matches. He would open the door of his plane and, with the motor cut, shout down to the men below to "hang on, help is coming." He would route the little plane time after time through channels over which marooned hunters could follow in skiffs.

Conrad tells a poor story, for he is modest. Harold Eastman, of Winona, meter superintendent for the Mississippi Valley Public Service Company, tells Conrad's story—and his own—better.

"I was hunting with R.J. Rice and Richard Guelzer. The wind caught us on a bog. The oarlock broke. Dick said 'we camp here.' We turned up the skiff for a windbreak. We tried to light a fire but everything was wet and it was too windy. At 9:30 a.m Tuesday we heard a plane. We fired our guns. The plane did not see us. At noon the plane saw us. It was Conrad. I know him. He saved our lives.

"Conrad yelled down to us from the open door of the plane: 'Sit tight! We'll get you out of here!' In five minutes he was back with a tin of food and cigarettes and dropped it. He kept flying over us, then hollered down 'start out and go in the direction I am!'

"We took our shotguns and started. Conrad said 'Leave your guns and take the skiff.' We did. We broke through ice several times, then we would hang onto the skiff and work it along the new ice. The *Throckmorton* picked us up. Conrad saved our lives. I feel all right except for the smoke in my eyes from the fire."

Over at the Conrad home four small daughters, Judy, Jane, Betsy and Molly and their mother waited for their dad. He came home all right. Then he slept hard, for today he took up the patrol again—looking for three skiffs and men, dead or alive.

Conrad says the river shambles was bad because pan ice piled up on banks and islands, so skiffs could not get through. He says he saw dogs alone on boggy islands. He says "the guys who used their heads built windbreaks with their skiffs and then built fires." He says a lot of fellows "lost their heads." He is a kind man. He will not even guess at how many are dead. It will take days to find out, he says.

Some of the dead brought in, like those at the Louis Stantz river landing and boat livery, had their faces and hands blue and bruised. It was not possible to park a car at this spot for the cars of anxious relatives—waiting. The bruises, they said, were from the men in the bitter night beating each other to keep warm—shadow boxing and sparring, likely even when their hands were frozen clubs and were without feeling.

Thus they died on the Mississippi on the night following Armistice Day.

Out of town a way is Calvin Volkel. He helped bring in 17. Likely saved their lives. He was sleeping Tuesday night, in the back of his tavern. He awakened and talked:

"At 9 Monday night it began to look bad to me. I needed a good big fast boat to save those fellows out on the river. I was looking especially for Eddie Whitten. I went to town and got Al Squires. We got a 12-horse outboard and started out. It swamped. Then we rowed, each with a pair of oars, shouting to each other 'one-two, one-two' to keep the stroke.

"Our backs became ice coated. I had put on an aviator's suit. We got to the place I knew Eddie was hunting. There were 16 others there! We got Eddie back ashore, and called the police for help. We needed good oarsmen. The men on the island were lying on top of the fire. Not beside it. On top of it. They lay on top of it!

"They had been shooting off boughs for fuel with shotgun shells. Two men would shoot at once and knock off a bough. I came back and brought off a fellow named Anderson. I brought a hatchet for wood, and whisky. Then we worked it this way. Every man who got ashore in the rowboat went back and took off another, and the one he took off went back and took off the next.

"It was in what we call Dark Slough..."

Also in the hospital is 14-year-old Ray Sherin, whose father, Torge Sherin, was in the rescue party that saved him from the bottomlands death after an all-night search.

The boy has a frozen purplish foot, encased in a special tent. He is not coherent. His eyes stare wildly at the ceiling and sweat stands on his smooth, boyish forehead. He will be all right. His foot may be all right, doctors say. He is very lucky.

Next to him in the room is Bob Stephen, Winona, with a frozen hand. He will be all right. Older, he tells the story that will be told up and down this river for years to come—"the river, the wind, the cold, the fear—and rescue."

Hundreds made it ashore under their own steam and men stood, white and shaking on solid ground and looked back on a river running four-foot waves. They came ashore and home and put down their guns and looked at them hardly believing there was a safe, warm world and they were in it.

There were long prayers by the Mississippi's banks Tuesday, the day after Armistice, when the ducks came and men died.

Red Legs Kicking

BY ALDO LEOPOLD

1946

WHEN I CALL TO MIND MY EARLIEST IMPRESSIONS, I WONDER whether the process ordinarily referred to as growing up is not actually a process of growing down; whether experience, so much touted among adults as the thing children lack, is not actually a progressive dilution of the essentials by the trivialities of living. This much at least is sure: my earliest impressions of wildlife and its pursuit retain a vivid sharpness of form, color, and atmosphere that half a century of professional wildlife experience has failed to obliterate or to improve upon.

Like most aspiring hunters, I was given, at an early age, a single-barreled shotgun and permission to hunt rabbits. One winter Saturday, *en route* to my favorite rabbit patch, I noticed that the lake, then covered with ice and snow, had developed a small "airhole" at the point where a windmill discharged warm water from the shore. All ducks had long since departed southward, but I then and there formulated my first ornithological hypothesis: if there were a duck left in the region, he (or she) would inevitably, sooner or later, drop in at this airhole. I suppressed my appetite for rabbits (then no mean feat), sat down in the cold smartweeds on the frozen mud, and waited.

I waited all afternoon, growing colder with each passing crow, and with each rheumatic groan of the laboring windmill. Finally, at sunset, a lone black duck came out of the west, and without even a preliminary circling of the airhole, set his wings and pitched downward.

I cannot remember the shot; I remember only my unspeakable delight when my first duck hit the snowy ice with a thud and lay there, belly up, red legs kicking...

Memories of Mallards

BY MARTIN BOVEY

1947

MINNESOTA HAS GOOD MALLARD SHOOTING, BUT I HAD MY FIRST REAL fun with mallards in Manitoba.

I had taken a year off from college to winter in Northern fur posts and was living at a little post called Oxford House, which stands on the canoe route the fur brigades from the Far West followed in going from Norway House at the head of Lake Winnipeg to York Factory on Hudson Bay.

The time was September 1922. Later there would be snow and ice and dog-team travel, but now golden leaves hung on the birch, and the water was open for canoes. Bound on a moose hunt with Isaac Mason, a full-blooded Cree, my seventeen-foot freighter raced down the sparkling rapids of Trout River.

At the western end of Knee Lake we pitched our tent.

When we left camp in the morning, my .250-3000 Savage and 20-gauge Winchester pump were loaded and ready.

Quietly we cruised the shores of spruce-rimmed bays and poked our way up tiny creeks. Our eyes swept the marshland which flanked the stream, studied the willow clumps, explored the shadows reaching out from the edge of the timber. Our ears strained for the sound of splashing water or the snapping of a twig.

At last the creek was no wider than the canoe, and behind me as we floated motionless I could feel Isaac coming slowly to his feet, knew his keen eyes were scanning the marsh. At last he whispered, *"Nemona moosa; seeseepuck pukko* [No moose; just ducks]."

My hand shifted from the rifle to the shotgun, and we moved forward again. Then we rounded a bend, and there was a confused splashing, a protesting "quack," a rush of wings, and thirty or more mallards roared up from a circle of open water.

I pulled myself to my feet and emptied the gun. Three birds slapped the water, and I went overboard to pick them up. Two were dead, but the third was thrashing around in water not over six inches deep. I headed directly for the cripple but did not watch it closely. Before I reached the spot where the bird had landed, the thrashing had ceased, and I found only a few feathers.

Isaac shoved the canoe toward me, then rolled up his trouser legs and stepped over the side. Together we took up the search. The rushes were so short and sparse, the water so shallow and clear, it seemed impossible to lose that bird. Yet at the end of twenty minutes we gave up and paddled down the creek with only two ducks.

I had begun to learn something about the cunning of the mallard.

For three days we hunted moose and shot jumped mallards. On the evening of the last day we put a bunch of birds out of a little marsh just at sundown. The water was covered with feathers, so we shoved the canoe into the short grass and waited. Back they came, winging in over the spruce and sideslipping down a golden sky. I killed one of them and waded after him.

Then suddenly the air was filled with mallards, and the sequence of events is blurred. I recall sinking hip-deep into mud and water and struggling to extricate myself, while trying frantically to get shells out of a trouser pocket that was under water. I remember fumbling to load an empty gun, while mallards tumbled out of that golden sky to land not twenty yards away. I remember struggling against the mud, getting almost free of it, then sinking back when I ceased fighting mud long enough to shoot. Finally gun and pocket were both empty, and I floundered over to the canoe, with ducks pouring out of the sky, to find we had left the rest of the shells at camp.

Back at camp I rolled my eiderdown out by the fire and lay in it watching Isaac putting himself to bed. He spread one of his two small rabbit-skin robes on the ground, placed a pack-sack of clothing for a pillow, and lay down on his back with knees drawn up and head so high that he was almost in a sitting position. Then he pulled his hat far down over his eyes, drew the second diminutive rabbit skin over him, and called out, *"Minou tipiscow* [Good night]!" and moved no more.

Isaac had been asleep a long time, but I still lay looking up at the stars and seeing again those ducks tumbling into the pothole. Black spruce fingering the golden west, and out of the west the mallards coming. Black bodies on black wings—black against gold. Northern mallards flighting in for the night to the Northern "honey hole."

South Dakota gave me my first taste of mallard shooting over decoys.

Father and I were working out of Breton, dividing our attention between the pheasants and the ducks. Up near Kidder a friendly farmer put us on to a ten-acre slough in the center of a full section of corn.

It was late afternoon of a balmy mid-November day when we first tramped in. The slough was bare of birds, and the sun went down without our having fired a shot. We were nearly back to the car when we saw them coming out of the west, high-flying arrows that broke to bits and came tumbling down the afterglow to the slough.

At dawn we were back, sneaking in through the corn, on frost-firm ground. The water was black. Then a cornstalk snapped, and the surface of the slough became a wild, protesting mass, swirling up and away to the sanctuary of Sand Lake.

Certainly not less than five thousand birds had used our "honey hole" that night.

Hunting pheasant that day, we kept a sharp eye on the weather. Once a cloud bank began building up, but it melted away under a bright warm sun, and the wind blew lazily out of the southwest. At sundown we sat in our car and watched the mallards stream in and spiral down to the corn-rimmed slough.

Not till noon of our last day did the weather change. Then the wind swung north, and the sky turned gray. We lunched as we drove, and as we parked the car and started in through the corn three mallards winged over our heads and coasted down to the slough. The signs were right.

Another hour and a sea would be running on Sand Lake.

"They ought to come early this afternoon," we agreed and moved on through the corn. Eight mallards jumped as we came to the slough.

From the north side of the slough a point ran out—a thumb thrust into a bowl of dirty gray water. There were tall weeds out to the first joint, but the tip was bare save for foot-high grass. Father settled himself in the weeds, using a pail we had brought along for a seat. The location was definitely second-rate, but at seventy-five you can't lie on your face and come to your knees in a hurry to shoot.

"Get out there and let me watch you hit them," Father insisted. "I'll try to get any that cross the point."

"We should have built a blind on the tip," I said as I poked weeds into the mud around his pail. "Three days would have given them time to get used to it."

Four crude decoys from the farmer's shed floated out front of me as I lay on my stomach on the point. The ground felt like a cake of ice, and the wind blew up my back.

Then they started coming, and I forgot the cold. They circled twice high in the air, searching for any hint of trouble. The kink in my neck was a full-grown ache when they swung far off to the south. I dropped my head to relieve the strain, then slowly raised it again. They looked big as geese coming in, sailing on set wings into the eye of the wind. I jerked myself to my knees and fired twice.

They flared and paid off down the wind untouched.

The next flock saw me move in the grass as I twisted a bit to ease the strain. I fancy those keen-eyed rascals can see a meadow mouse twitch his whiskers. Waiting for mallards where cover is thin is no game for a fidgety fellow.

There were ten in the next bunch and six in the third. They acted exactly as the first flock had—circled high, swung wide to the south, then came drifting down, riding the wind on rigid wings, growing bigger and bigger until they looked immense. But when they had gone there were four more empty shells in the grass and not one feather drifting down from that cold gray sky.

A pair came, circling lower. As they swung behind me I heard Father shoot and rolled over in time to see a limp form land with a thump in the weeds.

Five minutes later I missed clean on a fourth flock. I was plumb fed up. I walked back and picked up Father's bird—a fat, sleek greenhead.

"What the devil's wrong with me today?" I asked as I held that fine drake up for Father to admire.

"Try my gun," he said, offering me his beautiful 12-gauge Purdy.

I fondled my little 20 double. "Nothing wrong with this gun," I assured him. "If you were out there, you'd knock them cold with a .410. They practically land on my hat."

But when the next bunch came I began to wonder if the range really was so short. Didn't they shrink in size as I came up on them?

Thinking it over, I began to realize that against gray sky ducks look bigger than they are. And here I was lying down, my eyes almost on the surface of the water. I remembered how, crouched in a Currituck battery, incoming ducks had looked simply tremendous, how surprised I had often been to come to my feet and find them still out over the foot of the stool.

When the next flock came I let them keep on coming. My neck muscles were crying in protest as those five old busters came sliding downstairs, but not until they seemed about to hit me in the face did I grab my gun. A second later a drake and a hen were on their backs near the decoys.

I got three more with the next four shells.

"You've got the range all right now," Father declared as I brought him a bird he had crippled.

The wind died away, and only one more flock came to me. At sundown I had six birds. If it had not taken so long to relearn an old lesson, I should most probably have ended with my limit.

"This business about being too old for such a trip is nonsense," I told Mother over the telephone. "His notion that just because he'll be eighty next month he's not up to this sort of stuff is silly. You make him come. It'll be the best shoot we ever had."

"It would be wonderful," her voice came back. "You leave it to me."

Mother's salesmanship is tops, so five days later I was waiting in the lee of the elevator as No. 3's headlight stabbed through the darkness.

The long train rolled to a stop. The brakeman's light flashed on the porter's white coat, and as I ran I saw the familiar old green duffel bag, the gun, and the package of shells come down the steps from the lighted vestibule.

"Welcome to Brooks, Alberta—and mallards," I said as we shook hands. "Since when does Mother have to sell you on the idea of going hunting?"

"She's a pretty good salesman," Father declared.

"You won't regret it," I assured him, leading the way to the car.

We piled his stuff into the rear end and climbed aboard.

"This is Stonewall Jackson," I told him. "Make, Pontiac; vintage, 1934. Call her Stonewall because she stops as though she had hit one. Brakes grab a bit, but I'm learning the trick. Can stop her in four feet now instead of all at once."

"Where do we breakfast?" he wanted to know.

"D.U. cabin. Neither the hotel nor the Chinaman's is open until seven-thirty."

We rattled up the main street and swung around to the Ducks Unlimited cabin, which had been home to me during ten weeks of photographing.

"How about sleeping a couple of hours?" I suggested as we dug into the oranges. "No need to be out at sunrise here in order to get a good shoot. You're probably tired after two nights on the train."

"I came out to shoot mallards," he declared, "but I must say I didn't sleep too well last night. An upper is a little crowded with half a case of shells in it. I didn't dare leave them under the berth."

"Out here the fellows keep their shotgun shells in the vault and their War Bonds in the desk drawer," I told him.

We finished breakfast and poured his hunting clothes out of the duffel bag. He got into the old gray shirt that he has worn ever since I can remember, pulled on the breeches of the whipcord hunting suit V. L. & A. made for him thirty years ago.

"When I bought this suit they told me it would last a lifetime," he said, pointing with pride to the innumerable places where invisible menders and less skillful workmen had toiled over rents and tears.

"If you take it easy crawling through barbed-wire fences, it should last until you're ninety," I told him.

He slipped into his vest and strung his watch chain from pocket to pocket. The lead disk I had worn around my neck in World War I was on the chain next to his knife.

"Still carry the old dog tag, do you?" I remarked.

"It's my good-luck piece," he said.

I held his coat for him and commented on the leather elbow patches.

"Don't you remember the time I hurried too much trying to retrieve a pheasant you knocked down near the School House Slough?" he laughed. "I thought you'd have to borrow a pair of wire cutters to get me free of that fence."

To him the patches on that old suit were like a diary. No wonder he was sad when any part of his hunting or fishing outfit *had* to be replaced. His rubber stockings, shell bag, leader box, fly book, Hardy reel—even his green wool necktie—had all shared with him a host of adventures.

"New things raise no memories," he keeps telling me.

Ready at last, we climbed into the car and hurried north.

It was just sunrise as we rolled through a gate in a barbed-wire fence and headed off across the sagebrush prairie.

"I call it Hopi Lake," I explained, pointing ahead to a horseshoe slough, "because Hopi and I found it when we were camped up north a few miles in our trailer in '41. I've made pictures here, but there hasn't been a shot fired on the lake this season. See that?"

For a long time he couldn't, but then he picked them up as their wings caught the early sunlight. Big flocks of mallards coming from the east, from an all-night banquet in the grainfields, to sleep it off in Mallard Heaven on Hopi Lake.

We parked on the edge of the water, and I got the duck boat out of the rushes.

"Keep your eyes open," I ordered as I started poling down the lake. "You might see some ducks before long."

We hadn't gone more than a few hundred yards before they began getting out of Mallard Heaven. Father's eyesight is not what it used to be, and he saw only the few that swung over us, but he could hear the din as they left the water.

"Good Lord," he said. "You do have some ducks out here!"

We poled into that shallow little bay, shoved the boat into a clump of heavy rushes, and I started setting the decoys. The water was about ten inches deep and covered with feathers. They really liked this place.

The wind, what there was of it, being out of the north, I strung the decoys along the west side of the blind so that we could shoot with the sun at our backs.

A couple of bunches looked us over before I was back in the boat and had laid an oar across the gunwales for Father to sit on. I wanted him high so his feet would be under him. He was loading his gun when six green-winged teal plunked into the decoys.

"We're hunting mallards," I told him as I screwed a telephoto lens onto my movie camera. "Steady! Here they come!"

They were glorious in the morning light, driving high over us, heading west and on west till I thought they were passing us up. Then they started sliding down in a long, slow swing that brought them around into the wind, and suddenly they were there, hovering over the decoys, and the sun was bright on green heads and orange feet.

But Father had been looking too far to the left, and they were going away in a wild, mad rush when finally his gun went off.

A moment later a flock hurtled over the blind and was gone before he could squeeze the trigger.

"Pintail," I said. "We don't want them anyway."

Then the mallards really started. They followed the same pattern—passing high overhead westbound, then banking around and sailing in for the decoys. It was terrific! Sometimes there were a couple of hundred of them over us. Twice a dozen or more dropped right in among the outer decoys.

I made a few pictures, but mostly I tried to help Father see them. "Coming in at nine o'clock," I would whisper. "Now they're at ten, eleven. Right over you now. Take 'em!"

But he just couldn't find them, or if he did it was too late.

He must have shot a dozen shells without knocking out a feather.

"I simply can't see them in this bright light," he kept telling me. "I wish it would get cloudy."

He always sees better on gray days, when the light does not dazzle him, but today there wasn't a cloud in the sky. I was already down to my shirt, and the sun was getting brighter and hotter.

Then I had an idea. "We'll move to that island of rushes," I said, indicating a patch twenty yards to the north.

Five minutes later I had the boat in place and was busy shifting the decoys. I set them dead to leeward. Now the mallards would have to come straight into his face.

Two minutes after we were squared away, about forty threw their feet at us. Father saw that flock all right, but his 6's did no damage.

"You're so eager to have me hit something that I'm all tensed up," he said when he had missed a couple more shots. "You shoot, and let me sit awhile and relax. I'm not used to being swamped by mallards."

By the time I had killed three or four, he had smoked his pipe out and was less wound up.

I stowed my gun in the bow, and Father picked up his Purdy. Five mallards came down in a long glide.

"Straight over the stern," I whispered. "Just like the last bunch. Now!"

His second shot folded up a drake that landed stone-dead in the decoys.

"What a beauty!" he said as I waded back with that fine old greenhead.

"Pretty well greened up for so early in the season," I said, smoothing down his head and neck feathers. "You're over the hurdle now. Let's collect a few of these fellows for Mother."

He killed clean with his next two shots. The tension was gone, and his eyes were behaving better. It was like old times.

I picked up my 20-gauge.

"I'll work with you on a few bunches," I said.

We passed up a couple of teal. Then a hat-high single hurtled over from behind, and I shot fast as he zoomed.

"Pintail," I said as the bird hit the water. "Sorry to break the rules."

A dozen mallards roared in, and we cut loose together. He pulled one down from the left of the flock, and I took two from the right. They were all drakes and all stone-dead.

"We never had a better shoot than this," he exclaimed, tickled as a ten-year-old. "It's marvelous!"

It was better than that. It was like living over in a couple of hours those countless, golden days that thirty-eight years of hunting together had brought us.

We had a long smoke. Things seemed about over for the morning.

Then out of nowhere they came, and suddenly the air was filled with mallards coasting in on cupped wings, mallards wheeling into the wind, hovering over the decoys, driving over us from behind, and far above more mallards, like fighter planes flying top cover for the bombers.

"Don't shoot," I whispered. "This is too good to spoil."

He saw the ones that were trying to land on our hats and the ones that plunked onto the water just beyond the decoys. I told him about the ones banking around down-wind and the big bunches high above us.

I tried a few pictures, but it was no use. I couldn't hold a bird in the finder. It was too thrilling having him there to share a day like this.

"Let's take 'em," I shouted, and we let fly at a bunch of beauties hanging over the decoys.

We didn't touch a feather.

"We've done that before," Father laughed.

"Not often," I laughed back, thinking of the regularity with which he had pulled them out of the sky in younger days.

At eleven o'clock we picked up. We had ten drakes, three hens, and my pintail. They made a lovely string. There had been days when we had headed home with bigger bags, but none that had ever represented more of a sheer joy of living that comes to old shooting pals on gunning days.

You Got to be Crazy to be a Duck Hunter

BY ROBERT RUARK

1953

THE DAY WAS SLATY, AND THE WIND WHIPPED THE SOUND INTO A FROTH. The clouds tumbled low and menacing, with a suspicion of snow to come. My ears seemed to catch fire when we came into the warmth of the house, and little droplets clung to my nose. My hands were wrinkled from cold water and as red as radishes. There was no feeling whatsoever in my feet, inside their muddy hip boots. I was never happier in my life.

"Just look at the pair of us," the Old Man said. "Froze stiff, probably going to die of pneumonia, wet, muddy, and miserable, and both of us grinning at each other like Chessy cats. We're crazy as loons, but then you got to be a little crazy to be a duck hunter. Nobody in his right mind would get up before dawn to sit and freeze in a blind on the off chance that some old buck mallard full of fish will fly close enough to get missed."

We had had quite a day. The wind that tumbled the waters had broken up the enormous rafts of ducks—you know, the ones that sit so maddeningly in the middle of the bay on a bluebird day. The low ceiling had 'em well down within range, and the wind had also blown the water out of the little secret pools. As happens only once in a while, the ducks were hunting for a place to sit, and they came to the decoys like cats to catnip.

"There ain't nothing," the Old Man said, "as smart as a black mallard when the weather's with him. He can see from here to Japan, and he can spot a phony decoy from a mile high, which is generally where he's at. But you let that weather change and blow up a lot of wind, and mebbe a little snow, and there ain't nothing as stupid as a duck. That goes for geese too, and I reckon the old honker is generally smarter than the duck. You get the right weather, and you have to bat 'em out of the blind. How about that fellow today that lost his mama?"

The Old Man was talking about a two-thirds-grown Canada goose that had strayed off from the V, up there in the dirty gray sky, and was making pitiful sounds. The Old Man had snickered at it. "Some of them big fellows are tougher'n whitleather," he said, "but this little fellow will be real fine for your grandma's oven. See, now, how I call him down. I am going to make some noises like his mama."

He got out his goose call and began to talk like a goose's mama. I have no way of writing down the sounds, but you could see that lost goose stick his neck down as soon as the Old Man's wheedling call reached him. He dropped his flaps and came down out of the sky like a hawk after a fish. He came practically into the blind, and I took a whack at him and discovered I had done one of those things you do once in a blue moon—shot my gun dry and plumb forgot to load her. The goose took off, and the Old Man said, "Don't worry. Load her up and I'll call him back. Shoot him good this time, or we'll have him in the blind with us."

He set up a gabble again, and the goose turned and came right back to the blind. This time I was loaded with 4's, and I delivered a mess right into his head and neck, and he came down like a rock.

"It's a mean trick," the Old Man said, "but you can always call a lost young goose with that mama noise. And they do eat better than the old ones."

The Old Man had shot behind live decoys in his time; it had been legal. You'd have a hen mallard tied to a stick that was stuck in the mud, and she had more conversation than a woman. She would stand on her tail and flutter her wings and talk sexy to the passing flocks, and they would turn on a dime and come in with their feet hanging out and wings cocked. There is no easier target than a fat mallard or pintail grabbing for water with his feet and his wings locked.

Well, the wind stirred the water to a devil's broth, the ducks poured in, and we filled our tickets. The mallards were the prettiest, of course, but it was the pins that the Old Man admired most. "The French duck is gaudy," he said, "with his yellow shoes and all those colors of his plumage and that big yellow shovel for a bill, but you can't trust him. He's a puddle duck, and if you don't give him enough grain he'll double-cross you and eat himself sick on fish, just like any old merganser. But not the pin. Look at the gentlemanly clothes he wears, while the mallard looks like a pool-hall sharpie. You'll never find a pintail eating fish. He'd starve first.

"I know you read a lot about the canvasback and how fine he is to eat, and how all the politicians in his neck of the woods won't eat anything but terrapin and canvasback at their big dinners, but the old can ain't got any more morals than a mallard about eating fish. The only big duck I can absolutely certify is the pintail. And amongst the little ducks, I never ate a fishy teal so far. As a matter of fact, when all is said and done, for the dinner plate you can't beat a teal.

"Ducks..." the Old Man said. "Now, take teal. They fly faster'n greased lightning, and on a teal in a tail wind you got to lead him thirty foot. But they will skitter in amongst the decoys right while you're blam-blamming at a bunch of other ducks, and swim around like they owned the pond. It don't make sense. Once you got a teal on the water, you practically can't scare him off it, 'less you shoot at him."

I mentioned casually that we seemed to waste an awful lot of ammunition shooting cripples, and that the few belts I had at teal, sitting, usually resulted in the teal's taking off to Mexico.

"I can't explain it all to you," the Old Man replied. "But you got to remember that a duck in the water is like an iceberg. About eight-tenths of him is under water, and water sheds shot like a tin roof. You practically got to hit him in the head to kill him, because his wings are folded and the wing feathers and the back feathers'll shed shot just like water. I've noticed that in all sorts of bird shooting it's a heap easier to shoot a flying bird than a sitting bird, all question of sportsmanship aside. A flying bird opens up his vulnerable parts, his softer-feathered parts, and he spreads his wings enough to give you a chance to bust one. Sitting, wings folded, he's damned near armor-plated.

"And there's one thing more: standing in a boat or a blind and aiming down at water does something to the shotgun pattern. Don't ask me what or how, because I dunno. But shotguns were made to shoot either up or straight out, not down. A smarter man than me could probably tell you. All you got to do to believe it, though, is to watch, on the next cripple, how irregular the pellets strike the water."

The Old Man and I were not steady permanent-blind boys. He was against it. Said the ducks got to associate the blind with noise and the sudden death of a relative, and would skirt it just enough to pass outside good range, unless it was such a dirty day that they completely lost their minds and became as crazy as duck hunters.

"The way to do it," he said, "is in a *bateau*. The Cajuns call it 'pirogue,' but *bateau*—which is French for 'boat,' my ignorant young friend—is a flat-bottomed skiff. You pole her out to where the wind and water seem right, and stick her in a bunch of reeds or rushes, and you cut yourself some *roseaux*, or *tules*—which is French and Spanish, respectively, for 'reeds,' and build your blind around your boat. You always wear a khaki hat to match the reeds, and you keep your face down until you are ready to shoot, because anything but a teal or a bluebill will see your white face or bald head from as high up as he can fly, and all the decoys and calls in the world won't get him down—unless, like I said, the weather's so lousy they've quit caring. You peep through a little hole in the reeds, and you let them circle your blind twice, unless it's a very clear day, and on the second circle they'll decoy like cream.

"A man with patience will kill an awful lot of ducks, because when they drop those feet and lock those wings you get the first one automatic, and all you got to do is like the Cajun said—aim at the nose when the other half is climbing. A mallard looking for sky when he's just left the water is not really moving very fast, because he's fighting for altitude and his centrifugal force is all out of kilter."

I didn't ask the Old Man what centrifugal force was. Like I've said so many times, if you asked him he was apt to tell you, and it would take an hour or so, and everybody from Julius Caesar to Einstein would get mixed up in it.

The Old Man read me a lot of lectures about trash ducks and ducks that ought to be conserved. He wouldn't ever let me shoot a wood duck, because he said they were too pretty and too little, and besides, there weren't enough of them to go around. He never would shoot a gray duck or a spoonbill if anything else was flying, and when I complained that they looked like hen mallards at a distance he said I ought to sharpen up my eyesight or quit mingling with grown men. I took a crack at a swan once, and the Old Man took a crack at me. He said they weren't any good to eat and there were dodlimbed few of them around and what there was ought to be left in peace.

Come to think of it now, even in those days of practically nonexistent game wardens, abundant game, and large limits, one thing stands out about the Old Man. He never willingly took more fish or game than we could eat or give away, and he never shot a gun—or allowed me to shoot a gun—just to hear it go off and kill something useless. He was absolutely firm about leaving a nucleus of game, whether it was quail or deer, and of never shooting females if the females were identifiable. This sex definition did not, of course, apply to quail or ducks, because unless it's mallards close at hand or a quail flying at you, there just isn't time enough to tell.

But it seems to me I've been rattling around all over the place, and what I really wanted to concentrate on was what the Old Man said first, which is that it takes a crazy man to be a duck hunter. As we stood in front of the fire, steaming out our wet clothes, after having risked death by drowning, exposure, and pneumonia, after having been up since black night, after having rowed and poled miles, after having frozen fingers setting out decoys and having frozen feet from inactivity—after having been uncomfortable constantly in the quest for a few pounds of bird meat that I didn't like to eat too terribly well, I concluded one thing: if you have to be crazy to hunt ducks, I do not wish to be sane.

Christmas Hunt

BY TED TRUEBLOOD
1960

EACH SECTION OF AMERICA HAS ONE SPORT THAT IS, MORE THAN ANY other, associated with the holiday season. In some states it is deer hunting. In the South it is quail or turkey hunting. In the Pacific Northwest it is steelhead fishing. In numerous places it is rabbit hunting. Where I live and in many other regions as well, the sport of Christmas time is duck hunting.

Boys out of school go duck hunting. Town men with a few days' vacation use them duck hunting. Country men, enjoying their slack season, go duck hunting. More new guns and coats and mittens and boots are initiated during the week before Christmas and New Year's than at any other time of the year.

One of my most vivid duck-hunting memories concerns a certain Christmas afternoon. I was a grown man of thirteen or fourteen but my little brother was only seven or eight. After we had opened our presents in the predawn darkness, lighted the candles on the tree, and eaten breakfast, Mother got busy in the kitchen. Our country doctor and his wife were coming for dinner. We boys were spared the usual chores—our father did them all that morning—and we went out and wore the newness off our gifts. Eventually dinner was ready and it was wonderful, as Christmas dinners always were, and Dr. and Mrs. Hopper brought still more presents to be opened.

After dinner the grownups sat and talked. Burtt and I were outside playing when I noticed that ducks were flying to the barley stubble across a forty behind the house. I hurried in and asked if I could go hunting. I wasn't allowed to hunt on Sunday, and I wasn't sure about Christmas.

To my delight, my mother said, "Sure. Go ahead. Maybe the Hoppers would like a few ducks to take home."

I got my gun and a pocketful of shells and set out across the fields toward the barley stubble. It was a bright, sparkling winter day with about four inches of snow on the ground. The colors of a flock of mallards passing overhead toward the barley were so vivid in the brilliant light that I was tempted to shoot at them, but they were far out of range.

On the way I watched the ducks circling the 10-acre barley patch and decided that the ditch at the upper edge would provide the best spot in which to hide. I hiked toward it as hard as I could go, frightening away several hundred feeding mallards and a few pintails as I moved along.

I found a spot on the upper bank where I could sit on a tussock of grass, facing the field, with my feet in the ditch and my back against a weed clump. I dragged up more weeds and put them on each side of my seat, and I was ready.

When mallards are feeding in the stubble they select one particular field, and all the ducks in that area work on it until they clean it up. Then they pick another, possibly several miles away, and feed there until the spilled grain is gone. I felt sure that I wouldn't have long to wait, and I was right.

The first flock of possibly fifty birds came within a few minutes. They circled several times, never close, and lit near the far side of the field. I could soon hear their contented chatter as they shoveled up the spilled barley kernels from beneath the snow. The next flock came over on one of its circles, the green heads of the drakes glistening in the sunlight, but they were too high.

Finally a dozen birds swept past, directly in front of me and low over the stubble. I killed a drake and missed another by shooting under him as they flared. Quickly retrieving my duck, I crouched between my weeds once more and admired his plumage. A mallard drake that is dropped in dry stubble or on snow is a different bird from one that falls into water. He looks much bigger because his feathers are not matted down, and his colors are bright and clean.

I was still admiring him when two flocks began to circle simultaneously. One of them passed directly overhead, though rather high; so I fired only the full-choke barrel, and killed another drake. The solid thump as he hit the sparkling snow, the wonderful odor of the wisp of smoke that curled upward as I broke the gun to reload, and the remaining ducks, rapidly becoming black specks against the dark-blue winter sky, are fresh in memory yet. It was a perfect afternoon, and the mallards were still coming and still circling when I heard my father call.

By that time I had five ducks, all greenheads. I tied them with a scrap of bootlace, threw them over my shoulder, and walked down to the house, hoping to come back to the field but resigned to the possibility that I might not. The Hoppers were ready to leave when I arrived. By the time they had started home with a pair of fat grain-fed mallards it was chore time, and when the chores were done it was too late to shoot.

Mallards don't often fly to stubble on a sunny day, even when there is snow on the ground. Maybe that's the reason why I remember this Christmas hunt so well. The best time for field shooting nearly always is when snow is falling. With a big storm coming on—a condition ducks seem to sense—a little snow on the ground, and more coming down, they seem to lose all caution. They are overpowered by the desire to fill their crops while they still can. Then, if you are lucky enough to find the field they're using, you can shoot all the law allows and stand up and shout and wave your hat, and still they'll pour in. Nobody who has been in the right place at the right time can ever forget such a sight.

Another memorable Christmas hunt was of an entirely different kind. Actually, it took place on the day after Christmas. Al Miller, my companion, and I both have families, and we don't hunt on Christmas any more, but there was nothing to prevent our going on December 26, and the wonderful odors of warm fir needles and candy and oranges and just plain newness were still heavy in the house when Al drove up at the appointed predawn hour.

We unloaded on the riverbank and put our decoys and guns and lunch into Al's canoe. He told Bing, his Brittany, to get in, and then we got in ourselves and paddled out into the darkness. We put out our stool in a foot of water over a bar at the point of an island. Then we found places to hide in the reeds nearby. We took our guns out of their cases and opened some shells, and by then, so perfect had been Al's timing, my watch said we could shoot.

And the ducks came. There was no long wait that day. They came in singles and pairs and flocks of five or ten. This is the kind of duck flight that makes good shooting. You have two shots with a double gun, and you are as well off with two ducks within range as you would be with a hundred—and sometimes better, because unless you are an old duck hunter a hundred mallards with their flaps down are all but paralyzing.

There was an upstream wind. The ducks, mostly flying up the river, would see our decoys and swing around into the lee of the island, coming down without preliminary circling. They were anxious to reach the comfort of the bar, and they came at us with their wings cupped and their feet out. We did the best we could.

On such a morning the shooting is over all too soon. The sun was barely up by the time we had to stop. Then we simply sat and watched the ducks. There were thousands of them and we were where they wanted to go. It was wonderful. Now that Al and I had killed our limits we were free to enjoy them.

It was a wild day. The wind was driving up the river, rolling white-caps and hissing through the reeds. Masses of angry-looking gray clouds were scudding eastward toward the red sun. We could sense, and almost smell a storm approaching on the raw air, and apparently the ducks could sense it too.

The small flocks of early light were replaced by larger ones as the morning wore on, but still they flew before the wind and, when they saw our decoys, pitched in to the bar without caution. They lit in the sheltered water and gabbled happily. They climbed out on the bar and sat there, some of them dozing with their heads beneath their wings.

Some flocks, their thirst satisfied, left the river and beat their way back to the fields to feed again, a sure sign of an approaching storm. But others came to take their places, and at times the sky was literally full of ducks and the river black with them.

Al and I enjoyed it to the fullest. The time eventually came, however, when we had to go. The wild December sky was still filled with the whistle of wings when we picked up our decoys, loaded the canoe, and paddled back downriver to the car.

Whose Swamp This Is

BY RON RAU

1978

W HEN I WAS VERY YOUNG, I OWNED A SWAMP. OR PART OF A SWAMP. It was too big and I was too small to own it all.

I owned it only during the summer months and then only in the afternoon when the lake was rough with whitecaps or noisy with water-skiers. I owned parts of the lake too, when it was worth owning, in the early morning hours before the afternoon wind came up and again at sunset after the water-skiers had retired for the day. The parts of the lake that were mine were a lilypad-covered cove where black bass lurked, an off-shore patch of bulrushes where bluegill and sunfish hung out, and a sandbar "out in the middle" where you might catch anything.

I owned these places because I fished them more than anyone else. The remainder of the lake, as far as I was concerned, was up for grabs.

The swamp was mine during the summer because no one else ever went back there. It was a half mile from the lake, down a two-tracked trail through green ferns which grew jungle-like in the Michigan sandhills under the birch, aspen and pines. The ferns grew everywhere in the shade of the woods, and glistened in the shafts of sunlight seeping through the leaf cover. When you broke their stalks, they smelled green and juicy. Recently a friend who lives in Kansas mentioned a trout fishing trip he had taken to Michigan. I asked what he remembered about the trip. "The ferns," he said. "The woods were full of ferns." It had been a long time since I'd seen summer in Michigan and mention of the ferns brought it all back like an old black-and-white photograph unearthed in the bottom of a desk drawer.

Before you even reached the swamp, the ferns had you in a jungle fantasy. Leopard frogs lived in their cool darkness; leopards, of course, to a small boy with a BB gun. One of the cinematic frames left in my mind from childhood is of black-and-white tennis shoes standing among fern stalks, a leopard frog sitting so still on the ground, its throat beating like a heart.

Frogs. At that time they were the main attraction of the swamp. And solitude, which, sometimes when I went alone, was scary. I never went to the swamp looking for solitude, it was just there.

Usually I didn't go alone to the swamp. There was my cousin Jack (whom I soon lost to the water-skiers) and a dependable assortment of vacationing boys whose parents had rented cottages on the lake. I was the swamp guide.

My swamp, unlike the image the word elicits, was not a dark and dreary place. Coming out of the shaded green woods, it bloomed in a vast expanse of open sunlight. The duckweed sparkled and the black water avenues in between had a polished sheen. The cattail stalks were shiny and green with firm, brown tails. Coming out of the summer woods to the swamp was like walking into a lighted room.

With the innocent, single-minded purpose of young boys, we stalked the frog population of the big swamp. Pushing a blue heron into flight was not as significant as finding the nose of a bullfrog sticking out of the water at the end of a rotted log. Bullfrogs were crocodiles, or simply, *crocs*. When a croc was sighted, everyone with a BB gun was summoned to the area and after a whispered count-down I can still hear the *kutunk! kutunk! kutunk!* and then watching to see where the big frog dove, if he did, and searching through the muck with our hands to find him, if we could. Occasionally, I would take on a croc by myself, but the BB guns did not instantly kill them, unless you hit them in the brain. It was best to have reinforcements.

Stirring it up, searching for a wounded croc, the black ooze smelled wonderful, like the mixture of cow manure and sulphur. It seeped through your shoes, through your socks, and got between your toes, somehow always making the white rubber of your tennis shoes even whiter.

In addition to the crocs, we shot two other species. The most common was a fairly large green frog with a mottled speckled belly. I forget what we called him. And the leopard frogs which you were just as likely to find in the ferns as in the swamp. But the crocs were the prize. Big, fat bullfrogs with yellow bellies like a field of goldenrod in bloom.

Had we smoked, we would have sat down for one after the killing of a croc.

I knew and owned only that side of the swamp nearest the lake and it took all afternoon to properly hunt it. We put our dead frogs in a small burlap sack and took them home with us. Then we cut off their legs on the fish-scaling board and someone's mother would fry them up for us. I remember the legs hopping in the fry pan and the delicate, transparent white bones after we sucked the meat off.

I remember the broods of black and mallard ducks in the swamp during frog days, but a croc was more important.

The next gun I carried into the swamp was a bolt-action .410 shotgun. Owning this, rather than a mere BB gun, was a weighty matter. So too, now, was ownership of the swamp. The three hunting clubs, which shared it on paper in bank vaults, knew of the ducks too. With varying degrees of vehemence, they littered their trees with signs and posters and proclamations of what would happen to anybody who tried to shoot ducks in their swamp.

Somehow I persuaded my father to ignore the threats and climb over the fence with me. We hunted off the property of the swamp's largest landowner, a rich man from Chicago who had his own airport and was fond of circling the lake at a low altitude before landing, finally disappearing into the trees beyond the water. These people did not hunt ducks very often and there is something less criminal about hunting on the property of a very rich person. I doubt that my father would have crossed the fences of the two local hunting clubs.

At that time I held a cosmic view of the swamp's ownership. I knew it really wasn't my swamp, but figured it belonged to everyone. It just didn't seem right for a few people to own such a wonderful piece of the planet and not share it with the rest of the world.

My father, of course, did not share this philosophy and became nervous when there was shooting nearby. Sometimes we left early when the shooting got too close, leaving before the morning flight had ceased or leaving before sunset, before the ducks had come in to roost for the night.

It was here that I first heard the *peep peep peep* of duck wings, lifting my eyes so slowly to see a flock of dark silhouettes moving against the ashen evening sky. And the pleading throaty call of a hen mallard, already safely into the water for the night, calling to other ducks still circling overhead. It was here that I shot my first duck, one of six that passed above me like bombers in near darkness, me surprised at the burst of fire belching from my shotgun, and then surprised again to see the black form folding up and coming down out of the sky, hitting the water directly in front with a death-like *kerplock!* And then stepping out in my hip boots and removing the warm creature from the cold water. In the fading light I could still see the shiny blue iridescence of the speculum and realized that my frog-hunting days were gone.

At our cabin, there was a poster-calendar, outdated by four years, hanging on the tamarack-log wall. Illustrations of wild ducks framed the months of the year 1953. From the drawings I determined that mine was a black duck, which I later learned is the wariest of wild ducks.

Occasionally, I was allowed to hunt the swamp by myself. My father would leave after the morning flight, taking our two or three or no birds with him. I could hunt the swamp all afternoon and meet him at a pre-arranged hide for the evening shoot. Once again, I owned the swamp, this time of a fall afternoon. The other hunters had all left when the sun rose over the trees and took away the morning chill.

It was during these sunny autumn afternoons, sneaking around the perimeter of the huge swamp, engulfed in the smell and color of a Michigan Indian summer, that I really got to know my swamp. I looked around, and ahead, and above me instead of merely peering into the duckweed for a frog nose. I found deer runways and old beaver cuttings. I found two abandoned beaver lodges, yellow aspen saplings growing out of them. I noticed three huge pines that had somehow escaped the lumberman's saw. Once, while sneaking along the edge, I passed beneath an owl sitting in a deadfall, his head turning with my movement, his fierce yellow eyes cutting right through me. It was the first time I really felt like an intruder in my swamp.

Not many ducks spent the afternoon in the big swamp, and those that did were very hard to approach. You had to be very quiet and very lucky to get within shotgun range.

Sneaking and stalking along the edge, I never did walk all the way around it. The swamp was even larger than the crocodile hunters had imagined. I would walk until late afternoon and then retrace my steps to meet my father. Usually I showed up with nothing more than increased respect for the wary puddle ducks.

After my uncle had been caught trespassing at the swamp, my father stopped going. He hasn't hunted ducks since that evening we watched my uncle walking ahead of the jeep, watching and secretly following along in the twilight woods like criminals while the bouncing headlights guided his brother all the way out to the county road.

This embarrassment took something out of the swamp for me, too. For a couple of years I avoided it and learned about ruffed grouse haunts in the brown, dried autumn ferns. Occasionally, I came back with a duck or two, when the temptation became too great, and I could hear no other shooting in the swamp.

One Saturday evening in late October, I felt bold enough to carry a burlap sack full of decoys into the swamp. It was the first time I'd been back there that season and I wanted to do it right. I walked out to the end of a prominent point. Before my uncle got caught, my father and I had grown attached to this place, watching many sunrises and sunsets from it; the skyline trees as familiar as our kitchen-window view and the ducks passing over this finger of land almost unavoidably since it stuck so far out into the swamp.

I set the decoys, and with brush and brown ferns rebuilt our blind on the small hillside although there was another blind near the water's edge. Spent shotgun shells, the brass still fresh and shiny, told me that someone else had been hunting the point that fall. I didn't care. The old swamp didn't seem to care either. This particular peninsula had always been good for frogs, too.

Sitting there, soaking in the late afternoon sun, happy with my decoy set and happy with life in the late 1950's, I heard a twig snap behind me. And then another. And the rustle of ferns. Blood and anger and frustration flashed across my face. I didn't turn around.

"What are you doing here?"

"Hunting ducks," I replied, still not turning around.

"This is private land."

"I know it."

"You'd better pick up your decoys."

I did, wordlessly. I put them in the burlap sack, taking time to wrap the anchor cords properly. Then I flung them over my shoulder, the noise of their shifting breaking the silence. I looked into his eyes, this man who owned part of the swamp and would not share it. He was short, old and thin. He wore old hunting clothes and had, crooked under one arm, an automatic shotgun equipped with a polychoke. I looked him in the eye the way the owl had looked at me once, on the other side of the swamp. And then started past him.

"You're kind of a young smart aleck, aren't you?" he said.

"I guess so."

"What's your name?"

I told him.

"I don't want to see you back here again."

"You won't."

I walked away from my swamp, unescorted; walked all the way out to the county road with my arm hurting from the weight of the decoy sack. No way was I going to set them down and rest.

Fifteen years later I got a craving for a black duck and the old swamp. It was two days before the opening of deer season. I knew the chances of finding ducks were slim, being so late in the year. And although it didn't make any difference, I knew that the rich man who flew in from Chicago had crashed at his airport and died and the man who chased me off was in a wheelchair in Detroit. My folks, now retired and living on the lake, knew of these things.

Mostly I wondered how the old swamp was. It had been a long time. I got my shotgun, now a twelve-gauge pump, and drove to the other side of the lake in the pickup.

It surprised me how little time it took to walk back there. The big oak in the clearing looked shrunken, but sturdy.

I sneaked haphazardly across the peninsula where I had been run off.

There were no ducks. There were no shell casings scattered on the ground and I had to kick away the leaf mold to find the old empties, one a .410, the brass green. A colony of beaver had moved in and trees lay strewn about, some of them felled into the water. The beaver sign was nice. It made the swamp seem youthful. The cold grey November sky moved across the open expanse above the dead swamp trees. Snow was coming.

So who owns the swamp now? I wondered.

I never have walked all the way around it.

Missouri River Sandbar Geese

BY CHARLES L. CADIEUX
1979

"Like any close relation between two people, there will be an occasional clash of intents if not of wills, and you must work this out without loss of intimacy."

George Bird Evans, *Troubles with Bird Dogs*

When the spring thaw broke up the ice, the Missouri became a raging torrent, carving the river banks anew with huge chunks of ice—rearranging the geography so that we had a different river to hunt over every year. Sometimes those spring torrents brought down a motley collection of decoys, which had been left on sandbars the fall before.

Some of these were tire decoys. An arc was cut out of the body of the tire, becoming the body of the goose. A head and neck were sawed out of one-inch pine, and the whole works was painted flat white or flat gray to simulate blues and snows. From checking hunters, I knew they worked. I got a chance to hunt over them with Jake Gottlieb.

Jake stood six foot six in his waders, and weighed in at 290—40 pounds of which was fat. We floated over to a sandbar in his aluminum john boat, carrying guns and ammo, forty tire deeks, lunch and coffee and a double armful of dried cottonwood branches to make a rude blind. Butch, a bucket-headed Chesapeake retriever, scorned the boat and swam alongside across 100 yards of swirling water to reach the bar.

We set the decoys facing the northwest, which was also upriver. Cottonwood sticks with the leaves still hanging on were poked into the sand to form a blind. "Just enough to break our silhouettes," Jake instructed. It would have taken quite a few branches to mask his huge form, even when he was lying flat.

With everything arranged, Jake waded out to the other bank and tethered the john boat. Then he waded back. "Even if they do spot the boat, it'll help us," he said. "They'll shy away from it and move closer."

Our first customers were a flight of green-winged teal, which Jake disdained. "Not enough meat with the cost of shells what it is today!"

Next came a duo of mallard hens. "Take them if you want to," Jake offered. I was slow getting up and dropped only one of the hens—out there a "fur piece" in the swirling current of deep water.

Butch stood up, almost yawning, and looked at Jake. "Fetch," and Butch trotted down to the downstream end of our bar, plunged into the fast current and swam strongly to intercept the duck. Snapping it up, he reversed and vectored across the current back to the bank about 150 yards downstream. Without stopping to shake, he trotted up the bank to the quiet water and walked across to the blind. He dropped the duck, then shook heartily, spraying me thoroughly.

"Good dog you got there," I offered.

Jake looked pleased, but he said, "The bastard is too hard headed to suit me."

About 9 o'clock Butch was staring to the south and we heard the distant honking of whitefronts. Eleven geese were beating their way upriver against a light wind. Jake said, "I believe I can talk to those specklebellies." He did, giving as good an imitation of the "toodle-doodle" high-pitched quaver of the whitefront as I'd ever heard. The birds went on past, swung to the call and came in upwind, looking for a landing spot.

"Wait till they're over the bar," Jake whispered. I knew what he meant. It would be rough for the dog to retrieve geese dropped out in the current.

We jumped up and started shooting. I dropped two—one in the shallow water to the west of the bar, the other on the dry ground at the south end of the bar. Jake dropped two in the shallow water.

Butch raced into the water and started retrieving. He brought both of Jake's birds, dropping them alongside the hen mallard. Without hesitating, he headed out for the bird I had dropped in the water. As he picked it up and started in, Jake was grinning broadly. "I'd rather eat speckles than all the Canadas in the world," he said. "This calls for coffee. Whaddaya say?"

He was pouring coffee into the red plastic cups when Butch dropped the third bird with the others. He was blowing on the hot coffee when he saw that Butch was returning to his waiting position.

"What's the matter with you, you dumb bastard?" he yelled at the dog. "Can't you see that goose in plain sight there on the sandbar?"

Butch turned to look at the goose, but flopped down on the sand, one watchful eye on his oversized master.

"Oh—ho!" Jake bellowed. "So we're gonna be like that, eh?"

"Probably can't see it," I suggested, although the goose was in plain sight less than fifty yards away.

"The stubborn bastard sees it all right," Jake snorted. He walked over and stood beside the dog, which rose to all fours, warily watching Jake. Giving the dog a line with his forward-swinging arm, Jake commanded, "Fetch!"

Looking back a quarter of a century later, I can still hardly believe what happened. With a savagery totally unanticipated, Butch leaped for Jake's throat! Only the big parka saved Jake from that initial leap. Now, I've seen dogs being playful and sometimes playing rough. I've seen dogs bluffing, and they can be realistic. Butch was neither playing nor bluffing. He was trying his damnedest to kill!

Knocking the dog away with a mighty sweep of his arm, Jake faced the second attack. Butch roared back, again leaping for the throat. He was met with a right uppercut from Jake's mitten-clad ham-sized fist. The punch knocked the dog sideways. Before he could scramble to his feet, Jake dove on him. Swatting ferociously with his big mitts, Jake batted the dog's head, somehow avoiding the savage snap of those big jaws.

Grabbing a thick fold of hide on the scruff of Butch's neck, Jake slammed the dog repeatedly against the sand. Then he knelt on him. Whaling away with his free hand, Jake wore himself out on the dog, which finally stopped trying to get loose and lay still, absorbing fearful punishment.

Arm weary, Jake struggled to his feet, still holding onto the thick fold at the back of Butch's neck. Jerking the dog into the sitting position, Jake roared, "Sit!" Butch sat!

Jerking the dog ninety degrees to the right, Jake pointed him toward the dead goose. "Now, you sonofabitch," he yelled, "fetch!"

Butch took off at the dead run, scooped up the whitefront on the gallop, returned it stylishly to the pile, then went back to his position and flopped down to watch the swirling river.

I had stood there motionless, my shotgun at the ready, all through the battle. I guess I had in mind to defend myself, if need be. "My God, Jake! What got into Butch?"

Jake waited till he quit puffing, took a sip of his coffee and looked at Butch with a tolerant grin. "'Bout once a year, me and him go to the mat," he said. "Got to show him who's boss, then he's okay for another year or so."

"I wouldn't keep a murderous bastard like that ten minutes," I said. But Jake answered, "Geese!" and dove for his blind. I got hidden in time to see a small bunch of blues and snows riding the wind downriver, making knots. They made a half-hearted turn toward our spread, so I put out my imitation of a lonesome snow goose. They circled, but the circle didn't get any smaller. "We better take 'em," Jake exclaimed. "They ain't coming closer!"

We fired a total of four shots. One loner slanted down, wing-tipped, but trying mightily to stay up with the flock. He lost altitude in a long, flailing glide across the current, slammed into the undercut clay bank and fell into the river. Once in the water, he righted himself and began to swim up against the current.

"Fetch." Butch showed his intelligence by running 100 yards upriver before plunging in. True to his proud Chesapeake Bay heritage, he swam with great strength, but the mighty Missouri was pushing him southward with greater force. He kept his eye on the goose, changing directions when it did. When the goose became aware of the dog, it turned to swim downstream.

Swept up with the fast current, dog and goose went out of sight around the next bend, and Jake splashed over for the john boat.

"He'll never get that one," I said.

"Let's see if we can give him a hand," Jake said. "That water is fast and cold—cold even for a Chesapeake!" We fired up the little outboard motor and sped down with the current, searching the water far ahead. We had gone more than a mile when I caught a movement of white out of the corner of my eye. There was Butch, walking north along the bank carrying a very much alive snow goose!

Heading back upriver, Jake yelled over the noise of the motor, "What was you saying about not keeping a dog like Butch around?"

Bayman's Solstice

BY NORMAN STRUNG

1980

A LITTLE BIT OF HEAVEN." THAT'S HOW JOHN AND RAY DESCRIBED THE shack. The roof leaked; and when the north wind blew, you sat on the south side of the stove. But it was lonely and free and part of the marsh, and they wanted it to be a part of me as well.

"We'd better do it this season, though, before somebody torches it, or the town pulls it down."

So in mid-December we loaded the stool and the supplies in Ray's old Pacemaker, snubbed the two duckboats up close to the stern, and threaded our way through the creeks of Baldwin Harbor on our way to the shack and the wetlands.

An anachronism. We knew it, but never spoke it, for to do so would have been a partial admission of defeat. We were ten miles from the New York City limits. Launching ramps, super highways and solid suburbia encircled the shack. If all we wanted were blackduck, it would have made more sense to trailer the boats and hunt by the day, and then be warm and sensible and secure at home by the night. But such pragmatics exact a compromise. You lose the richness of truly being there. Of being part of the thing you are hunting.

The creek opened to the bay, and you could feel the freedom. One moment we were prisoners of a narrow waterway, and the next we were on the marsh—open and salty and wild. The hundred-thousand-dollar homes stacked up like standing dominoes, the black and foreboding bulkheads, the forest of pilings and the fiberglass cabin cruisers all ended at the beach head and marshlands. No easy transition; it was like a time warp, or perhaps it was more like a battlefront.

"Drop the boats back, John. I'm gonna take her up to 15 revs."

Outside, beyond the canvas curtain, a nor'wester was freshening; cold, clean air tumbling down from Canada. Inside, it was warm and moist and the heat of the engines and the dampness of the bilge, thick with the elusive yet distinctive odor of an old wooden boat—mold and gas and oil and salty, wet wood.

John payed out the painter on the starboard duckboat, then the port, as Ray eased the throttles forward. The bow rose, and the motors pitched an octave higher, a trifle out of sync but relaxing in the throaty, rhythmic thrumming. The boats found their place just beyond the crest of the second stern wave and planed smoothly in the flat water of the wake.

I glanced astern as John entered the cabin. The houses on shore had become indistinguishable individually, melting into a solid white wall that encircled the bay. Ray was absorbed in the intricacies of the twisting, winding channel. John poured a cup of coffee and watched the wake and the duckboats.

The shack...its status was hard to define. It was legally owned by George Combs, who has eeled and clammed and run a line of killie pots for as long as anyone can remember. He built it as a kind of line shack, a place of shelter and food in the days when the run from his pots to his house was often complicated by fierce nor'easters and cranky outboards and ice making up. It was always stocked with food and blankets, and the coal bin and kerosene lamps filled, but it was never locked. If anyone was in trouble, they could always count on the shack. That's what it was there for. And if you knew George, or knew someone who knew George, it was yours for the asking when the blackduck flew. You just had to keep the lamps and the coal bin full, and put a few bucks in the kitty for what you used.

But George didn't own the marsh and mud where the pilings were sunk 60 years ago. He never dreamed of owning it, of filing deeds and such, for it was of the sea, and what fool would lay claim to that? The Town of Hempstead asserted its ownership of the marshlands and now leases the right to the mud that lies under the shack. There were other such shelters on the bay, but one by one they fell to the match and the stone and the scavenger and the bureaucracy. The shack is one of two left on the marsh—proud and defiant.

We rounded the bend of a narrow neck in the bay, and a small frame building broke the straight horizon. The network of islands and water stretched before us—crooked checkerboards of golden meadows laced by whitecapped creeks and channels.

We were laying off the shack in a half-hour, two hooks in the muddy bottom to hold the 30-foot cruiser against the wind and the tide. We loaded the duckboats with coal, water and grub, stool, shotguns and decoys. Ray battened down the canvas drop and jumped into his bouncing boat. Then we were off across the channel.

The wind had risen to plus-30, and it was whipping up a stiff chop—nothing dangerous on those protected waters, just a staccato beat against the thin hulls as we ran into the teeth of the blow. The shack loomed ahead, and a dozen blackduck leaped out of the calm lee, struggling against the wind, then wheeling gracefully to run with it, becoming mere specks against the gold of the marsh in a matter of seconds.

John's boat bumped the floating dock in front of the shack and six more birds rose and wheeled two hundred yards away.

"Lookin' good," he announced, more to himself than us. "The tide's dropping and they're moving out of the Sanctuary to feed. We'll have some good gunning this afternoon."

We hustled the provisions into the shack, each of us glancing over his shoulder to watch the birds aloft. The staples and gear were simply plopped down. Order would come later. Birds were moving, and that was the priority.

In a matter of minutes we were skipping down the creek in front of the shack, bound for Huckleberry Lead. The place was a dead-end creek, a backwater, where the blackduck could find water right for feeding, no matter the tide. John pointed to two fresh cuts in the shoreline: eroded channels from when a nor'easter had coincided with a high tide. The islands were covered waist-deep then, and the flood of water that moved on the ebb had carved the cuts into the face of the marsh.

"Right there, Ray. Inside the hook."

...A room-sized nick in the shoreline surrounded by high grass. Easy hiding, where the boats would conform to the contours of the marsh. Decoys were set quickly, nothing fancy or extensive. Seven oversized, handmade cork blackduck stool, four in one bunch, three in another, with a hole in the middle. John and Ray were of the mobility school, which holds you are better off to move with the moods of the blackduck than to try to change their minds with a huge spread of decoys. The boats were tucked into the bank, pinned with a stake, and they disappeared.

"...Meeep...meep...meep." A burnt umber apparition appeared at the periphery of vision, coming from behind, gliding into the wind. John replied by mouth. "Meeep...Meep," not a loud quack, but a reassuring, low grunt. The bird dropped low on the water, wanting to land outside the rig. John's assurance drew him nearer; he rose on the wind, slapped his wings three times, and continued to glide.

No words were spoken nor signals given, but simultaneously, as the black reached a point predetermined by 70 collective years in the marsh, both men rose from the waist, and John shot. There were no adjustments of lead, no tracking; John was up and on the bird the instant the stock was nestled against his shoulder. The blackduck crumpled, fell and was stone dead before it hit the water.

"...Better get him. I usually let them blow into a bank, but the tide and the wind are working together and he'll drift fast and far."

John stepped out of the boat and struggled through the soft sand and mud of Huckleberry Lead. He reached the bird, and halfway back two more blacks approached.

"Down!" Ray hissed.

John curled into a ball, hugging gun and dead bird to his breast, crouched low on the water, watching the pair from under his hatbrim. It didn't work. The birds hovered on sky hooks just out of gun range for 15 seconds, then they were gone with the wind.

"...Happens every time you get out of the boat," John grinned. The black landed on the afterdeck with a thud, John climbed aboard and we closed the grassboards around us again.

Four birds approached from the northeast. Wind drift vectored them well outside the rig. John called, but the blacks showed no interest. Instead, they landed 300 yards away, in the lee of the large hummock.

"Keep your eye on them. They might swim into the rig."

We settled back and talked in hushed voices, watching hopeful birds trade across the sky. John recounted other days on the marsh—when the blackduck were more plentiful and limits more liberal; a week at the shack when they were locked in by ice; gunning mentors who are dead and gone.

John Magnus, 51. A 30-year man with Ma Bell. Thirty years of wires and poles and telephones and The Public. On call 24 hours a day for ice storms, accidents or poor service. But a bayman at heart, who shot his first duck at age eight when Long Island was rich with game and open lands.

Ray Milek, 64. Salesman, draftsman, engineer. He works with figures, but his deft fingers belie that calling. I have never seen a rope more lovingly handled nor more deftly coiled, a knot more swiftly tied. Like John, he is a bayman at heart. But there was just so much work for baymen, so they succumbed to sad reality, and dreamed of their days at the shack.

"*Quack...Quack....*" A fat mallard hovered over the stool, dropping in like a chicken to cracked corn. He was the product of some freshwater pond on the mainland, raised on white bread and birdseed, and dumb. No need to call him. He was an obvious sucker.

He crossed the threshold and Ray snapped up like a jack-in-the-box. The mallard, too, was dead before he hit the water.

"Boys, I hate to say this, but we'd better scoot." The water was ankle deep as John retrieved the bird. "This nor'wester is blowing all the water out of the bay, and this whole creek is gonna be dry in an hour."

Just as the wild storms from the east flood the marshes on a high tide, a strong wind from the west empties them at low. The workings of wind and tide and water. Adjust to the rhythms or stay on the marsh until nine. Too cold. A salt marsh at 35 degrees feels like Montana at 20 below. The tips of my fingers and toes were getting numb, my sinuses swollen.

"Let's go then."

John was right. The creek was already too shallow for the outboard, and the boat had to be poled to the shack, but we were running with the wind and the tide, and the poling was easy.

Ray moored the boats, I hung the birds, and John laid a fire in the pot-bellied stove. By the time the sashweight fell and the door closed sung behind me, the cabin was tainted with the sour, sulfury smell of burning coal. Coal crackling and hissing, red and glowing behind the ash box.

At first, we stood and sipped sherry, feeling the warmth of the fire grow without and the warmth of the wine grow from within. They met each other somewhere beneath our first layer of clothes, and the heavy jackets came off, then the sweaters and then the heavy boots, until we were seated around the oilcloth-covered table in wool shirts and pants. Then the warmth drew out another odor—the boat-smell but now with kerosene instead of equal parts of gas and oil. Old, salty, damp wood. A meadow mouse scurried across the floor.

John stretched, took another sip of sherry, and leaned back in his chair. "A little bit of heaven," he announced to his glass. And he was right once more.

The dining area was its biggest room, and obviously the first. Two bedrooms angled west and north as an afterthought. The paint on the cabinets was at least an eighth of an inch thick, flecked and stippled with the peeling remnants of preceding layers. On the walls were dozens of yellowing prints: "Calling Mallards," "Greenwing Teal Buzz," "A Blackduck Set," "A Turnback Whistler," "The Brant Are Back," "Canvasbacks and Redheads on a Tidal Flat," "Bluebills in a Snowstorm," and boatman's charts of Gloucester, New Bedford Harbor, and the Great South Bay.

I walked over to the dirty, dusty windows, and looked beyond the boardwalks and the collected driftwood, the eel and the killie pots, and saw that blackduck were now pouring into Huckleberry Lead. The water was only inches deep, and draining down from the shoreline to expose mud flats and sea cabbage and all the creatures large and small upon which blackduck dine. If we could be out there, we would all limit out; but the tide had dictated otherwise, and so be it. We had a place to eat, to sleep, to keep warm and to dream—satisfaction of the most basic needs without the complications of social living. The shack was our retreat.

We bagged three more birds in the morning. The wind had swung to the southwest overnight, and water poured into the bay at the turn of the tide. By nine it was clear that the blackduck wouldn't fly until the ebb; they were now dipping and gabbling, preening and paddling, in the Sanctuary by Jones Beach.

"Wanna take a run west and see George?"

"Sure. Maybe he's got a line on where the blackducks are tending."

In half an hour we entered one of the hundred-odd mainland creeks that fed into the bay. Four clapboard buildings stood on pilings clustered at the end of a dock and boardwalk. Two Garvey skiffs, a Maine Lobsterman, and a half-dozen grassed duckboats tugged at their moorings. Ray's air horn bellowed twice, and a figure appeared on the dock.

I was introduced, and immediately forgot the man's name, for he had far more memorable attributes—hard, outsized hands, a shock of white, tousled hair, eyes blue and deep as the sea, and a face the color and texture of raw roast beef. A bayman. And with no more to go on than a how-do-you-do, I was aware by the touch of that bucket of a hand that I was surely among friends, and welcome.

We hobbled down the rickety boardwalk, heads bowed to the bite of the wind, turned a corner, and went through a door. The room beyond was a wealthy cousin to the shack, but undeniably of the same blood, and alive with warmth and conversation and rough laughter.

I shook hands with old George and young George and Fred and five other people whose names I cannot remember either, for they all seemed cast from the same mold: hands as hard as horn, beefsteak faces, wool pants and the knee-high rubber boots that are symbol and sustenance of their trade; they are baymen all.

Ushered to a place next to the stove, a fresh cup of coffee in hand, I listened to the conversation, and watched the comings and goings through the heavy, black door, its seal against the gnawing, searching wind assured by the same pull of sashweight, rope and pulley that closed the door of the shack to the weather, yet left it open for all who wished to enter.

"Hell, it's the weather that's ruining the blackducking. Fred's still catching striped bass down by the bridge, that's how warm this fall's been."

"There's a pile of birds in the Sanctuary, but they're natives. No redlegs down yet, and that little nip we had last night was like a fart in a hurricane. It'll take more than that to move the blacks down from Canada."

"George had a party last week, and they had 11 birds toll inside Huckleberry Lead, but the sports couldn't hit 'em."

A young teenager wearing wool pants and black rubber boots burst through the door with a lone bird. "Missed the other half of my limit," he said, proud that he'd hit his first half. "He landed right next to me as I was picking up the stool."

I finished a second cup of coffee, then it was time to go. The tide was dropping, and the shack lay on a creek that was too shallow for an outboard at low water.

"Good luck, boys, and if the birds fly, let your conscience be your guide."

The tide...the comings and goings of the tide, and how it orders your life on the sea. Lunar time, a different rhythm. If the world clocked itself by lunar time, eight-to-five jobs would be one hour and 23 minutes later each day—a natural way out of the bondage of the regular and the ordinary. I suspect that is one half of the reason why people become baymen—to heed that different-tolling bell.

We killed two more blackduck that evening. One was a pass shot that was no more of an accomplishment than hitting a thrown tin can, but the second bird tolled from 300 yards up, and with such cupped-wing grace and confidence that you could hear the wind whistle through his feathers as he descended. We feasted on roast duck that night, and raw hard clams and steamed soft clams.

Before bed, I went outside. The lights of suburbia twinkled from every direction. The bay and the marsh were a soft, black velvet, waves gently lapping on the shore. A jet approaching Kennedy passed overhead, gliding into the light west wind. I felt as if I were in a black hole, the center of a tiny universe.

In the morning, a thousand brant with their course, gutteral prattling, flew over the shack as we made the boats ready. Brant season had been closed for three years, so the birds continued to trade all day long, coming into our blackduck stool like flies to sugar. It was particularly frustrating because the blackduck didn't. We saw them on the horizon, miles distant, and they swarmed like bees over the Sanctuary, but it was a bright, warm day, with only enough south wind to riffle the water.

We hunted from sunup to three, and Ray finally managed to scratch down a black who came too close to the rig. He didn't have the slightest intention of decoying, and Ray's shot was satisfying for that reason.

We packed it in well before sundown. Loading the boats, transferring the gear to the Pacemaker and cleaning up the shack were chores that would be complicated by darkness. By the time we were done it was nearly sunset...the last day of autumn, the longest night of the year.

The sashweight fell behind me, and I walked to the end of the dock for one last look at the shack. The sun was gorged fat and sped doubly on its way by heat mirage, moving so fast that I could witness its ebbing toward the horizon. Behind me, a full moon was rising. Standing there, on the jellied and quivering marsh, I thought I could feel the earth spinning.

The Goose Place

BY RON RAU

1982

I FOUND THIS PLACE TWO FALLS AGO, IN MID-OCTOBER. I WANTED TO, BUT I didn't, make it back there last year. We had other things planned that took us out of Alaska and down to the States at that particular time. Whatever other plans arise this fall, I am going to work the goose place into them. In fact, any other plans are going to gravitate around the goose place.

You can't find a place like that and then miss it two hunting seasons in a row.

Here is how I'm going to get there.

I'm going to pack the pick-up here in the yard and then drive a half-mile down to the harbor where the boat is moored. Hopefully, I'll have someone with me I really want to take along this year. When I found it, I was alone. You can't go alone to a place like that two years in a row.

Then we'll transfer our gear to the boat and you ought to know about her, briefly, right now, because we couldn't do it comfortably without her. She's my fishing boat. I troll commercially for salmon. She's 28 feet long and draws about five and is planked with Norway spruce with ash ribs. She holds a ton of ice and has a 1963 Saab diesel engine, a two-cylinder gem that uses only a gallon an hour at cruising speed. Both the engine and the boat were built in Norway. I bought her in Seattle as *Karen* but re-named her *Bluegill* before sailing up to Alaska. It's not bad luck to change the name of a fishing boat if you also change her fishing grounds. I re-named her *Bluegill* because I liked the image of a small scrappy boat chasing king salmon around the mid-northern Pacific. I even painted her like a bluegill: white hull, light blue cabin, scrambled-egg yellow deck trimmed in black.

"You must be from back East," is something I occasionally hear out on the fishing grounds. Evidently, so are they, I reply. And then we tell each other about catching bluegills, when we were kids. Inevitably, we end the conversation agreeing that a bluegill tastes just as good as anything in the Pacific.

The Alaskan fish buyers write "Blue Gill" on my fish tickets. I quit correcting them the first season I fished her.

We'd better get going to the goose place. Never let a commercial fisherman start talking about his boat.

So we'll load our junk onto the *Bluegill* and she'll smell musty and fishy from the season but we won't notice it after the first few minutes. I'll prime her with starting fluid and hit the starter and she'll turn over for a long time because she's been idle for a week. Then I'll prime her again and one cylinder will fire, and then the other, immediately. Then there will be a thud on the hatch cover from the tin can blown off the stack. It rains a lot in Southeast Alaska and a tin can over the exhaust stack is a good idea.

Then we'll do some of those little boat chores while she is warming up, at least put the food away in the cupboard, and then we'll leave the harbor. If she needs fuel, we'll run along the shoreline six miles into town.

If she doesn't, we'll cut straight across for Elephant Nose, which is the northern projection (of that shape) of the island I look at from my kitchen window. If the wind is blowing out of the river valley (the Stikine), we'll hit choppy water at the Nose, and maybe even put the stabilizers down. You've got to take the waves against the starboard side for this crossing— five and six footers sometimes. If the poles get to bending too much with the stabbies out, I might back off the rpms, even though I don't believe we would ever break one. Something just tells me not to run full bore with the stabbies out.

We'll sail around the Nose and run toward the north shore of Zarembo Island, maybe picking up some relief from the wind when Vank Island swings to the stern. There will be another crossing over to Zarembo and then we'll run along Zarembo for about 15 miles, and just after we pass the logging camp, we'll come to that god-awful five-mile stretch where Clarence Strait comes through Snow Pass and joins Sumner Strait.

You can count on that crossing being nasty in October.

We'll say nice things to the *Bluegill* thinking how comfortable it is in her compared to a skiff. We can sleep in her too, whereas if we had only a skiff, we'd need a tent.

Now we'll be looking at Prince of Wales Island, a Rhode Island-size beauty where the goose place is. If the boat would hold still, and if you had good binoculars, and if you knew where to look, you could see the cut in the shoreline where the river comes out. There are a couple small islands out there, and some rocks, and we'll angle just south of these. That will line us up with the river mouth. We'll look closely at these islands, at the white water around them, to gauge how hard the wind is blowing over there. Sometimes you pick up relief from the group of islands to the southeast, but don't count on it. Usually, it just gets worse.

But the sloppy crossing is only seven miles wide, and we'll cross in an hour, and the closer we get, the less it will bother me. I'll be thinking back to two Octobers ago.

It started out as a fishing trip. I took the *Bluegill* into town, had the hold filled with ice at the cannery, and headed out for one last trip that fall, hoping for maybe five or six hundred dollars extra to take into winter. Hell, maybe even a grand. I was pretty much counting on the five hundred. I could fish a full ten days with that much ice aboard in cool October weather.

After four days I had one fish. I was going crazy out there. I hadn't seen another boat. I had left the harbor confidently and had tried every trick I knew and all my favorite lures, and still had only one fish. Forty dollars. My head felt like an over-sized water-balloon. My brain had atrophied. I was chasing a flock of sea birds working on bait fish, but I'd been chasing them around all morning, without even a strike.

I actually banged my head against the bulkhead, repeatedly, in frustration.

"Enough! Enough!" I said aloud.

And then I pulled the gear and shut the engine off. I sat on the bunk and just stared at the stack of dirty dishes in the sink. It was nice to hear the *laplaplap* of waves against the hull.

And then I looked at the shotgun case leaning between the cupboard and engine cover. It was like seeing an old friend again with both of you having time and money to spend, and nothing better to do. I usually don't have the pump gun aboard, because of the dampness, but I had figured maybe I would want it.

I knew of this place nearby, less than an hour away. In fact, that's why I was fishing here. I'd only *heard* about this place. And I'd been eyeballing it on the chart that summer, thinking of duck season. There was a salt marsh three or four miles long that cut back into the island and then ran out again. And a salmon stream that flowed into the salt marsh. I had heard there was some good goose hunting in there.

So I took the *Bluegill* in at high tide, up the river mouth which was swollen to the treeline, and then made the dogleg turn that goes toward the marsh. As soon as you make that turn, you can see the open expanse beyond the trees. The river channel narrows here and the trees begin closing in on the boat. I watched the fathometer closely.

(Actually, I came in an hour before high water so that if I got hung on a rock, I might still float off.)

It was like sailing up a jungle river with the sunlight breaking through the rain forest and giving the narrow channel an aura of heavy yellow-greenness; the huge cedars really closing in and leaning out over the boat from either side; running tide-water swaying the lower branches with an easy current. I felt like Bogart on the *African Queen*. The diesel was turning only five or six hundred and going *ka-phock-ka-phock-ka-phock-ka-phock*.

It would have been more relaxing to have had someone on the bow watching for rocks. I love that boat. I sure didn't want her on the rocks again. I almost lost her once.

At the narrow entrance to the marsh, the fathometer shot up to about eight feet, which in turn shot a charge of electricity through me. I had her in full-throttle reverse, and then it dropped down to 20 feet just as suddenly, even before she responded to reverse gear. I would get to *see* that rock in three or four hours. Then it dropped gradually to 30 feet and I knew there was a nice hole underneath where the marsh turned into river channel. I tried to picture what it must look like at low water—I do this a lot, but it is never right.

Over the hole, after checking it out with the fathometer, I kicked her into neutral and watched a few mallards getting up way out in the marsh. It was the first time I'd really had a chance to look around. You could tell they were mallards because the sun shone on the white underwings, and the wings on a faraway mallard always look like they are set a little too far back on the body. There were other ducks flying around too—teal, widgeon, probably a few pintails, and small divers. I wanted to shut her down and just *listen,* but thought better of it. It would not be a good place to be if, for some reason, the engine wouldn't start up again.

The marsh was flooded and more resembled a lake.

For a while, I toyed with the idea of anchoring in the thirty-foot hole. There would still be ten feet after the water went out and it would save a half-mile walk. Something said *no, don't do it* so I decided against that, too. It was a lot less hectic on the way out because I knew we could get through okay. I took her out almost to open water and dropped the anchor 40 feet. I went inside and shut her down, then climbed back outside and looked at the quiet sky. It was full of darkish-gray cumulus with patches of blue. We were protected from every direction but the northeast, and even then it was only seven miles to the large island of Zarembo. It looked like a good anchorage. It was just after noon and the sun was shining on the boat between the clouds, and it felt great to be going duck hunting again. I crawled into the bunk for a nap. Screw a bunch a king salmon, as Denny Donders, my old deckhand, used to say when fishing was poor. I wished he was along. He would enjoy this.

I woke with a start, not knowing where I was.

I woke in a cold sweat with the faces of the people I had been dreaming about swirling around inside my head, their images fading in the last stages of private seance. I wanted to keep them there, I hadn't seen any of them for so long, but they always fade too quickly. Then I am left with the feeling that one of them has just died.

So it happened again, is what I think.

I can count on three or four of these charmers every summer, especially when I am fishing alone. I can deal with them, too. It has gotten to the point where I welcome these dreams and enjoy dealing with them. I've developed a method.

First, I lie there in my bunk and force my eyes open, wide, unblinking. I try to recall the dream-plot but the events soon become jumbled and intertwined and I close my eyes but that doesn't help and when I open them again, the dream-plot is gone. The people are still there, people I know and love, or people I knew and loved, but they too fade quickly away, popping out of my mind like soap bubbles. Then everything is gone and I am left staring at the cabin ceiling. I ask myself questions that require undue heavy concentration. *Where am I?* Here. *Yes, but where?* On your boat. Oh yeah. Then I let my eyes play over the cabin interior; the chart rack, the CB radio, the exhaust-pipe fitting where is goes through the ceiling, the purple-tinted stainless-steel stovepipe from the cookstove, the boat's papers, the pots and pans hanging from a bulkhead, the sink, the engine cover, the VHF radio, the fire extinguisher. After it is all refamiliar I ask more questions. Sometimes, *What year is it?* I can always get that answer from my permit card tacked to the ceiling above the bunk. *Where are we anchored?* And then I think that one out carefully which sometimes requires the retracing of a couple days' fishing. I think it out pretty good because I don't want to be surprised when I stand up and look. It happened once. I had lost a day and woke up anchored 20 miles away from where I thought.

So I lay there getting it all together again, replacing myself within the time and space flow, and then I stood up.

It was still a shock. When we anchored, the boat was pretty much level with the base of the trees on either side of the channel. Now it was way below them. The channel was almost too small and the trees, looking up at them from below, seemed enormous. For a moment, I thought I was still dreaming. While I slept, time and tide had done their usual thing.

I loaded the dinghy and rowed to shore. It felt strange stepping onto the rocks after having been on the boat for four days. It felt as though the rocks were moving. I pulled the skiff up to the trees and got into my chest waders. I had brought them along too, along with a backpack and a dozen *el cheapo* inflatable rubber decoys. I also had a single cold beer in the pack.

It smelled different being on shore. It smelled green. I put on the pack and began walking toward the marsh, looking back once or twice at the

Bluegill swinging just slightly with the current now flowing *out* of the salt marsh. She was below me in the channel and looked pitifully small and insignificant. But I knew better.

I cut into the forest, cutting off the dogleg bend in the channel. The greenness inside was like a weight, as though the air itself had been over-laden with green and then hung from the trees. A solid carpet of moss covered the ground and grew partway up some of the larger spruce—moss growing up the trunk and hanging bayou-like from the lower branches. Moss covering the skeletons of fallen giants on the ground; moss growing green and hairy from the remnants of stubby limbs stick-ing up from rotted trunks; moss covering tipped-over trees which never made it to earth—fuzzy green artifacts leaning against living trees. Green on the ground and green above with yellow-green sunlight piercing the canopy and creating vivid chartreuse patches on the dark forest floor. The New England poet had the right idea but the wrong location. *This* was the forest primeval.

Here and there I crossed deer runways, trails made by the small Sitka black-tailed deer, their tiny hoofs cutting through the moss to the rich black muck underneath. I came out of the forest about where I wanted to, and the smooth swollen channel we had sailed in on was now more like a small river, rippled and running fast and occasionally breaking white against rocks. It looked like a healthy trout stream, but you wouldn't want to wade it just here. It was too deep and fast and the footing would be treacherous with the slippery rockweed.

I walked close to the trees, well above the running water. Ahead was the openness of the marsh with brown sandbars forming between shin-ing rivulets. Above this, the dark green line of the evergreens, and above these, the blue-grey afternoon sky and ducks criss-crossing in it. Mostly singles and doubles, but occasionally a small bunch. Every so often, I could hear a hen mallard far out in the marsh, and farther out yet, or so it seemed, Canada geese.

Picking my way among the rocks, I hurried toward the opening, the entrance still four or five gun ranges away. A movement against the trees ahead, and on the other side, caught my eye and I stopped. Two drake mallards approached, flying just above the water, just a bit higher than my own level. I waited until they were beside me, pulled up and simply swung with them as they passed, realizing that if I dropped one, or both, there might be a problem retrieving them. They passed without knowing I was there, without flaring, which they would have done had they known, beating straight down the gut of water between the trees, and then lifting above them at the dog-leg bend, visible against the sky for a long time. I watched until they were just two specks, disappearing, re-appearing, disappearing. When I turned back toward the marsh, there were five or six more mallards entering the gut, higher, on my side, just above the trees.

I crouched and waited, then shot at a bird directly overhead. Hit it, but it climbed, brokenly, straight up; shot again, hit it, and it dropped, reluctantly, and came down in the forest with a crackling of small branches. I ran downstream and then cut into the forest and stopped, listening. I heard it on the ground and ran to the sound. It was a hen mallard that died in my hands before I had to rap its head against a tree.

It was the first duck I had shot in two years.

Spooked by the shooting, there were more ducks in the sky, out over the marsh. And ducks, mostly mallards, a few teal, two mergansers, streaming from the open marsh down the channel gut. It was a natural flyway. I crouched again among the rocks, next to two red, spent shotgun shells. Feeling cocky. Two shots and I had hit the bird both times. Five minutes later there were six shotgun shell casings on the rocks and only the sickening image of a wounded drake fighting his way down the gut, flying below his comrades, barely clearing the trees at the bend, only to fall dead into the forest a few seconds later, an impossible find.

Then I heard geese. Would they too come down the gut? It seemed to be the natural passage out of the marsh. I saw them, 15 or 20, huge birds compared to the ducks, crossing the opening where the 30-foot pothole was. They turned momentarily to fly down the gut, but then disappeared over the trees on my side of the channel.

No, things hadn't changed much in two years. Geese never flew over you at that level. I lay against the rocks listening to them and recalling that I had taken only two or three in my life—we had never really hunted them but got an occasional shot while hunting ducks. I lay there listening to their lovely, wild cry, not getting more distant, actually seeming to get louder...how many times had I experienced this before?...*if only they would have flown*...strange that their calling was not becoming more distant, it *was* getting closer, by God, and then I began shaking and looking up the channel for strays or another flock and then their calling was just too loud and they broke over the trees, directly above me. I picked one out and missed missed missed. And then watched them climb, scattered and high, disappearing quickly over the trees across the channel. The calling finally became distant, and then it was gone.

There were now nine empties at my feet and a single mallard to show for them. Waterfowling really hadn't changed much in two years. In fact, not a bit.

I walked the channel to the entrance into the salt marsh. It was totally unbelievable that I had brought the *Bluegill* in here just three or four hours ago. Below me, far enough that it would be a nasty fall, the water rushed with a white froth over a rock that was beginning to appear in mid-channel. I looked around for the rock we had passed over at eight feet and oh my God! was that it just ahead? A rock ledge ran out from the trees ending with a double-peaked jagged horror that fell off, straight down like a cliff, into the water. I calculated the tide and sure enough, we had crossed over this ugly bastard. If you hung up on it, and rolled off when the water went out, you'd have the boat upside down wedged in among the rocks below. I got a second adrenalin rush along with chills in my spine. Seeing that rock in person was even scarier than seeing it on the fathometer.

Ahead of this rock was the 30-foot pool, now about half that deep. It still didn't look like a bad place to anchor, although the outcurrent was building. I wondered what it would look like in another three hours, after six or seven feet more water had left. On the way out, at darkness, I would see for myself.

I cached the mallard inside the lower branches of a spruce and walked the narrow channel into the open, sunlit expanse of the marsh. I followed the channel, which soon divided, and then waded across a large, but shallow, tidal pool. Exposed as I was, small bunches of mallards got up well ahead of me. I did walk up on teal and diving ducks, neither of which I wanted. I could still hear the geese, somewhere out in the open marsh.

That was what I wanted.

I tried wading the main channel toward two tree-covered islands but turned back with the water only a couple inches below my chest waders. I slogged back to shore and sat next to a piece of driftwood. I might have made it across; in fact, I almost had. But it would be a short wait. I watched a rock next to the water's edge, and you could see the water level dropping. I sat for maybe 15 minutes, looking over the pretty meadow that flooded and emptied twice a day, seeing just a few flying ducks but getting a good location on the geese. They seemed to be in a pothole, on the far side of the second little tree-island. They were generally quiet, but every few minutes you would hear a bird, and then maybe another, and then nothing. Sometime soon, as it is with wild geese, a single bird would begin honking, then another, and a third, and three or four more, and the entire flock would be honking and then they would be in the air, traveling again. I tried the channel again. Now the water was only waist deep, and I made it across easily and jumped two single mallards before I got to the first island. They jumped out of range, but I wouldn't have shot anyway. It looked like I could make one hell of a good stalk on the geese, coming out of the trees right on top of them if their pothole was close enough to the island. I had the feeling it was. It looked like a set-up.

Inside the first island, I removed my packsack and leaned it against a cedar with a three-foot trunk. There were some other trees that large and many more smaller ones. I could see them all and the brightness of the marsh outside. It wasn't a very large island.

I walked to the edge of the trees and ahead of me, just a stone's throw away, was the other island. It was even smaller. Between the two islands was a deep muddy cut containing only a trickle of water. I heard the geese again, or rather one goose, deliberate and resonant and close and unaware. Just beyond the trees in front of me.

Crouching and half-running, I left the cover of one island for the next. I had not taken more than five or six steps when a pothole I hadn't seen, on my right, just out of shotgun range, exploded with geese. Jumping with that quick, shrill, unmistakable warning cry. I ran toward the island hearing the flock I was stalking answering, questioning, and then I heard a powerful splashing of water and the sound, the heavy sound of wingbeats. I froze and looked straight up, over the trees. The air was full of goose noise, and I waited, waited, waited, and a single, absurdly low, broke over the trees barely clearing them, and I fired and he folded violently and hit the ground just a few feet away with a force I felt in my feet. I was ready for another, but the wild lovely sounds grew fainter and fainter. They were almost out of earshot before I walked over to my goose and looked down. He was dead and huge and wonderful to look at. I retrieved the packsack, opened the beer, lighted a cigarette, and sat next to him a long while before I ever touched him.

When I walked out just before dark, the 30-foot hole was a large gentle whirlpool, not the sort of place you could sleep without fear of dragging anchor. A fast current left the whirlpool and just beyond that there was a 15-foot waterfall.

The next day, I walked into the marsh before daylight. It was noisy with birds and the tide was out and all you could see were the outlines of trees against the faint sky. I was too early and jumped ducks and geese, well within range, without even seeing them. At nine o'clock I had nothing and was feeling sheepish about having come in so early, spooking all the birds. I waded across the pothole to the spruce island where I had killed the goose, going slightly over my waders because the tide was already rushing in. According to the book, it would be the highest tide of a month of high tides, rising to 18.8 feet from a minus 3.2. I would spend my day on the island, stranded by water.

I built a fire and dried out some (it wasn't cold) and then built a little blind, close to the pothole as I could get. It wasn't much of a blind, all I did was roll a sawed log over to a little spruce Christmas tree on the edge of the brush that grew around the island. I crushed down some of the brush and sat on the stump behind the little tree. There was a tiny spider hanging from a thread, suspended in front of my face where I looked through the branches, and I kept mistaking it for faraway ducks in the sky.

The geese came in a couple hours before high water. They came from the direction I was watching and they came into the basin flying very low and unaware. They circled quickly, always in shotgun range had you been underneath, and sat down on sandbars and also in the water before cautiously swimming to the shore to feed. They came with their music flying before them. You would hear them coming, and not see them for a long time, and then you could finally see them against the trees across the marsh, lightbrown in the sunlight.

With tall trees surrounding it, the basin was a natural acoustical chamber. Four or five geese sounded like twenty. Twenty sounded like an invading army. It was confusing to be looking for a very large bunch, and then realize that only a half-dozen birds were coming into the basin.

There were mallards too, flying into the basin with the flow of high water, but there were more geese then anything else. I shot a drake which strafed the island pothole, and he fell dead just beside the blind. All the geese which had set into the basin spooked with the shot, but that was what I wanted. When more geese came in looking for others, they flew over me and I took two from different flocks that passed too low, watching them drop from the sky, watching only the falling bird, not even thinking about a double. Every time I shot, the geese that had already set down in the marsh got up and left.

But others kept coming. I let a flock land in the pothole, and then let them swim into shotgun range. I sat, motionless, watching the preening and social interchange between the birds. Then I experimented with head movement, hunkered over the stump behind the little spruce. A bird 20 feet away finally caught it, gaped incredulously, and burst into the air, splashing and honking. The entire flock got up with panic-honking, but I only watched. I had been watching them too long, too close.

The water poured into the marsh, running with a powerful current that carried branches, logs, seaweed, foam, and diving ducks past my blind. The blind flooded and I was stranded on the island with a feeling of loneliness and despair. It was as if God was angry and flooding the world. The geese stopped coming and so did the ducks and finally the current stopped and the marsh was a quiet lake, the silence broken only occasionally by the hissing landings of divers setting in nearby. Foolish ducks that swam close to me for a better look. Then the current started flowing the other way, carrying the foam and debris and diving ducks back toward the big water.

I remembered someone else in town who would appreciate a wild goose and decided to shoot another. Two hours went by with only a couple small bunches entering the marsh and setting in immediately, out of range.

Then I really wanted a goose.

I heard a flock coming from behind me, from the river channel. I stood up and turned around against the high wall of trees on the island. The goose noise got louder and louder and I looked to each side of the island, expecting to see them pass by. Then it got louder still, their callings bouncing around in the basin. It was confusing and I expected to see them break over the trees any second, or maybe pass just beside the island, but still in gun range. The noise got louder and louder, like a goose freight train bearing down on me. I flung my hat off thinking the bill had obscured my vision and maybe they were right above me. The goose noise shrieked all around me and I turned my head quickly from side to side, looking for the birds, positive they had gotten by somehow. It was like a bad nightmare.

And then the entire flock broke over the trees, filling the sky, 20 or 50 birds, you couldn't tell how many, and I picked a single and fired and he came down into the pothole, striking the water with an incredible splash like dropping a bowling ball from an airplane.

That was the last goose I shot. I sat on the stump and picked two of them, waiting for the water to go out. Finally, it did, and I walked back to the boat well before dark. I put the geese and ducks on the ice next to the lone king salmon and it all looked pretty good. I left the next morning because you couldn't stay in a place like that by yourself for more than a day or two. It was just too perfect and clean and lonely. You could lose your soul if you stayed too long.

Calling Ducks

BY GENE HILL

1983

ULYSSES S. GRANT ONCE REMARKED THAT HE ONLY KNEW TWO TUNES. One of them was "The Star Spangled Banner" and the other one wasn't. And compared to me, General Grant was a musical prodigy. Be that as it may, I am getting my hands on as many duck and goose calls as I can. I intend to learn to call waterfowl even if in the process I offend every ear in the country—-and I just might. Even my Labradors have started to slink into the dark recesses of their kennel, and the rest of the world around the farm becomes dumb and silent as I tune up my "highball" and "feeding chatter" out behind the barn.

I thought I had a goose call working pretty good—and I did except the one I had down to an acoustical fine point was the danger call, a single, piercing honk that I can reproduce with such fidelity that no goose ever hearing it has stopped climbing until he has reached his maximum altitude, which I believe is somewhere in the neighborhood of 28,000 feet.

My duck calls, on the other hand, are such a curious combination of unnatural sharps and flats that more than one mallard has succumbed and warily circled over my blind, no doubt only out of an incredible aural curiosity rather than what I hoped would be a verbal promise of feathered companionship, great food, or a torrid love affair.

Like most of us, I tend to quickly shift any of my own personal shortcomings over the area of blaming them on faulty equipment and go out and buy something new. Right now I have four different calls, two duck and two geese—and a pintail and widgeon whistle that I won't count, because I haven't gotten around to working on that yet. I'm not sure if anyone makes an instrument that can begin to compensate for the fact that I'm about as tone deaf as a post—but I'm trying them all. And to give myself the pat on the back that I truly deserve, without out-and-out bragging, after only a few months of practice I have come up with a very recognizable version of both "Mary Had a Little Lamb" and "Silent Night" on the harmonica.

There are few things I enjoy more than waterfowling and all that goes with it. The deep envy that I radiate when the weather-tanned guide nonchalantly hauls some birds down within range with a few casual notes on his call has become more than I can control. When I'm out behind the barn practicing to the sheep I constantly have this mental image of myself, dressed in hip boots, my old and battered but very distinguished ducking cap pulled just slightly down over my eyes, my three-inch magnum 1100 casually tucked in the crook of my left arm and about four assorted calls strung around my neck. My weather-tanned face warily scans the cold and shallow light of just dawn on a real weather-making morning. My experienced eyes pick out a small flock of ducks—still so far away that the other men in the blind have no idea of their presence.

"Blacks," I say casually. "About two miles off, twelve hundred feet high, at eleven o'clock."

"How can you tell?" ask the greenhorns with me in the blind.

"Count the wingbeats," I whisper, and start to finger the Olt call I favor for distance work.

"He thinks he can call those birds in," followed by not too muffled laughter, comes from behind me in the blind. I turn, silence the chattering with a scowl and put my call to my lips. In spite of the incredible volume, there issues forth a sound so ancient, so pure, so wild, so magically entrancing that even before the lead black starts to turn I can hear the quick snapping as the gunners check the safeties and the rustling of heavy gunning clothes as the men instinctively crouch lower in the blind.

I smile to myself and shift to another call, a gleaming masterpiece made from soft glowing Osage orange. A subtle series of chuckles follows that sounds like a hen mallard reading the menu of a duck's version of the 21 Club. The flock is swiftly closing in and is about to turn upwind and scatter in the blocks. I give the signal for the other guns to stand and take their shots. And after all have missed, I rise and pull a pair of drakes, stone cold, at 55 or 60 yards. Then without a word, I send my perfectly trained retriever into the bay. My weather-tanned face permits itself a slight but manly grin of satisfaction as I turn to the other men and promise that I'll call the next bunch in a little closer—if they'd like. I bring out my pintail whistle and start to work a flock that they have yet to spot, as the Labrador brings in the second duck and puts it in my hand.

So this fall if you should happen to see a weathered ducker in hip boots, a nicely flavored cap pulled down just slightly over his eyes, an automatic magnum tucked in the crease of his left arm, a perfectly mannered Lab at his side and enough calls strung around his neck to make him look like a pipe organ, stop and say "hello." It's me imitating a duck hunter.

Russian Agents on the Chesapeake Bay

BY J. H. HALL

1985

CARTER DEWHART, LESTER HARMON'S FRIEND, HUNTING COMPANION, and possible slight relation, had a varicose leg, and so while Lester dispersed the decoys, Carter busied himself on the shore tidying up the blind and keeping an eye out for Russians. It was a system the two of them had used successfully for many years.

They were setting up on the lee side of a slender spit of sand and grass, known locally as Harmon's Hook, that extended a quarter mile out into the creek. Lester scattered twenty or so blackneck decoys to the incoming ducks' left of the blind and a dozen jinglers, also known as goldeneyes, to the right. The idea, which he had plagiarized from *Sports Afield*, was for the real ducks to land between the two flocks of decoys.

When he finished with the decoys, Lester hid the skiff in a tall stand of sea oats about 200 yards from the blind. Before he left the boat, he covered his ten-quart bucket of corn with a burlap bag and shoved it up under the bow. The corn would be for later. Lester never put the corn out until after he had finished shooting, and he always quit baiting a day or two before he planned to hunt. Knowing exactly when to quit required delicate timing and the careful weighing of several factors, i.e., the size of flock you were feeding, species, what the competition was offering, and so on. It wasn't as simple as it looked. If you quit too late, you'd risk shooting over a lot of incriminating evidence; quit too soon, and the ducks would simply take their business elsewhere.

Baiting, before it was outlawed, has a long and honored history in that part of the country. Even after it was outlawed it had a long and honored history, thanks mainly to the efforts of such traditionalists as Lester Harmon and Carter Dewhart. And if their friend C.E. Lee had gotten himself in trouble baiting ducks, it was not because he baited, but because he baited in excess. Carter and Lester baited in moderation. There was a big difference, if not in the eyes of the law, certainly in the eyes of the Almight.

What made baiting so effective and therefore so tempting to traditionalists was the ducks' almost pathological love of corn. Not just puddle ducks either, which might have acquired a taste for corn legitimately by feeding in fields, but also diving ducks, whose legs were located so far posteriorly they couldn't even walk on land. Most diving ducks would swim through 20 feet of water for a few grains of corn. To Lester it was one of Nature's great mysteries, one to which he had devoted several years of painstaking study. He'd even done some original research in the area (nothing elaborate and never published) and over a period of several seasons he had performed a few uncontrolled experiments in which he compared the relative effectiveness of a number of varieties of field corn, dried sweet corn, pop corn, ornamental Indian corn—he even tried field corn on the cob, because the cobs wouldn't fit into the small scoops the wardens used to collect their bottom samples. Unfortunately the ducks seemed to have trouble removing the kernels from the cob, and a few varieties of cobs have a dangerous tendency to float. He finally settled on loose kernels of an Agway F1 hybrid (XJ290) which combined acceptable flavor with excellent sinking characteristics.

When Lester arrived back at the blind, Carter Dewhart was pouring two cups of coffee from a corrugated aluminum thermos. That was another of Carter's contributions to the hunt. He provided coffee and conversation; Lester furnished labor and materials. And each man was more than satisfied with each other's contribution.

The early morning sky was a dense grey canopy that stretched from one horizon to another. The wind snarled out of the northeast and spit snow down the backs of both men's necks. In other words, it was a perfect morning to hunt, and yet the sky was devoid of ducks, as it had been more often than not for quite a few years. At one time ducks had been so plentiful in the area, they had been harvested like a crop, trapped or shot, then packed into barrels like potatoes and shipped north, redheads for fifty cents a pair, canvasbacks for seventy-five. Even after the market hunting ended and seasons and limits were established and licenses required, the sport hunting held up for many years. Then more and more people up North started draining marshes where the ducks bred, and plowing and planting the reclaimed land, so that what you ended up with a few years down the road was an excess of wheat and a shortage of ducks. Which meant even shorter seasons and stricter limits in the south. But no one, as far as Lester knew, ever suggested re-flooding the marshes. No. Instead what happened was the government bought up the surplus wheat and sold it to the Russians, and used the profits to pay more game wardens—in rubles!—to enforce the laws down South. At any rate, that was how Lester heard it, and he believed it too. He knew it for a fact.

Just as Lester was finishing his first cup of coffee a small flock of buffleheads entered the creek from the hunters' right. (Lester could remember when they wouldn't shoot buffleheads; there wasn't much more meat on one than on a quail.) After a brief long-range flirtation with the decoys, the ducks veered off on what would turn out to be the downwind leg of an ellipse.

"Les, I think this bunch just might do it," Carter Dewhart said.

"Yeah, they look a little interested," Lester answered.

"But first they got to talk it over."

"I believe they've decided in our favor."

"You say when, Les."

There were six shots heaped acoustically so close on top of each other they were inseparable, except by the ducks, five of which fell dead or injured.

"Dagonnit," Carter Dewhart said, "I couldn't catch up to that last one."

"I better get after those cripples," Lester said, pushing through the back of the blind and heading down the beach to the skiff.

Three ducks were killed outright; a fourth was able only to flop and was easily captured, but the fifth could do everything but fly. He made a series of long dives aimed erratically at the other shore, and when he emerged for air he showed only a sliver of back and a slight bulge of head and beak held low to the water, a silhouette almost undetectable in the choppy seas that became even choppier the farther the duck led Lester out into the creek. Lester hated chasing cripples around that creek. With all the new houses along the shore and all the city people sitting in them with binoculars, it was like being in an arena. He could feel a hundred eyes on his back, all pulling for the duck. It was fifteen minutes before Lester finally made the right prediction as to where the duck would surface and, with a single shot, put an end to the chase.

When Lester was not more than 150 yards from where he would have hidden the skiff, a small green plane with pontoons passed low over the pines to the south, then swung directly into the wind and landed on its first approach. Lester knew immediately that it was the Russians, probably alerted by their agents on the shore. A uniformed man hopped out onto a pontoon and lowered something, probably a dredge to check for corn, into the water, while the pilot taxied the plane through the gap in Lester's decoys right up to the beach. Lester guessed that would be the last time he'd use that particular pattern of decoys. His first inclination was to hold his course and return the skiff to the tall grass and find a better place for the corn than the bow of his boat, but before he could implement that plan, the agent on the pontoon was motioning for him to come over there. Then in a minute the other agent was out on the beach seconding the motion.

When Lester arrived on the scene, Carter Dewhart, who didn't move well because of his leg, was just getting out of the blind. He and Lester exchanged quick criminal glances, then Carter turned to the wardens. "Kind of rough morning to be flying around in, idn't it?"

"Yeah, a little bit," the older, heavier agent said.

"And what can we do for you gentlemen this morning?" Carter asked.

"Aw, I don't know," the heavier one said, "I guess as long as we're here, we might as well go ahead and check your licenses." Lester thought he could smell vodka on the agent's breath when he talked, and see black flecks, probably caviar on his teeth. And his southern accent sounded like it had come off of language tapes or maybe television. The young, quiet one probably didn't even speak English yet. Lester surrendered his license without a struggle.

"I see you boys are using automatics," the agent said after he'd finished with the licenses. "What's that, an eleven hundred you got there?"

he asked Lester.

"Whatever it says on there," Lester answered. He wasn't helping anybody arrest him.

"Don't mind if I check the plug, do you?"

Lester hesitated, then handed him the gun. While the agent inspected it to make sure it would only hold three shells, Lester stood there staring off into space remembering the days when that same space had been black with ducks. Now it was green with game wardens, foreigners. Then it occurred to him that under the right circumstances there might be as much pleasure in shooting one as the other. The little green plane with its pontoons looking as plump as a pair of mallards' breasts did make an inviting target. One load of number fours in the right place and those two boys would be walking back to Moscow. Just under the gas cap looked about right to Lester, and then maybe one more round to the cowling. Wouldn't do to have a crippled airplane fluttering around the creek; might upset the city people. The image of him chasing that wounded airplane around the creek amused Lester—he could see it so clearly in his head—and a small outburst of laughter escaped his lips. He had a life-long habit of laughing at the wrong time.

The agent looked up. "Something funny?"

"No, sir," Lester said. He almost said *"Nyet."* He had a habit of doing things like that too.

The agent returned Lester's gun and took Carter Dewhart's. Carter was a tall man and he sort of hovered over the agent as he shucked three shells from the gun, re-inserted them and tried to insert a fourth. "Captain, that's all she'll hold," Carter Dewhart said. "It's against the law for a gun to hold more'n three shells, you know."

The agent just smiled and gave Carter back his gun. "You boys got a license for this blind, don't you?"

"Yes, sir," Carter said. "You've got to have a license on a stationary blind. It's the law."

"You don't mind if Billy here checks, do you?"

"Help yourself. That license is just inside on the left."

Lester almost choked when he called him Billy. If that boy's name wasn't Vladimir, Lester's wasn't Harmon. High cheek bones, squinty blue eyes, big dumb jaw. These federal people treated you like fools, then expected you to jump up and lick their hands. They could turn a man into a criminal just by how they treated them, just by how they looked at them.

"It's all right," Billy reported from the blind. Probably the only English phrase he knew, Lester figured.

"Okay if we look around a little?" the senior agent asked.

Carter Dewhart said, "Go right ahead. You tell us what you're looking for and me and Lester'll give you a hand."

"Well, you know how it is. Sometimes a man'll accidentally kill an illegal duck and feel so ashamed of himself he'll hide it in the bushes. Some others might hide a bucket of corn. We know you fellows wouldn't do that, but they make us check everybody."

"Aw, don't feel bad," Carter said. "Les and I aren't the type to take that sort of thing personally. We know you're just doing your job."

The one called Billy backtracked Lester's trail all the way to where Lester had originally stashed the skiff and then tramped around in the tall grass. Meanwhile the senior man followed a series of paths that radiated out from the blind, most of which led to places where Lester or Carter had at one time or another urinated.

"Those two would make a right nice pair of bird dogs, don't you think, Les?" Carter Dewhart asked.

Lester said, "Yeah, that fat one's got a good nose on him, for some things."

"Not very rangey though."

"No, and he's not real stylish, but he'd do for an everyday dog."

"Is that corn still in the skiff?"

"Yeah, it's up under the bow. You think they found anything with the scoop?"

"I believe they would've said something by now, don't you?"

"I guess."

When the two wardens reconvened, they just looked at each other and shook their heads indicating that neither had found a thing. "You mean you fellows haven't killed a duck all morning," the senior man said.

"No, my word," Carter said, "we've killed ducks."

"Well why didn't you say so?"

"We thought you were just interested in illegal ducks, and all our ducks are legal."

"We still have to check them."

"They're in the skiff," Lester said. "I'll get 'em for you." His sudden outburst of cooperativeness struck a false note.

"Don't trouble yourself," the warden said. "Billy'll check 'em." Lester was sure he had given them away.

When the one called Billy climbed into the boat, his rubber boots actually touched the burlap bag covering the corn. When he squatted down to inspect the ducks, his leg brushed against the side of the bucket. Lester's heart flapped like a frightened duck caught in a trap.

"Five buffleheads," Billy reported. "Three hens and two drakes."

"Anything in their necks?"

"If there's corn in 'em," Carter Dewhart chimed in, "it probably came from back of the marshes. That's the direction they were coming from, and they tell me those boys down there bait pretty heavy. Why I bet you could go down there and catch a dozen this morning if you hurried.

"I heard a terrific amount of shooting down there this morning. Sounded like a small war, didn't it Les? That's what it sounded like to me, like they'd chosen up sides and were shooting at each other."

"The necks are clean."

"They're probably from around here then," Carter said.

Then Billy climbed back out of the skiff, and Lester's heart subsided and his respirations returned to normal. He and Carter had been spared by Slavic stupidity. Lester was amazed. Anybody could've found that corn. A retarded child could have found that corn, but this pair of experts had missed it. He felt like pointing it out to them just to show them what a couple of fools they were. And to think he'd been so afraid of Communists.

"Well," the older agent said, as he got ready to leave, "it looks like you boys are all right this morning."

"And you'll find us to be all right each and every morning that you check us too," Carter said expansively.

"Good," the agent said. "That's how we like to find people."

"You ought to be ashamed of yourselves for even troubling us,"

Lester said.

The agent wheeled around. "I beg your pardon."

"The likes of you checking on the likes of us."

"Now listen here, you got no need to talk to us ike that. We're paid to do a job, and we're..."

"I know you're paid," Lester said. "I know who pays you too."

Carter Dewhart came over and put his arm around Lester's shoulder. His hands were powerful from a lifetime of handling crabpots, trap stakes and oyster tongs. He surreptitiously drove his thumb into Lester's shoulder, the one he knew was troubled by bursitis. "Ow," Lester complained.

"Officer, he doesn't mean any harm," Carter said in a voice so soothing it seemed impossible to be coming from the same person who was applying such painful pressure to Lester's shoulder. "No need to take offense. You have to understand, some people strive so hard to live an upright life that when they're accused of doing..."

"We're not accusing anybody of anything. This was just a routine check. That's all in the world it was."

"We understand that."

The older agent looked at Lester's grimacing face and said, "We know you Harmons are good people..."

"The best there is. Proud people, maybe a little too proud sometimes," replied Carter, simultaneously applying pressure, again, to Lester's throbbing shoulder.

"And Dewharts too, and you fellows shouldn't be taking this personally."

"And we don't, either."

But Lester took it personally. He took it very personally. Still, the agents were leaving, walking down to the plane, and he knew Carter Dewhart was right. There was no point in provoking the Russkies now. Besides, you couldn't afford too much righteous indignation when you had a bucket of corn stashed under the bow of your skiff.

Lester thought too what a fine thing it was to have a friend like Carter Dewhart who could talk to people. Russians, Chinese, Japs, Germans—it didn't matter to Carter. He could talk to anybody. Then the two agents climbed back into their plane, taxied downwind, and turned back into the wind. The engine roared furiously as the plane headed back toward the sand point on which Lester and Carter stood, then lifted off the water and soared over their heads.

"Make a right easy shot," observed Lester.

Marsh Tales

BY WILLIAM N. SMITH

1985

From an Interview With Monroe Todd
Chesapeake Bay Guide

One Christmas Eve years ago me and a couple of my buddies was rigged out for geese in a blind we kept on the Nanticoke River. It was a great spot for gunning geese—water on one side and a big cornfield that the birds fed in on the other. Anyway, it was getting toward dusk. It was cold. Snow was on the ground, in the air, and wind blowing hard. We were going to make sure that we brought home the Christmas goose that year so we brought one of those portable record players that we used for calling in ducks and geese with us. We had it set up and calling real pretty when in come a flock of nine birds—they set their wings and started coming in, and we let 'em have it, killing all nine. Just then this damn warden appears out of nowhere from behind the blind. Taps me on the shoulder and says, "Say, would you mind telling me what that is you're playing on the record player?"

"Well, I wish it were 'White Christmas,'" I answered, "but it isn't."

That was a real expensive Christmas—cost each one of us five hundred dollars and a year's hunting probation.

From an Interview With Bucky Clark
Long Island, New York, Guide

One real cold morning, Alfred Tuthill, Joe Avona, and me were down at Shell Beach Point shootin' whistlers. Alfred and I were shooting a double-barrel and Joe had his old Model 11. We were really cutting 'em down until Joe's Model 11 froze up. He tried thawing it out by puttin' it under his coat, holding it in his gloves, and blowing on it, but nothing would work. Finally, he came up with the idea that if he pissed on it, the warm piss would free it up. So, he laid her down and pissed all over it, and damned if it didn't free up. He was some proud of himself for doing it, too, until the next bird flew by. He raised the gun, shot it, and piss went flying all over him!

From an Interview With Leonard Ward
Crisfield, Maryland, Waterman

Bill James had this fourteen-by-sixteen-foot gunning shack on some property he owned down near St. Pierre Island. It was a nice, tight little building, and if it got cold, you could always go inside, light a fire, cook yourself a meal, and have a little nap. See, we always kept some local moonshine in there and usually a little food of some sort. Now, back then you could buy a gallon of this murky looking stuff which was pretty potent for three dollars or a gallon that was clear for five dollars and just as potent. We'd buy a gallon of each and mix 'em together. Hell, it made no difference if you got into them pretty good anyway. Now, this one time I got a deal on some sardines from a man around here. He was selling cases of them damn cheap, so I bought two for the shack. One was packed in mustard and one in oil in these little wooden boxes. He told me that there was twenty-four boxes to a case, but when I went to unload 'em it turned out there was fifty to a case! Now, that is a hell of a lot of sardines no matter how you look at it. We also kept the place pretty well stocked with ammo and sometimes a gun or two and on this day had at least five hundred shotgun shells, plus a real nice rifle of mine and a load of cartridges.

Now, before I get ahead of myself, let me tell you that Bill lent the shack to these two local boys for a couple of days to do some gunning. These boys were real characters and loved to get into the 'shine once in a while. They were doing real good down there, killing a mess of birds till this one day Peeler, which was the name of one of the boys, got cold and went inside to warm up. He left his buddy, King Cole, outside in the shore blind to shoot. Peeler stoked up the fire real good and got himself pretty well into the bootleg as he sat and looked out over the river. Sitting there, he saw these seven canvasbacks pitch into a nearby cove and drunk as he was decided he was going after them, so he picked up his shotgun and headed out after them. "Draggin' belly" he called it as he pulled himself across the ice and through the marsh till he just about got himself within range of them. Then they jumped up and flew off. Now that surprised the hell out of him 'cause Peeler could drag belly with the best of them. In a blind he wasn't much of a shot, but I'll bet he killed more black ducks by sneaking up on them than anybody around. Anyway, figuring something else must have spooked them, he sat up to take a look around and damned if he didn't see smoke billowing out of the shanty like crazy. Getting up, he ran just as fast as he could towards the shack to try and get the ammo and rifles out and just as he got up on her, he could see the flames starting to leap out of the door. He swung it open anyway and just as he did, heard the most god-awful noise through all that smoke. Then all hell broke loose as the sardines, which were in wooden boxes and soaked in oil, started going off like little rockets, shootin' all over the damn place. He hit the ground and got out as fast as he could and him and King Cole sat and watched the place burn to the ground with the ammo going off and those rifles inside. He said it didn't take long, no more than a couple of minutes and the whole place fell in and that was the end of that old place.

I Don't Know Why I Hunt Ducks

BY AARON PASS

1985

S OMETIMES I'M NOT QUITE SURE WHY I HUNT DUCKS. IT CAN'T BE FOR the meat, for I must confess that I'm not overly fond of duck. To be sure, I've eaten some fine ducks—teal with a vinegar and oil sauce, spiced with soy and ginger, char-broiled over coals; wood ducks roasted on a bed of sauerkraut; and mallards shrouded with bacon, smoked over hickory in a steam of apricot wine. Each was a feast. But, put my back against the wall and I'll pick venison, wild turkey, grouse, quail and rabbit over duck as my most favored wild meats.

This is all just as well, because of all the things I shoot at, none are so likely to survive the experience as are ducks. Particularly big ducks which have decoyed perfectly and are hanging almost motionless with wings cupped and feet down, suspended like balloons 30 yards from the blind— I miss those especially well. In fact, I shoot ducks so poorly that when one does fold off my gun barrel, I ask around the blind to find if anyone else was shooting at that bird before I claim it.

So perhaps it is just as well that I am not passionately fond of eating duck flesh. My shooting skill would not assuage a more hearty appetite.

Obviously, neither do I hunt ducks to show off my prowess with a shotgun. I don't really know why I can't hit ducks very well. I think having to spring up on cold-numbed muscles, through overlaying brush on top of the blind; there to pick out a target and shoot quickly amidst a maelstrom of flying ducks, gunfire, and a wet, 80-pound Labrador trying to get between my legs to see what's going on, is more than my powers of concentration can handle.

Also, I came to duck hunting rather late in life and had previously hunted quail and grouse—birds which are shot while flying up and away.

In duck shooting, the target is still descending toward me as I rise, but will reverse, without notice, that attitude at some point while I am in the "pick one out and shoot" phase. I will just have to live with being a mediocre duck shooter; other men have borne worse burdens.

So it is neither the meat nor the ego gratification (at least on a superficial level) that drives me, but still I do hunt ducks. I hunt ducks with vigor and enthusiasm, if with little skill. That is about the only way you can hunt ducks—with vigor and enthusiasm.

Duck hunting is hard; it is physically tough. Duck hunting is getting up, out of a warm bed, at 2 or 3 a.m. on a bone-chillingly cold morning to stumble about a dark house trying to assemble all the gear you should have gotten together the night before. Duck hunting is a long drive in the dark, bolstered by a cup of too-strong coffee that is having its way, none too gently, with your innards. Duck hunting is meeting your partners at sleazy all-night diners and all of you trying to act just as if it were a perfectly reasonable hour.

Duck hunting is a long run uplake in a small, open boat in 17° F temperature against a stiff northwest wind that puts a chop on the water. It is carrying your gun and gear plus a bag of magnum decoys through gumbo mud that coats your wader boots with a fresh quarter-inch casement at every step. Duck hunting is an outboard that won't start, ice in the fuel line, and an O-ring made from a section of leather bootlace to get you home.

Duck hunting is racing daybreak to put out 50 decoys because you clung to the warmth of the sleazy diner for one more cup of coffee. It is also knowing that you'll have to pull in each one of those blocks, each dripping with cold water and sporting a little apron of ice at the end of the day. Duck hunting is those droplets of water that instantly freeze into little pellets of ice on your parka. Duck hunting is tough.

Duck hunting is also every man's brush with adventure. The sport, besides being physically demanding, also holds an element of danger. Small boats, often overloaded; cold weather and cold water; winter storms (during which duck hunting is often best); and the sheer "aloneness" of it all, make for a quaver of caution in the prudent man considering duck hunting. But prudent men seldom duck hunt or at least seldom during the really rough weather and on their own in vast and deserted winter marshes. Prudent men stay home and watch the Superbowl.

You don't have to be Indiana Jones to get a slight rush of adrenalin when you break ice for 100 yards to reach a wind-swept point blind where the grating of flexing ice sheets and the bite of a north wind will be your daylong companions. It is not the same degree of danger as facing a wounded grizzly bear in an alder thicket, but neither is it inconsiderable.

And, too, duck hunting has its magic moments. Duck hunting is that quiet 10 minutes before shooting time with a cup of thermos coffee and whistling wings in the pre-dawn gray above you. Duck hunting is the storied sunrise in gold and violet and all hues in between. It is the marsh waking up and a flight of ducks, just twinkling specks in the distance, illuminated by those first rays of golden sunlight. It is a high flight of mallards breaking up and whiffling down, losing altitude at your call. It is a squadron of cans showing their silver backs as they make that last downwind turn before they sweep into range over your blocks.

Duck hunting is the sunset-red sky of Louisiana filled—*filled*—with mallards deserting Arkansas on the evening before a hard freeze. And it is the incessant and strident keening of a "Reelfoot-style" caller sawing its way through a Tennessee River fog from the direction of the old man's blind. (The old man was at the launch that dark morning. He had a Dennison Stradivarius that had been "tuned by Earl hisself—never had it apart.") Duck hunting is hoping the ducks work for the old man hailing on his bronze-reed call over there beyond the fog.

On the question of killing ducks, for that is ostensibly what all the rigamarole thus far described is all about, I also have moments of doubt. Although not a great duck shot, as I have already mentioned, I do, now and then, hit one—a fact which causes me some mixed feelings. On the one hand, there is the exhilaration of a shot well made, the sense of accomplishment from a planned-for result achieved, and the vindication for all the trouble and effort expended. On the other hand, there is the realization that a life which began on the prairies of the far north and flew 2,000 miles against the odds, successfully contesting the perils of migration, has just crumpled at my shot. It is a sobering and humbling reflection.

This is a great paradox, the mystery within the mystery of hunting. In

Meditations On Hunting, Ortega, a Spanish philosopher, noted, "Every good hunter is uneasy in the depths of his conscience when faced with the death he is about to inflict on some enchanting animal." That hunters are appreciative of natural beauty and do also esteem and appreciate the wild things they will ultimately kill, is a complex relationship that defines the hunter's role within the spectrum of the hunt. The hunter chooses to make himself a part of the hunt. This includes the sharing of burdens of the hunt and the sharing of both the triumph of and the responsibility for the hunt's successful conclusion—which inescapably calls for the death of the quarry.

To sum up, Ortega concluded that hunting is a sport where the goal is not the game taken, but the activity by which that game was taken. The game is integrally important not as a goal itself, but as an authentication of validity—the seriousness—of the hunt. Ortega: "One does not hunt in order to kill; on the contrary, one kills in order to have hunted."

Few hunters perceive this at the conscious level, though almost all do viscerally. However, it has always been, is, and forever will be a complete bafflement to the non-hunter.

In short, it is not so much what you get but what you have to go through to get it. In this aspect, duck hunting excels. Few other pursuits put you through so much, and as a consequence the rewards are much sweeter. Not just the ducks taken, although as we have seen they are an honorable part of it, but all of the cumulative sights and experiences that are part of and often unique to duck hunting as we know it. The sunrises seen, the obstacles overcome, the dangers avoided...all are part of it—in fact they are the whole of it.

It may be argued that these sights are not the sole province of the duck hunter—the sun also rises in suburbia. And anyone willing to go can see the marsh wake up; but so few do, particularly when it is 17° and there is a brisk chop on the water. When it is really rough, when sheet ice and snow are giving the pre-dawn atmosphere that peculiar pink-violet cast, when "red sky at morning (sailor take warning)" gives the sunrise an unusual intensity, when the sky if full of "V" formations as ducks ("new" ducks that decoy easily) flee an approaching storm—these are the sights reserved for those willing to tough it out to see them.

So whenever I question my motivations to go duck hunting, I call my accumulated images to the fore: the big greenheads dropping through the willows in a Louisiana backwater; the old man with his "Stradivarius" on the Tennessee River; a Labrador bitch named Brute, who would filch a can of Vienna sausage, crush it in her jaws, suck out the contents and then deposit the compressed mass of shredded aluminum in the corner of the blind. And I always remember that high flight of ducks, mere twinkling specks, illuminated by the morning sun that had not cleared my earth-bound horizon. This is what duck hunting is all about.

Each of these impressions is an image of the duck hunting I have known, captured by my mind's eye for instant replay on demand. Doubtless your own memories are just as vivid. For we were there together, you and I, though perhaps a thousand or so miles apart. In the wild fowler's way we were together to break the ice, to slog the mud, and to witness the daily explosion of sunlight—while prudent men slept safe and warm.

The Naming of Sawbuck Point

BY STEVEN MULAK

1985

W E LEANED INTO THE WIND AS WE WALKED BACK ACROSS THE SAND flat. It seemed no matter how we twisted around and ducked our faces behind our hat visors, there was no escaping the sting of the blowing sand in the January wind. Finally, John stopped and unslung the load of eiders from his shoulder and pulled the hood of his parka over his head. He tightened the drawstring until there was only a tiny opening around his eyes. I followed suit. It was when we started off again that we first noticed the car parked next to my brother's old Blazer far ahead of us, and the person standing next to it watching us through binoculars.

Earlier, the trip out to the beach had gone much easier. In the pre-dawn darkness the wind had been at our backs, and all that we carried then were our shotguns and a box of shells in each pocket of our parkas. Without all our usual duck hunting equipment, John's dog probably throught we were out for an early jaunt along the beach. I should say here that one of the attractions waterfowling holds for me is all the nifty para-phernalia connected with the sport; camouflaged boats and decoys and blinds and canvas bags full of "stuff," all of it of the heavy-duty kind, guar-anteed never to let you down. I like it all. But it's refreshing, too, to go pass-shooting every so often where none of the above is necessary: Just hunker down and blast away and have a ball—and bring plenty of shells.

Flocks of eiders followed the surf line around our point in order to get into the shallow bay beyond. They have a disinclination to fly over land, so their flight paths are fairly predictable where a sand spit or breakwater juts out from the shoreline. We didn't need a blind, just a place to blend into the beachscape. Ice floes can make a perfect hiding place, but the morning's wind and tide had combined to completely clear the beach. There were a few pieces of eroded salt marsh on the point, looking like great hunks of sod. They put us farther from the water's edge than we would have liked to be, but we crouched behind them and waited. Unlike hunting blacks and other "civilized" ducks, there is a certain prehistoric aspect to eider shooting, founded in the not-remote possibility that we might be the first humans ever seen by these ducks. It must be something like what all waterfowling was like a century or more ago.

Some flights stayed farther out at sea, but most cut the corner sharply and passed right in front of us, just a few feet above the breakers as they fought the wind. It was easy to pick out the strikingly black-and-white drakes from the drab hens and V-neck-marked immatures, but much tougher to hit them in the conditions of high wind and maximum range. They're far from wary, but they do have something of a collective instinct that will cause a flock to ease away from the beach if we were up and moving around at their approach. Deliberate and in cadence, their formations paraded by. When we'd spill one of the big birds, the others in the flock wouldn't flare or hardly miss a wingbeat. Rather, like the 18th century soldiers they so reminded me of, they would simply close ranks and push onward. Fife and drum music would not have been out of place.

Despite the cold, despite the wind, despite the blowing sand that quickly turned our automatics into single-shot guns that complained "Clean me!" in a gritty voice each time the action was worked, despite my needing more than two boxes of shells to take seven ducks, despite my having to put up with my brother singing snatches of "Sylvia's Mother" all morning long—despite all that, I managed to have a wonderful time. There is something rare and spectacular about duck shooting on a clear day, and the sky was the sort of cold blue that goes all the way to the horizon. The morning was full of visual images and Technicolor memories of big ducks and long distances and full choke words like "wallop" and "magnum." On one shot, I dropped a drake in the surf that was down but not out. When John's dog went after him the duck dove into an oncoming breaker and I could see the duck swimming inside the rising curve of the transparent wave. The birds were plentiful: Enough so that the serious fun that waterfowling usually is with its long waits between too few shots turned into whoop-'n'-holler sort of fun normally associated with catching pumpkinseeds and plinking rats at the dump. Eiders are big, durable ducks, and in the wind even our tightly choked loads of fours didn't always kill them outright and we had to chase several. We limited out before ten.

At this point I should say something about the table qualities of eiders: They are nonexistent. Eiders are the ducks they were talking about when they made up the "cook 'em with a brick" joke. Once we tried preparing them as dog food, but all we got was a dirty look from John's retriever. But if you'd like to try them, send me your address. I warn you, though, there'll be no backing out: Once I've got your name, you've got my eiders.

"Who's that?" I had to raise my voice to be heard in the wind. John squinted a fast look at the person who had parked next to his rusted-out Blazer and shook his head. We plodded on toward the foot of the beach road, walking the Neanderthal-like walk of wader-wearers everywhere. In spite of the recent popularity of camouflage clothes and all things outdoor, we hardly looked like a page out of a fashion magazine: Our parkas were tattered and bleached out from one too many seasons on the salt marshes; our guns looked the way once-lovely guns always do after spending a few hours near salt water; our noses were running, and even John's dog was fighting off a late-season case of the mange.

As we approached the parking area, it became clear that the person who had been watching us was a middle-aged woman, and that she was very unhappy about something: Her frown radiated anger from 100 yards away. As if in juxtaposition to our appearance, she was nattily dressed in an expensive-looking trench coat with a matched set of Icelandic wool accessories. And, conspicuous by its absence, was the duck blood, sand, and feathers we both wore. Even her Saab seemed to make John's old duck hunting car seem all the more dilapidated. We stepped across the wire cable at the road's end and she came forward and lit into John: "You men are a disgrace! I've been watching you. There is no useful purpose in killing eider ducks. I should turn you both in! I even saw that one..." She pointed to me but I didn't look... "kill a duck that the dog retrieved by

The Naming of Sawbuck Point 279

slamming its head on his gun butt. You're disgraceful—both of you! Eiders are peaceful ducks..."

She pronounced "eider" with a long "e," but other than that she was right: My shooting *had* been disgraceful! And maybe I should be reported: If the guys at the skeet club ever found out how lousy I'd shot, they'd ban me to the trap range forever. We were in every way legitimate: in season, within the limits, legally licensed, sufficiently stamped, properly plugged, earnest, square and forthright—even if we didn't look it. But hunters everywhere are on the defensive when they encounter someone like the Binocular Lady. I muttered a little prayer of thanks that she had cornered John and not me and snuck around and opened the tailgate of the old Blazer through the broken rear window. I piled both shoulder loads of ducks into the back. Right on the top, one of the eiders had his tongue protruding from his beak at a right angle, almost in a cartoon imitation of a duck that was down for the count, and another looked like we'd bludgeoned him to death. I closed the tailgate quickly.

Understand that my older brother is the sort of fellow who is so quiet that at times he seems to be killing time, waiting for something else to happen. I'm usually the one who asks permission to hunt or talks with game wardens or makes inquiries. He owns a restaurant, and should get used to dealing with people. At least, that's what I told myself as I cowered in the car, not daring to glance at the abusive scene playing outside the side window.

Right around the time I was beginning to seriously contemplate driving off by myself, John got in. He turned the ignition key (he leaves the keys in the Blazer, hoping someone will steal the old heap) and slid a ten dollar bill behind the overhead visor. He spoke without looking at me. "Don't say a word. Just look straight ahead." I didn't and I did. We drove off.

A quarter of a mile down the road John took a corner and pulled to the curb. "Listen to this..." He turned to me and the expression on his face contained the boyish delight I recalled from long ago—a look reminiscent of a time when little boys shared great secret plots and jokes together. He nearly giggled. "We'll have to give this sawbuck to DU, but you should have seen the look on that woman's face! Did you see it? It was great!"

I held up my hand. "What's going on. I don't know what you're talking about."

"This..." He held out the ten dollar bill. "That woman gave it to me —
I mean *GAVE* it to me, for Chrissake!" He laughed out loud.

"Why?"

"Why? Because she thought we were poor or on relief or something.
She said, 'I wish it could be more.' Why weren't you watching? It was
beautiful!"

I was certain I had missed something in the conversation. "Wait a
minute. The last I heard, she was calling you a 'wanton murderer,' for
God's sake. Now, I'm aware we both look like ragamuffins, but it's a big
jump from being a murderer to being somebody a do-gooder gives money
to. What the hell did you say to her?"

"I said..." He paused for effect, trying to look smug, but ruined it
when he started giggling. "I said, 'Honestly, Lady, me and my retarded
brother there only shoot enough to feed our family.'"

The Life of a Decoy

BY ZACK TAYLOR

1987

My FIRST EXPERIENCE OF LIFE WAS SMELL. A MAN I CAME TO KNOW AS Harry Shourds of Tuckerton, NJ with quick movements of his hands gouged out the nostrils on my bill and joined me to the world of scent.

What scents there were! The smokey smell of wood burning. Pine and cedar shavings as fragrant as flowers. The pungent odors of turpentine and linseed oil.

Then suddenly I could see. First from one eye, then the next. There was a man on his decoy bench. At hand were collections of knives and chisels. In the small room centered a potbellied stove, black as ink. Cans of paint and brushes were evident beyond counting. The floor was awash in wood shavings. And stacked on shelves were other decoys. A man was talking.

Suddenly he laughed. "Ducks don't have ears, Harry."

"Know it, John. But I like my decoys right." Defiantly he fashioned a nail on the end of my bill.

"Take them glass eyes. Others make 'em outa tacks. By the time any black duck gets close enough to see my decoy's eye, glass or tacks, he's in my boat."

"I just like 'em right. Like 'em to have a pretty shape. Like to have 'em to ride just right." His hands turned me over and molten lead poured into a cavity cut in my belly. "That'll keep him upright in a blow, eh, John?"

Then there was paint; black brown for my body, yellow green for my bill. Feathers painted on by a feather used as a brush. Finally a leather thong that a long lead was tied to was tacked to my breast. Then I was stacked on a shelf in the barn with a dozen like me and the long wait I

---

came to know and hate began.

One day Harry's coarse hands grabbed me. On the wagon I went in company with a round, brown, curious-looking boat—a sneak boat Harry called it. I was nestled breast down, tail up with a dozen brothers on the sneak boat's after deck. He clucked to his horse and down the sand road through the pines we went.

It was dark next morning when I felt the boat bob, saw Harry's dark shape begin weaving the boat through small channels in the marsh.

What a day that first one was. No sooner was I in the water with my brothers and sisters than I heard wings whistling in the dawn glow. Harry's gun barked and two ducks lay on the water. His retriever plunged after them. Then came other guns sounding over the marsh. Harry lay in the sneak boat craftily hidden in the grass; as ducks flashed by his call would reach out to them and I would use the wind to bob and weave as realistically as swamp cedar and pine and paint could. It was thrilling.

Many times the scene was recreated. Then came the long wait in the barn. Then the days in the marsh became fewer. "Slowing down are ye, Harry?" I noticed the other man too was creased and bent with age. "Reckon. It's a lot warmer and dryer just to carve 'em; 75 cents apiece ain't bad." His eyes lit up. He nodded at a small boy at his side. "But I'm breaking in young Harry here. Already he's a pretty fair shot."

Young Harry was a decoy's dream. He wouldn't quit. Day after day we hunted. In the storms he hunted the high marsh. On the low tides we staked out on the open points. We slept often under snow blankets. When ice covered us Harry would row past and *Whack!* with the flat of an oar; the ice would fall away. Nights when the full moon lit the marsh, young Harry would stake out on the ponds. Then all ears harkened for the sounds of whistling wings or the whimper of the dog that usually announced them. When ducks silhouetted against the moon, Harry's gun would shatter the stillness, long tongues of flame would seek out the duck that came tumbling down.

Nothing stilled the fire in this young hunter. If ducking was better on the other side of the bay, Harry set the sneak boat's sail and we could feel the rise and fall as winds took us to the gunning grounds and back again. Many waterfowlers feared ice. Young Harry sneered at it. Up he'd sail to the flows. Then he'd jam a hook into the ice and hobby horse the boat up on the surface. The sneak boat skimmed along as if on wings instead of the brass-tipped runners on the bottom.

There were stormy days when the ducks went wild and we all dragged our anchors. And there were "blue bird" days as Harry called them. With no birds flying we'd snooze in the sun and hardly a trace of a breeze to allow us to "work" on our leads. But they were all days of ducking. They were what my life was all about. Oh, life was good!

But the years began to take their toll on my master. Trips to the marsh were fewer. Then year after year we gathered dust in the barn. The sneak boat sailed no more; chickens clucked on her once proud decks.

There was a violent thumping and banging. A stranger entered the yard in a new contraption that ran without a horse. Harry came out of the carving shed to greet him.

"We're opening a new duck club in Currituck Sound," the stranger said. "Currituck is easy to get to now the railroad is in. Bought 10 miles of barrier beach with the prettiest broken marsh you ever saw. Need decoys. I was told you could fix me up."

"Sure I'll carve you up any kind you want; two dollars apiece," said young Harry, only he was young no more.

"Fine for next season but for this we've got to get going now. I'll give you a dollar and a half for all you've got in the barn." We were thrown in the back of the noisy contraption and rattled off.

Currituck was different. Bigger waters. Ducks by the thousands. We were stored in special buildings, branded on our bellies with our owner's initials. The sportsmen came across the sound in their stove pipe hats. Servants awaited them. Local watermen set us out and gathered us up. The sportsmen never wet their hands. Yet, we were out in the elements where we belonged. And I'll say this for them, bad weather never deterred them. Many were crack shots. They'd come and go. We'd work every day dawn to dusk for a week straight then take a rest. They brought guests. (One got excited and put three No. 4 shot in my side.) Still, along with my brothers and sisters, I was doing what I was created to do. Ducks by the score, even the hundreds, spotted us and came pitching in to join us until the guns spoke. The retrievers were busy and they, too, loved their work.

Then things went wrong. There didn't seem to be any young men. We heard talk of war, heard explosions at sea off the barrier beach. The club was boarded up. My owner died. A local man offered four dollars apiece for us. We went off to another barn. Instead of storms and blizzards and ice our bodies were shrouded in dust and cobwebs. The seasons slipped past. We stayed in our stacks.

One day all that changed. A stranger had me in his hands. "Even though it's branded, this isn't a Currituck decoy," he said to his companion. "Look, it's hollow with the inlaid keel. Been used hard. See the shot holes." Now the other man was examining me with a magnifying glass. "Original paint. Old as hell. Pine head. Glass eyes. Leather thong. Inlaid ballast. By golly a nailed beak! This is Harry Shourds' block!"

"Junior or senior?"

"From its age, I'd have to guess old Harry. I'm going to offer ten dollars apiece for this batch of blacks."

So I came to live not on a shelf in the barn but on a shelf in a den. It wasn't a bad life. Many admired me. Bragged about my graceful shape, the skill of my maker. "An artist, a natural folk artist." I smiled inside. Old Harry Shourds an artist! He probably wouldn't know what the word meant. Might take it as an insult. Sure he was proud of his blocks and like the other decoy makers carved in a distinctive way. Folk artists? The waterman way of life was too hard. It left no time for art.

One night in the den, cigars and brandy instead of winds and waters, I was on display. "This Shourds with the shot holes and the brand fascinates me. I've got to have it. Name your price."

"Well I do have a dozen like it. I won't be too tough on you. How's $500?"

There were more years on display, days in a sneak boat's decoy rack long ago in the past. Would I ever hear wings beat and guns again? Would the retrievers ever churn past? I was afraid I knew the answer. I did not approve.

I learned a lot at my first auction. Hollow "Barnegat-style" decoys were collector's dreams. Harry Shourds' name was magic. (If the excited novice could only know how his shot holes stood me apart!) Men could hold me in their hands and the marsh years of old sprang to life. I thought of Shourds' life lived on the edge of poverty. At $1500 the hammer fell. It would have been a fortune for him.

My last sale was different. I was x-rayed, examined under fluorescent light, the paint Harry made with lamp black and linseed oil and a spoonful of red lead (a secret he shared only with his son) was chemically analyzed. The exchange was brisk.

"This is an authentic Harry Shourds original circa 1890; certainly carved before the turn of the century. It is in fine condition considering years of abuse. (Abuse! What was I created for?) The museum simply must add it to its collection. I'm prepared to make you an offer you can't refuse—$7500." (I thought of Harry junior whacking me with an oar to rid me of ice, how carelessly he threw me on the stacks. He could have gone through college on $7500. Not that he'd have traded life on the water for a college degree.)

So now I sit in a glass display case. Hundreds who have never held a shotgun or even seen a duck fall from the sky march past me daily. Freezing winters on the marsh, blistering summers in the barn tempered me. Now the moisture in the air around me is monitored at a constant level; the temperature never varies. Every year my insurance value increases.

Never again will a sneak boat rock beneath me. No more will I nestle against my fellow blocks. The glowing dawn sun can no longer brighten my life. The wind in the marsh grass is but a memory. The slap of the waves against my breast is gone forever.

I've even heard the breed I was created to entice is vanishing from the skies.

The Drifter

BY STEVE WARD
DATE UNKNOWN

I'm just an old has-been decoy,
 no ribbons have I won.
My sides and head are full of shot
 from many a blazing gun.
My home is down on the river,
 driftin' along with the tide.
No roof have I for shelter,
 no one place I can abide.
I've rocked to the winter's wild fury,
 I've scorched from the heat of the sun.
I've drifted and drifted and drifted,
 the tide never ceased to run.
I was picked up by some fool collector
 and put up on the shelf.
But my home is down by the river
 when I can drift all by myself.
I long to go to the shoreline
 where the clouds are thick and low.
And feel the touch of the raindrops
 and the velvet soft touch of the snow.

Wax and Wane

BY STEVEN J. MULAK

1987

A T TIMES THE WATERFOWL SEASON SEEMS SHORTER THAN ITS ALLOTTED number of days...times when an entire season can be compressed into a single day on the marshes:

5:40 A.M. The silence is overpowering. Nearly straight overhead Andromeda and Pegasus shine boldly in the October sky, and although the first hint of dawn shows in the east, the starlight is still reflected brightly in the water. I continually glance upward in amazement. Crystal-clear dawns are not normally associated with promising waterfowling... except today. This morning we'll have fine shooting at unwary natives, and weather won't be a factor. It's opening day, and the hunting won't be as fruitful until a month from now when the first winter storms begin pushing the migrants down from the Maritimes.

I finish securing the boat, then pull the overhanging grape tangles over the gunwales. Probing ahead with an oar, I feel my way back along the river's edge. There is a fallen tree in the dark water that I bust my way through, a half-step at a time, being careful not to hole my waders.

My father extends his hand and helps me up the bank. He has set up our folding stools behind some low sumac five yards back from the bank. He works some imaginary stickiness out of the action of his automatic, and I test out my call with a few tentative clucks and quacks, then we settle down to the quiet business of waiting. I check my watch, not because I suspect that it is anywhere near shooting time, but because the first symptoms of the opening day butterflies have begun. If they ever stop, so will I. Under the clear sky, things will brighten up early, and I'll check my watch a dozen more times during the next half-hour. Our conversation is in low tones.

"Is the boat okay?"

"I tied it under some overhanging vines."

"Coffee?"

"Sure." At this time of the day, coffee is something felt as much as tasted, and it feels good. I rest the rim of the cup against my bottom lip, blowing through the swirling steam as I stare out at my decoy spread.

"The rig looks good," my father whispers.

I nod a thanks. The silhouettes of the teal and mallard decoys are still dark and colorless, but they *do* look good. Daylight will reveal a fresh paint job on each bird; rich browns and grays, crisp blacks, pure whites, iridescent greens. A season of use will wash and scuff the colors, and they'll never seem as fresh as this opening day. But today all is new; the guns show no signs of rust, my dad's "Father's Day" waders wear no patches, and even the brass heads showing in the shell box are shiny.

The sky grows lighter, and with it patches of fog begin to accumulate over the water. Across the river, several birches dressed in autumn amber emerge from the dark background of the woodland. When I can definitely see the color on the head of the nearest decoy, I check my watch and find that the season officially began more than a minute ago. I take a deep breath and flex my shoulder blades. Next to me, my father pulls back the bolt of his gun a half-inch, knowing full well there is a shell in the chamber but taking a small comfort from just seeing it there—nervous preliminaries.

We wait.

"Okay..." I've seen them. There is no need to say more. My father eases forward, crouching, and slowly turns to face the direction my eyes indicate.

The flock of ducks is silhouetted against the brightening dawn. They move quickly, and seem to be showing off their maneuvering skills. Teal. We lose them momentarily when they pass in front of the dark background, but they break the sky again much closer to us. There is no doubting their intentions—they come straight for the rig, skimming over the wisps of fog on the river.

The safety on my father's gun clicks off...

7:50 A.M. I've never before seen a whitecap on the swamp creek, but there's no denying it now. Close behind it is another, and out farther several more waves have their tops blown back upon themselves. In the shallow lee of a broken-down black willow, our eight decoys occupy half of the small triangle of calm water. If it were winter, this would be called a blizzard instead of a typical November storm.

We had brought enough decoys to lure the entire Atlantic flyway, but thankfully we'd come to our senses in the gale winds before dawn and had put out only a handful. Chasing down storm-dragged decoys is no fun, especially when ducks are flying, and on a perfect day like this, a waterfowler needs little more than to be near some sheltered water. Shooting in the gale is difficult, but we are getting plenty of practice.

The season has waxed full. The migrants are in, as attested to by the wide variety of birds that have attempted to join our eight black duck decoys behind the willow. The only redhead duck I've ever seen in this state lies on the sacks of extra decoys behind us. My eyes keep wandering to the drake, as if in disbelief.

A small flock of mallards, flying low with the wind behind them, swings around the willow. When they see the calm water they turn outward, climbing into the wind as they look the rig over. Two hens peel away from the group, heading farther downriver, but the rest sideslip toward us, their formation scattered. Heading into the strong wind, the birds are actually flying sideways and backward as they approach. The shot is confusing at best, and we both miss. In the gale, the mallards only have to think about flaring and they are instantly out of range. No second shots are possible.

We grin foolishly at each other and reload. There is more luck than skill involved in this sort of shooting, and misses need no excuse. We hunker back down into the rushes. The wind begins to spit tiny bits of ice along with the sparse raindrops.

I've read descriptions comparing the sound to ripping canvas, but those are from a time when duck hunters were full-time watermen on whom a strain-burst sail left a lasting impression. To me, the five buffleheads sound like an F4 accelerating close overhead after a bombing run. As with the watermen, the sound leaves a lasting impression. The buffs pass behind us, braking with an alarming din as they swing across the wind to come in lightly in the rough water beyond the rig. All five are drakes. They seem to sit on the water rather than in it, seemingly inflated imitations. Their crisp coloration and bright blue bills do little to dispel the impression.

We watch them intently as they swim into the rig. My partner cups a hand to his mouth and leans toward me to have his whisper heard in the wind. "This doesn't sound too macho, but they're really cute."

I nod. They are.

"What now?" he asks.

I glance out at the little black-and-white ducks. They have fluffed out their feathers and are resting at the rear of the rig. "Let's wait for more mallards."

He grins, and nods in agreement.

11:25 A.M. We watch a hovering insect land on the knee of my waders. "A mosquito. Amazing."

My brother shakes his head. "This is crazy. November duck hunting is supposed to look like a Chet Reneson watercolor. I'm half tempted to take off my shirt and get some sun."

Late November brings an abundance of waterfowl to coastal New England, even as the inland migration begins to wane. Dawn had brought fast shooting, but the tide and the unpredictable weather has left us stranded on the sunny salt marsh for at least another hour. We wait, talking the talk of idle hunters everywhere; tomorrow's game in Foxboro, stories about our father, speculations about where the ducks are and how well we'd be doing if we were there with them.

Then, because we have not paid attention for a sufficient number of minutes, a single black duck appears over the decoys. He is a rich brown loam color in the sunlight. Without announcement I stand and pump two quick shots at the bird, and although he sags noticeably, he does not fall. Instead, he flies a straight line out onto the salt flats, losing altitude as if the load of shot had not so much injured him as weighed him down.

We stand, shading our eyes. Although we never actually see the duck fall, when he finally sinks from view we assume he's down. My brother estimates the distance: "He's weynafug out there."

I nod. "Probably farther."

After a moment's thought, he brightens and turns to me, his hand on my shoulder. "Well, for once I'm glad you saw him first." He grins. Overeagerness has its accompanying penance: Although it had been his turn to shoot, I am the one with the hike across the marsh in front of me.

I start off and am halfway across the shallow tidal creek when my brother whistles "bobwhite." I freeze...wait...then hear a single gunshot and see two teal flare off. A third is at the center of a ring of ripples just outside the decoy spread. He floats on his back with one gray foot idly paddling the air. The damsel of fate who controls the fortunes of water-fowlers must be a sadistic old biddy. She keeps score, and extracts penalties for specific transgressions: Cripple a duck and pay by watching your brother kill cleanly a bird it would have been your turn to take. She's the same one who sends in the mallards when you're picking up after a fruitless morning.

My brother waves to me. "Hurry back!" There is more than the necessary amount of glee in his voice.

The muck on the far bank of the creek is exceptionally sticky. This must be part of my penance, too. Waders should come equipped with handles just above the heels—I'm always afraid I'll puncture them by pulling as hard as I have to to get my feet out of the mud.

Up on the flats, the summertime expanse of waving grass has been turned into a stubble field. The tides and winds of autumn sweep over the marsh and carry off the deciduous plant tops, leaving only short stems that are devoid of all resiliency. I crunch along through the brittle stubble, leaping the smaller cuts as best I can in my cumbersome waders and taking the long way around the wider channels through the marsh.

At high tide the salt flats are dotted with ponds. But they drain out with the ebb, leaving empty mud holes that contain nothing more than a puddle or two. My black is in the weeds at the edge of one such drained salt pond, and he springs into flight at my approach. He gives only the slightest indication that he is an injured bird. My shooting, never anything to write home about, is poorer than usual today: I fire once too quickly, then concentrate and center him with the second shot. The bird falls into the mud, but immediately rights himself and runs for the far weedy edge, waddling like some target duck in a shooting gallery. The pellets of my third shot strike all around him, but to complete the shooting gallery simile, he rolls over only to pop back up again and resume his escape. I fumble in my pocket and bring out another shell in time to reload and fire again, but the results are exactly the same. A walking duck, of course, is not nearly as vulnerable a target as a bird in flight, and my shots have evidently not penetrated the armor that is his folded wings.

As the bird runs, so do I, trying all the while to keep the gun loaded and retain my footing on the slippery mud bank. At last I succeed in falling. When I look up, the bird has made it into the weeds. I mark the spot in my mind. But to get there, I must navigate around several cuts in the marsh. I arrive at "the spot" but am no longer sure I know where it is. Weeds and cuts have a sameness to them, especially when viewed from a different angle. Davy Crockett ponders the problem for a moment, then looks for tracks. In the soft mud they are easy to find. There is blood among the webbed footprints.

But the surface is harder in the weeds and the telltale tracks vanish. I look for feathers or blood or any other signs of the duck; there are none to be found. I search farther in. The bird has been hit four times: He cannot be all that healthy, and must be hiding nearby. I look farther up the cut, then into the next one. Protected from the winds and tides, the dead marsh grass around the drained pond is still knee high. It isn't all that thick, but a black duck has the perfect camouflage for this stuff.

Ten minutes pass, then fifteen. I look back at my brother. His estimate of the distance was accurate.

The duck is going to die before morning. It seems a waste. Before giving up, I return and look again at the duckprints leading into the tall weeds. It seems a hopeless case, but I give Davy Crockett one last hearing. Squatting down like a golfer looking over a putt, I have a different perspective. There, as obvious as a finger mark on newly brushed suede, is my own trail through the marsh grass. And that of the wounded duck.

Eight feet into the weeds, the hidden path ends. I stare at the lump of mud for a long moment before I can see the mottled khaki bill and the shape of the bird's head hunched into his breast feathers.

At times like this, looking a live cripple straight in the eye, I wish more than anything else that I had shot slightly better...or slightly worse.

3:15 P.M. The dull yellow-gray of the high overcast sky is typical of New England winter days. There is no warmth, no brightness, no shadow from the thin sunlight. It is as if the December sun has all it can manage to simply illuminate the afternoon landscape. In the peculiar silence of times preceding a snowfall, each sound is magnified and thrown back at us from the woodline bordering the swamp. The new ice on the marsh will hold no weight today and breaks noisily, but the cold is such that within a week all but the swiftest flowing waters will be frozen solid. Inland waterfowling is in its waning days.

We tow our boat through the ice, then hide it in some flooded puckerbrush next to the open water created by a spring hole. The crescent of brush accommodates the boat as if it had been planted with that purpose in mind. In the spring hole I arrange a late-season rig of blacks, scuffed and in need of repainting, with a pair of baldpates thrown in for color.

With the solstice just two weeks away, sunset will come early. There is barely two hours of daylight left when we settle in and begin waiting. My shins hurt from being repeatedly knocked against the shelf ice on the way in. In my pocket, the latest in my extensive collection of handwarmers has quit working. In that respect, it is little different from all the others I own.

The quiet of the marsh is complete. The insects that buzzed and hummed a backdrop through the warmer months are silenced now, and there are no bird sounds save the occasional distant cawing of a crow. No breeze stirs the few remaining leaves. My partner feels the silence too, for he barely speaks above a whisper. "I saw a few flying out of here this morning. No reason to think they shouldn't be coming back to feed this afternoon."

"That'd be nice." I speak quietly as well. "You know, just once I'd like to be able to know ahead of time that we were going to have a gangbuster's day. That way, we could shoot selectively and not have the feeling that the first hen to show up might be the only thing we'd see all day."

"This might be it, with the snow on the way and things freezing up all over..." He ponders his own statement for a moment, then smiles inwardly. "Could be..."

There has been no agreement made, but minutes later neither of us makes a move when a pair of hen mallards circles the rig, then eases in among the decoys. Conversation stops. We don't want to do anything to scare off these volunteers in our decoy regiment. The pair wanders along the edge of our spring hole, muttering duckily as they feed on buttonbush seed balls.

Within minutes, my partner nudges me and nods toward a tall pine we have been using as a reference point. I search the sky and finally notice a flock coming down the marsh, much higher than my eyes had been focused. They pass in front of us, perhaps fifteen birds altogether. There are several black ducks mixed in with what appears to be a flock of mallards. I sweet talk to them with the call, but the only answers I get are from the visitors in our decoys. The flock makes the circuit of our end of the swamp; down into the frozen corner, around the meadow behind us, then back to our pocket of open water. They are low enough on the second pass for me to clearly tell the drake mallards from the hens.

Out in the black water, the decoys are the only color in the gray December landscape. The iridescent green wing and face patches of the two baldpates seem especially gaudy among the washed-out tones of the marsh. Sixty yards from the boat, the two suzies continue to feed, paddling about and clucking softly. When one of them rears back and stretches her wings, I know the circling flock is ours.

They pass behind us for the fourth time. My ears follow the sound of air through their wings, and my eyeballs strain at the tops of their sockets. The birds appear below the brim of my downtilted hat, banking around on their final approach.

Next to me, my partner takes a deep breath.

With cupped wings and extended feet, the flock begins its flip-flopping descent; gray bodies, white wing linings, iridescent speculums against the dull winter sky.

We shoulder our guns together, eyes skyward.

5:50 P.M. Coming back with the drone of the motor filling my ears, I wonder why the night is thought of as black: The sky and water are shades of cobalt and purple and ultramarine, and the passing shoreline is shadowed in tones of indigo. Some of the sky colors blend and change and darken even as I watch, but nowhere is there a color I can label as black. The water mysteriously continues to hold the twilight glow, even though the sky and landscape grow darker. Over the darkening treetops, the Dipper is at its low winter point, nearly touching the horizon. The first stars of Cygnus the Swan shine in the west above the lavender line that was the sunset.

Mine is the only boat returning. There are no other gunners out on this last day of the season. Even the bats and snipe that amused me on other, earlier evenings are absent, having headed for warmer climates. The season—which began with teal and native wood ducks on this same river, then waxed full during first the inland and then the coastal migrations, and finally brought in the late redlegs in its waning days—has ended. Blacks will be the local natives for the next few months. For some reason known only to themselves, they choose to remain on what little water stays open through the bitter New England winter. Two of their number lay on the sacks of decoys in the bow. They are impressive trophies on the wing, but right now look for all the world like a couple of dead cats— nothing is rattier looking than a dead duck that has spent a few hours in the bilges of a boat.

The reprieve from the cold that came with picking up and sacking the decoys is fading. I jam my hands deeper into the pockets of my parka, then finally hug them into my armpits and use my knee to steer the boat through the blue evening.

The work of hauling the boat onto the trailer goes quickly. I carry the gas can and the motor to the back of the truck, then use a hand lantern to check for things that might have been forgotten in the shadows. My fingers are so numb that I cannot push the switch to shut off the light. Normally, I am eager to be out of my waders and on my way toward home and supper, but on this last night of the season, I linger. I toss the lantern into the cab, then reach in and shut off the headlights and the engine. In spite of my cold feet and fingers, I walk back to the edge of the river. One last time before the season slips completely into the past, I want to listen to the silence and see again the stars reflected in the quiet water.

Reflections on a Wood Duck Pond

BY CHUCK PETRIE

1987

GIVING UP A SECURE JOB WITH THE GOVERNMENT AND A LOW-INTEREST G.I. mortgage on a new home in the suburbs may sound like a screwy thing to do, especially for a 39-year-old man with a wife and children. But it was a decision my wife and I made three years ago and we don't regret it—most of the time. We wanted a challenge, something different. We wanted to live in the country, where we would be free of the problems of living on the rim of a city. Besides, I needed a change from the tedium of a mindless, paper-shuffling bureaucracy.

And on evenings when I sit in my canoe, nestled in the bulrush cover on the wood duck pond, waiting for birds to fly over the tree line before they buzz the water on their pre-roosting security sweep, I don't regret the decision one bit.

I am alone on the pond, four acres of quiet water bordered by autumn-gold tamarack and surrounded by cattail and bulrush. I know the ducks will come. They do almost every night in the first three weeks of October. They are predictable. It is almost not fair, I feel, that I take advantage of their predictability. That's why I come here only four or five times a season, and then shoot no more than one wood duck each time—and sometimes none. I am rich here. I can have a duck almost any night I want one. It depends on my mood.

I put out only a half dozen decoys—four mallards and, well to one side, a pair of wood duck blocks. The woodies invariably head for that treacherous pair, and sometimes they come in so fast I don't even get a chance to shoot. Then I watch the meeting of the newcomers and their plastic brethren. Usually the encounter is short-lived, and the ducks, betrayed, will swim away or fly a short distance to another part of the pond. It is amusing but deceitful.

Wood ducks are not the only waterfowl that come to the pond. When the wind blows hard from the east, the big lake, only a few miles away, is churned into froth. Then mallards might come, or bluebills or ringnecks. But they are different and I feel no compunction about shooting at these transients.

And there are other birds. Sometimes a blue heron will stalk the shallow border of the pond. Migrating geese sometimes fly over, and, although I know they see the pond and sometimes gabble among themselves as if discussing it as a possible resting place, they evidently never agree on its suitability and continue south. I occasionally hear a grouse drumming in the thick, dark halo of woods that surrounds the water, and I know there are migrating woodcock out there too.

I don't hunt the grouse and woodcock. My agreement with the man who owns the pond is that I only hunt ducks. That's okay. I have many other places to hunt grouse and woodcock and, for that matter, ducks too. But this is a special place. It is only three miles from my home. The landowner lets me keep my canoe in the woods near the edge of the pond, so I can leave my house and set up here in just minutes.

There is a farm a half-mile away from the pond, and, except for the occasional bellow of a cow, when its udder is turgid at milking time, or the sight of a white contrail against the blue sky, I can imagine myself in the wilderness. This little lake is spring-fed, and some day it will be a bog; even now there are pitcher plants growing on the damp, wooded trail leading to the water's edge, and spongy bog moss is beginning to infiltrate the cattails. This pond could be in northern Minnesota, Quebec, or Alaska, and sometimes I let my imagination convince me that I'm hunting in one of those places.

There is a stream flowing from the pond, but the beavers have dammed it. This year, consequently, the water level is high, and the water spills over into the woods on the lower sides of the basin to the west and north. Some afternoons I can hear wood ducks calling, their shrill ascending whistles echoing from back in the trees.

The beavers' lodge is on the southwest shore. They have free rein of the pond from there and are not afraid to swim right into my decoys. Inquisitive animals, a pair will often come snooping around the blocks, inspecting them. Invariably, one will slap its tail on the water to express his disapproval of these strange objects, then swim away to pursue more serious endeavors.

On the west shore, two hundred yards north of the beaver lodge, lie the half-submerged remains of an old blind. Whoever built it went to great lengths to ensure comfortable hunting. It consists of two-by-fours and plywood with a roof. The sides are covered with tarpaper, and the roof is shingled. Inside, the blind had room for three hunters to sit and shoot out of the large open port that faces the pond. Now, though, the blind sits cockeyed in the water, its wood rotted and shingles brittle with age and exposure to the heat and cold.

Occasionally I find myself staring at this decrepit blind, wondering about the people who hunted in it. Who were they? Where are they now? When did they build the blind?

I entertain myself by making up answers to these questions and envisioning three men sitting in the blind as it appeared years ago. The hunters look like they stepped off the cover of a sporting magazine from the 1930s. Two of the men have '97 Winchesters leaning against the wall of the blind; the other cradles a double-barrel—a weathered A.H. Fox—in his arms. The men's shells are paper and brass, and the decoys in the water in front of them are wood. Squeezed between two of the hunters on the blind's board seat is a Labrador retriever, looking forward, his eyes fixed on the empty space above the wooden blocks. Perhaps this dog was a distant sire of the old Lab sitting in the bow of my canoe. I imagine that dog sitting among the men, and then I look at my dog and notice that he, too, is staring at the blind, his brown eyes lost in concentration.

There are brook trout in the pond; I know it. Actually, I don't really know they are in the pond itself, but I know the outlet stream holds brook trout. It only stands to reason that the pond would have them too; it is cold and deep, except for the shallow rim that supports the cattails and bulrush. I've never tried to fish for the trout. I'm afraid if I tried, I might not catch any and decide there weren't any here. It's comforting to think the trout are here, though, and I'd like to keep it that way.

It's getting dark on the pond now. Shooting is allowed until sunset, but the pond, set in a basin and surrounded by trees, sees night early. The tree line is slowly eclipsing the sun, and the shadow of the tamaracks is crossing the water. When the dark veil reaches the other side and ascends to the opposite tree line, the entire basin will be enveloped in shadow. Still, it will be legal to shoot for another twenty minutes, until the sun sets.

It's time to anticipate the arrival of the wood ducks, but, instead, I look over the side of the canoe, into the water, at my reflection. My slight movement causes a series of tiny swells to radiate from the hull, distorting my image.

This leisure is one of the beauties of being alone in a duck blind. It allows me time to meditate, to relax and see things in other perspectives, to soften the images of the past, present and future. Reflections on a wood duck pond seem to take the harshness out of reality—not necessarily distorting it but softening it, at least temporarily. Sitting on the bank of a stream, watching the current go by, I often get a helpless feeling of being left behind in time. Here, though, where there is no current, just still water and solitude, my mind follows time in any direction, and I can believe that all is right in my life, that the future will be gentle, and my past, when necessary, has been forgiven.

Now it is too late to shoot. This will be a clear night, and the ducks won't come in before dusk like they do on cloudy, overcast afternoons. So, in the gathering darkness, I paddle out to the decoys, pick them up, and head for shore. But before I can beach the canoe the ducks arrive. They haven't disappointed me. In flocks of fives and tens they come in low, fast, circling the edge of the pond before finally pitching in toward the center of the circle of dark water. The dog and I sit quietly in the canoe and watch until it is too dark to see anymore.

The Almanac

BY CHRIS DORSEY

1989

WHERE'S A DAMNED PEN WHEN YOU NEED ONE, THOUGHT HENRY Ottman as he sifted through the papers littering his desk. The pencil with which he was writing snapped—a lousy reason to put his mind on hold, he thought. This morning, like every morning, Henry finished brushing straw and dirt from the chicken eggs that he had collected at sunrise and promptly sat at his desk to enter the notes of the day. It was his diary of sorts, thoughts and meditations collected from nearly a half-century of living on the farm.

October 26, 1983:

Felt like winter this morning. Frost didn't melt til almost noon. Decided to sit near the smoke house and brush the eggs. The sun kept the chill off, and it felt good on my old bones. My eyes aren't what they used to be, though, never saw a single duck heading for the marsh.

Henry put down his pen and walked to the living room window. He looked over the marsh, craning his head left and right looking for silhouettes against the cirrus. He wiped the dust that had accumulated on his bifocals from traipsing through the chicken coop. He looked again. There were no ducks as far as his eyes could reach. The sight of thousands of mallards circling the marsh like a feathered tornado ran through his mind's eye, his memory colliding with the reality of the moment.

Henry put his overalls back on and once again slipped his arms through his denim coat and headed outside. "Where were the ducks?" he wondered. He searched the sky again, turning around and around until he became dizzy and confused. An anxiousness came over him as he tried to remember when the ducks used to arrive. "They should have been here by now," he thought. He went inside to find his notes from years past.

Beside stacks of fading photos and yellowing magazines, was the box that stored his notes. The tattered pages became a time capsule and, just then, was Henry's most valuable possession. Was his memory failing him, he wondered, or were the ducks really gone? He shuffled through two decades worth of note pads before reaching his entries from the 1960s.

October 26, 1966:

The clouds were gray today, and the wind tasted like winter. Snow can't be far off now. Ducks must a sensed it too. Saw thousands of them today. Mostly mallards, but a few pintail as well. A few hundred teal also buzzed in, but they're usually too fast for my BBs. Hardly worth sending Angus on a retrieve unless there's more than one blue-wing to pick up—they barely make a meal for a chicken-hawk. Mrs. likes to cook teal, but doesn't want to clean them. Fred down at the hardware store sure likes the teal, though. Says he sells lots of shells when the blue-wings come through.

"What have we done?" Henry thought to himself. He blew the dust from his photo album—the archive where he stored snapshots from his hunting forays to the marsh. Each black and white captured a moment and mood otherwise lost in time. Angus was a pup in one photo, and Henry remembered the days when he and the Lab didn't need decoys to bring home a limit of greenheads. The flocks had faded, however, like the images on the prints.

Spring

"Henry must be on the sauce again," said Harold Stolman.

"Good thing Eleanor isn't alive or she'd have his butt in a sling," responded Wayne Mickelson.

The two drove past Henry's farm and couldn't help but notice the "overdue" alfalfa left standing in the field. The other farmers in the area already had their first crop of hay cut, baled, and stored in their lofts. Harold and Wayne shook their heads as they made it their business to notice the shortcomings of others.

Henry didn't much care what the others thought. He walked the field and found a half-dozen mallard nests in the alfalfa. It wouldn't be long, he reasoned, before the ducklings hatched and he could cut his hay without turning the hens and their eggs into fox fodder.

June 12, 1984:

One of the nests hatched today. Saw mama and seven ducklings scamper across the road on their way from the hayfield to the marsh. Could have been more duck-lings—tough to see them in the grass. The other nests should be hatching soon.

Henry couldn't understand his neighbors as much as they wondered about him. The government had succeeded in convincing the other farm-ers in the area that the only way to turn a profit on their land was to expand production. Henry didn't share in the ag agent's enthusiasm for the 16-bottom plow, nor would he sign a contract with his neighbors to allow them to run ditches through the marsh that bordered six farms. His was the only signature that held up progress. It was a silent veto for which his neighbors cursed him.

"Where would the hens go with their broods?" he thought to himself. "A few more acres of corn isn't worth losing the birds."

June 28, 1984:

The last of the nests hatched today. Found my mailbox smashed this morning. Neighbors must really want to plow the marsh. Wish Angus would have been here to rip the pants off the one who did it. Vultures...every damn one of them. They won't get the marsh...at least as long as I'm here.

Ducks to Ducks

BY HARRY E. HUGHES

1990

URING OUR DUCK HUNTING LIVES WE HAVE ALL HEARD STORIES ABOUT strange partners. But none can compare with the two I met in rural west Tennessee.

My story begins when I was transferred from outside the state. Being an avid waterfowler, my first priority was to find a place to duck hunt. So when a friend suggested that I contact Bert Henning and Jack Webster, I jumped at the chance.

The two were retired railroad men from the G.M. & O. Railroad and they appeared to be in their late sixties. A hunting partner's death almost a year before had left the men looking for someone to share the blind with them. They were also looking for someone young enough to help brush the blind and do "some of" (it amounted to "all of") the heavy work. I entered the picture anyway.

As the years went by I looked forward to hearing these old water-fowlers talk about their hunting experiences as much as I did actually hunting ducks. Though I didn't realize it when I got involved, I was replacing Al Parker, their best friend, and the greatest duck hunter who had ever lived. (Well, at least in their opinion.) Bert and Jack told stories about Al that made Nash Buckingham look like a kneebooter from Memphis.

During the years I spent with Bert and Jack a person could not have asked for better blind partners. They were willing to go duck hunting regardless of the weather; whether or not the ducks were flying at all. They were perfect partners except for one small matter...well, at the time I thought it a small matter.

I noticed that on each opening day, Jack brought out a box of shotgun shells wrapped in plastic. At first I thought he was afraid his shells would get wet on the trip to the blind. But there was something else odd about the box of shotgun shells.

After Jack unwrapped the box he would hand one shell to Bert, who then loaded it into the chamber of his Model 12. Jack took one himself, and put it in his Browning. He'd then wrap the shells up again and place them, ever so gently, back into his hunting bag. That would be the last I'd see of that special box of shells until opening day of duck season the next year. My two elderly hunting partners never said a word about the ritual.

By the end of our third season together, my curiosity was getting the best of me. On the last day of the season I finally got up enough nerve to ask.

"Jack, something's been bothering me for a while, and I have got to ask you about it," I said.

"Sure, Harry. We're all friends here," Jack replied. "What do you need to know?"

"It's about that box of shells," I said. "For the past three opening days I've watched you pull out that box of shells wrapped in plastic. You carefully take out two. You load one into your gun and Bert loads the other into his. That's the last I see of that box of shells until opening day the next year. What gives?"

A long silence filled the cold duck blind as Bert and Jack looked at each other.

Then Jack spoke up. "Harry...do you remember how you got into the blind?"

"Sure. Al Parker died, there was a spot available, and I got it," I said.

"That's right," Jack said. "Al died over three years ago and you got the spot."

"Jack, I fail to see the connection between that box of shells and old Al Parker," I explained.

"Let me continue," he said. "We were going to tell you but the time was never right. So since you brought it up, we'd better tell you the whole story now. Harry, those are very special shotgun shells and ones that we have a very special relationship with."

"Oh, I get it," I said. "Those shells belonged to Al. It's his last box and you guys are using them up sparingly each opening day."

"Not quite, son," Bert said.

"OK, if that's not the story, then what is?"

"All right," Jack said. "This is the whole story. Al Parker was not buried like most people around these parts. His body was sent to Memphis to be cremated. It was his wish to do it that way...he wanted to spare Virginia, his wife, the expense of a funeral. To make a long story short, Virginia was surprised when the funeral director showed up at her doorstep with Al in an urn. She didn't know what to do with it. She couldn't bear to sit it in the living room, so she stuck it in a closet in the upstairs bedroom. During one of our late-night poker games we decided it was a dirty shame that one of the world's greatest duck hunters should be locked away in some musty old closet for no telling how long. So, that night, after a few high-balls, we took matters into our own hands. We decided to do something about the situation.

"To do what?" I asked.

"To kidnap Al...or what was left of him...and replace his ashes with ashes from my fireplace," Bert said. "You know that they are almost the same color."

I couldn't believe what I was hearing. "Wait a second," I said. "You decided to kidnap Al and replace his ashes? What about Mrs. Parker?"

"We knew that Virginia would never open up that urn," Bert explained. "Hell, son, she can't even stand to cut up a chicken, much less look at the charcoal remains of Al. Besides, we felt that this is the way Al would have wanted it."

The two went on to explain that they made up a story about Al borrowing one of their duck calls. They told Virginia they believed it was in Al's old hunting coat hanging in the upstairs closet—the same closet, by the way, where Al was residing. So while Bert kept her busy downstairs, Jack went upstairs. He found the urn and made the big switch.

"We had originally decided to take his ashes to the blind and spread them on the water, but then Jack came up with this terrific idea," Bert said. "Why not mix his ashes with gunpowder and load them into a special box of shotgun shells? That way, Al could not only go hunting with us for a period of time, but he could help us—as he always did—to kill ducks."

"So you see, Harry, these shells did not belong to All at all," Jack said.

"These shells *are* Al."

I stood there in a state of disbelief, wondering how these two old geezers could have done such a thing. This was right out of Alfred Hitchcock. But then I thought some more. It was, after all, just two old men showing their love and affection for a fallen comrade. Nevertheless, I had to admit that it was a unique way to salute the passing of a fellow duck hunter.

The sun was peeking over the horizon when Jack reached into his hunting coat and brought out a three-inch shell.

"Harry," Jack said in a low voice, "this is the last of the shells. You might say it is the last of Albert Waynewright Parker. Bert and I would like for you to have it and use it this morning."

It felt like I was receiving the Nobel Prize for world peace, and to these two gentlemen, it was just such an honor. I took the long blue shell and slowly loaded it into the left barrel on my double.

"Guys, I really don't know what to say," I said. "This is quite an honor."

"Don't say anything, son. Just do old Al proud this morning and that will be enough," Bert said.

It wasn't long before Jack spotted a lone Canada goose headed down in our direction. "Get down!" he ordered. "A goose coming straight in from the river." With that alert, we quickly got down against the shooting rail of the blind.

"Harry, this goose will be yours and Al's," Jack whispered. "He's all yours—take your time."

That was all I needed. Not only had I never killed a goose in my entire life, but here I was with my shotgun loaded with the last remains of the World's Greatest Duck Hunter. (Well, at least in their opinion.)

The goose kept coming and all six eyes were fixed on his every move. The pressure now was great. It felt like I was in Yankee Stadium in the last game of the World Series, score tied, bottom of the ninth, Harry at the bat.

My cold hand reached slowly over and clicked the safety off. There was a large lump in my throat as I watched the goose make a high pass in front of the blind to start his final approach. At that point, a single thought kept running through my mind. *What if I miss? What if I miss?* The pressure was unbearable.

I watched the goose through the cane that lined the front of the blind, while Bert blew his call. The large bird was no more than 65 yards out and closing fast.

"Son," Jack said in a low whisper, "if you're going to take him, you had better do it now."

With that piece of advice I took one last look over the cane, raised up, leveled down, and slowly pulled the trigger. To this day I can't even remember the gun going off, let along feel the kick of the Winchester. Everything appeared to progress in slow motion when I pulled the trigger. The goose never seemed to blink. He flared up over the decoys and turned back toward the river. A cold, sinking feeling engulfed my entire soul. I looked over at my hunting partners and saw the disappointment streaming from their faces. It was the last of old Al Parker...and I had missed.

We watched in dead silence as the goose made his way back up river when all of sudden, to our astonishment and surprise, the goose folded in flight and fell half-way across the field, dead as a mackerel.

A spontaneous cheer went up from the blind and we all knew deep down that somehow Al had come through.

"You got him, Harry! You got him!" shouted Jack and Bert. "What a grand way to say goodbye to Al!" Ashes to ashes, ducks to ducks.

My relationship with these two marvelous duck hunters lasted only two more years as I was too soon transferred to another part of the state. But sometimes, just before the opening day of duck season, my mind still wanders back to that blind in rural west Tennessee, and the day that I shared it with Jack, Bert...and Al.

Gray Muzzles

BY JOHN R. WRIGHT

1994

OR THE FOURTH TIME SINCE TURNING IN, I RAISE UP TO CHECK THE glowing clock face. It is finally 4 a.m. and time to roll out. I swing my legs over the edge of the bed and the dog hears the springs complain. She pulls herself up with effort. She's wanted one of those L.L. Bean cedar dog beds for years, but the old couch cushion with a quilt over it seems to satisfy.

She passes me on the stairs as we go down, her joints all a-pop. Neither of our bladders is what it used to be, so she is as happy to be let out as I am to get to the bathroom. By the time I have the coffee started, she asks to come back in.

We're going out for ducks today, like so many times before. I've been a hunter for more than 30 years. She was born one. She'll be nine her next birthday, and I'll be 46.

Peach, named for the shade of her yellow Lab's coat, goes back upstairs for a few more winks before we head out. The dekes are already in the truck and the ancient, patched waders hang warming by the woodstove. Things were checked through and laid out last night, so I need little time to locate calls, whistles, shells, and fowling piece. But it does take awhile, at that.

The squashed disk in my neck is making itself known this morning, sending waves of dull pain down my right shoulder and arm. The recoil of magnum duck loads won't go unnoticed today. Then there are the less insistent naggings from knees, elbows, and other parts, all eager to remind me that football does, indeed, build character. Peach is not without her miseries, either. She seems to be a touch arthritic this season, packing her right rear leg at times, sitting with it shot out straight, and generally trying to keep her weight off it.

The coffee's ready and after an eye-opening, scalding slug, I return to the bathroom and the medicine cabinet to fetch an aspirin for the dog. She patiently accepts her pill by way of my finger poked down her throat.

I start the truck, then come back in to finish the coffee. My back is starting to loosen up and by now I can bend over enough to duct-tape my socks to my pant legs. If I fail to do this, the socks will be wadded into the toes of my wader boots before I've gone 50 feet. Peach hears the truck running and comes back downstairs. She, too, is moving a little easier and reminds me that she's ready for breakfast.

Outside, I drop the tailgate and open the door of her dog box. She waits politely for the command "load up." Her jump is good, but for that bad leg, which trails a bit behind. I'm standing by and give her just a little push—she would have made it anyway. In the cab I run my checklist once more. Decoys, calls, whistle, license, half a box of steel number ones, and the old double.

Ten minutes from home is the all-night market where I stop to fill my go mug. Somehow, their coffee is always better than mine. I get a couple of doughnuts I hardly need and nuke them a little in the microwave. Hunter and dog are better larded this season than last. I draw a stare from the wormy-looking graveyard clerk. I guess it's the lanyard and calls around my neck. Them's my "bonafidees," I think to myself. Man's gotta have proof of a good reason to be out and about this early. Don't want to look like some drunk who hasn't gotten to bed yet.

Back at the truck, I push a last bit of doughnut through the grill of the dog box door and watch it vanish. This produces a series of tail thumps against crate sides.

It's black as the inside of a bull when we get to the reservoir. I'm always early or late. The engine runs, the heater blows, and I drink more coffee, intimidated by the thought of setting out blocks in the waist-deep water. The small, persistent leak in the crotch of my waders remains unfound and so unrepaired. There's nothing but country on the radio at 5:45 a.m. and I finish the coffee as some unidentified down-home crooner laments his misspent youth. You and me both, Bubba.

The faintest dab of pink in the east spurs me to action. The dog jumps stiffly to the ground, but limbers up fast and is soon rolling on her back in the snow. While I heft decoys, bird vest, and gun, Peach rushes into the remaining blackness like the pup that still rules her heart. She checks back shortly before I reach the lake's edge and I heel her up to keep her out of the water. Her habit of swimming out with me as I set the decoys is too taxing for her these days. Better to spare that bone-wracking chill for honest retrieving.

One of the dekes has a massive fissure in its belly, so 11 will have to do. By then, I feel the magic fingers of ice water tickling at my nether regions and I'm very anxious to make landfall. My bird vest goes down in the cattails for the dog to sit on as I arrange spare shells and break off stalks that might impede my swing. No blind here, just the old "hunker down in the weeds" routine. Then I stand and wait for daylight. I have found that legal shooting time and enough illumination for the dog to mark usually arrive at about the same pace.

It's brightening fast now and I load up. The dog's ears rise at the snap of the closing action and again as I tune up on the call. No slowing of the blood there. Her anticipation is as strong now as in her first season. Mine too.

I'm cold, though, and it occurs to me that a certain amount of toughness has been lost over the years. Seldom anymore do I undertake the long, wet belly crawl to jump maybe one bird that was standard operating procedure a few seasons back. The great need to shoot the gun and fill the bag has drawn away some and simply being here takes on new dimensions. But for the dog to work, which has become everything for both of us, the odd duck must be killed and, as I was summoned by that thought, a bluebill sizzles by at Mach-2 with me standing tall and flat-footed. Raising the gun from a very relaxed port arms I mount it, release the safety, socket the butt into that shooter's sweet spot, swing hard, and in one oily smooth motion, shoot at least four feet behind the bird. Peach watches the duck, looking for a hitch or a wobble, but ultimately has no reason to leave her seat.

Birds are in the air now, and I kneel in the snowy cattails, recharge the right barrel, and send out a hail call to whom it may concern. My knees are soon a pair of burning pincushions, part from the cold and part from the reluctance to bend. So much has been left on the playing field. A glance at the dog tells me she feels it too, that suspect leg extended out from under her weight. And so it goes for the next hour. Another pass by. Another miss.

I am contemplating an organized retreat when that absolutely gripping sound comes to us from above and behind— wind slicing through pinion feathers—and I hunch down and crane my neck to see two drakes with bottle-green heads drop and turn out past the far edge of the stool, coming about into the wind and across the gun at 60 yards. I wait and fight to stay still, my heart doing that trip-hammer jig it learned long ago. As the birds cup wings and toe up to that invisible dead-certain mark, I get an instantaneous and totally dominating cramp in my right hip, causing me to lurch and come to my feet as if on strings. The birds flare at 40 yards, towering rapidly and putting distance between us.

Then in a slow-motion reversal of fortune, things begin to work. The pain fades as the gun lifts itself and tracks the high bird, tracing its bead along the stretched green neck, going past and building daylight. Swinging harder still, I pull the back trigger for the choke barrel. The kick is not felt, the report not heard, but I see the drake tumble and the dog go, both casting up diamond slivers of skim ice as they hit the water together.

He's a cripple, leading the dog on a merry chase out beyond the ice rim. At 75 yards she finally dives with him, going under, head and all. When she gets back she's winded, but has the duck and delivers to hand.

As always, she is very proud of herself and well she should be. She has broken through ice and fought her way to clear sailing. She has gone round and round with a diving cripple and done what all dogs hate—gotten her ears full of ice water on her subsurface retrieve. She has done a smashing good job and she knows it, jumping straight up and down as I praise her, pet her, and admire the duck.

It's a nice fat bird and she wants to worry it a little. I sack it and rub her up with the decoy bag. She likes it and thanks me with "that look." The birds, then, seemingly stop flying, so we elect to go home. Peach is happy, knowing that when she is wet and it's just the two of us, she gets to ride back in the cab with me.

At the cabin again she gets another aspirin and I get the whiskey jug down. She curls up behind the woodstove as I toss in a chunk. Soon she is twitching in dreams I wish I could see. Her face has turned almost completely white now and, wiping my mustache, I realize mine has too. But the marsh was made for two gray muzzles like us. And you know what? After our nap, there's the evening flight.